COSMOS

| POSSIBLE WORLDS |

Published by National Geographic Partners, LLC
1145 17th Street NW Washington, DC 20036

ISBN: 978-1-4262-1908-5
ISBN: 978-1-4262-2068-5 (special sales edition)

Acknowledgments and Permissions

Page 29: lyrics from "No Woman No Cry" (written by Vincent Ford, performed by Bob Marley) ©1974 Fifty-Six Hope Road Music Ltd & Primary Wave/Blue Mountain Music. Copyright Renewed. All Rights Reserved. Used by Permission. All rights administered by Primary Wave/ Blue Mountain Music.

Page 115: from Anna Akhmatova ["Here the most beautiful girls fight"] in *Complete Poems of Anna Akhmatova,* translated by Judith Hemschemeyer, edited and introduced by Roberta Reeder. Copyright © 1989, 1992, 1997 by Judith Hemschemeyer. Reprinted with the permission of The Permissions Company, Inc., on behalf of Zephyr Press, www.zephyrpress.org.

Page 115: from Anna Akhmatova ["Here the most beautiful girls fight"] in *Complete Poems of Anna Akhmatova,* translated by Judith Hemschemeyer, edited and introduced by Roberta Reeder. Copyright © 1989, 1992, 1997 by Judith Hemschemeyer. Reprinted with the permission of Canongate Books Ltd.

Page 171: excerpt from Carl Sagan, *Broca's Brain*, published by Random House, 1974. Copyright © 1974 by Carl Sagan. Copyright © 2006 by Democritus Properties, LLC.

Page 309: "When Spring Returns," from *Fernando Pessoa & Co.*, by Fernando Pessoa, translation copyright © 1998 by Richard Zenith. Used by permission of Grove/Atlantic, Inc. Any third party use of this material, outside of this publication, is prohibited.

Page 309: "When Spring Returns" from *Fernando Pessoa & Co.*, by Fernando Pessoa, translation copyright © 1998 by Richard Zenith. Used by permission of SSL/Sterling Lord Literistic, Inc. Any third party use of this material, outside of this publication, is prohibited.

Page 367: grateful acknowledgment is made to the following publishers for permission to reprint portions of the "Encyclopedia Galactica" from Carl Sagan, *Cosmos*. New York: Random House, 1980; London: Little, Brown Book Group Ltd., 1980. Copyright © 1980 by Carl Sagan Productions, Inc. Copyright © 2006 by Druyan-Sagan Associates, Inc.

Since 1888, the National Geographic Society has funded more than 13,000 research, exploration, and preservation projects around the world. National Geographic Partners distributes a portion of the funds it receives from your purchase to National Geographic Society to support programs including the conservation of animals and their habitats.

Get closer to National Geographic explorers and photographers, and connect with our global community. Join us today at nationalgeographic.com/join

For rights or permissions inquiries, please contact National Geographic Books Subsidiary Rights: bookrights@natgeo.com

Interior design: Melissa Farris

Printed in the United States of America
20/WOR-CG/1

For

Sarah,

Zoe,

Norah,

and

Helena

as you set sail for the stars

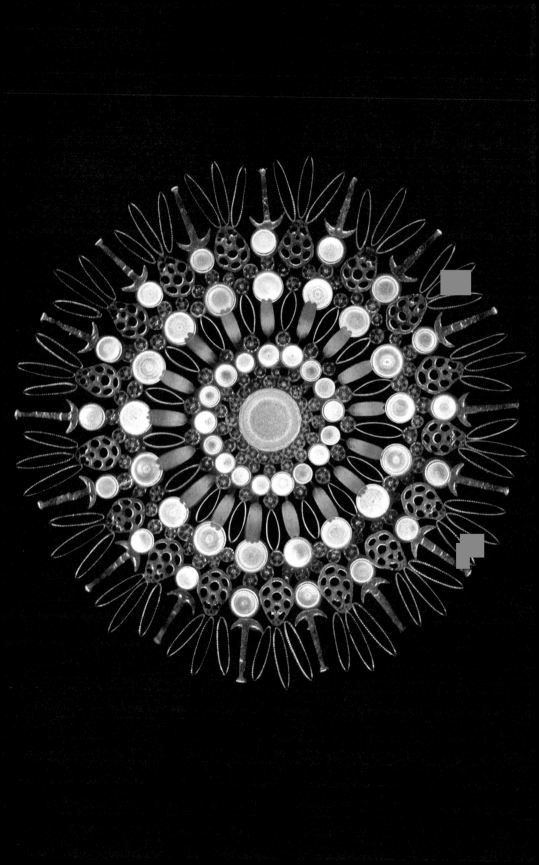

CONTENTS

| PROLOGUE | 15 |

| ONE | **LADDER TO THE STARS** | 28 |

| TWO | **OH, MIGHTY KING** | 60 |

| THREE | **LOST CITY OF LIFE** | 88 |

| FOUR | **VAVILOV** | 114 |

| FIVE | **THE COSMIC CONNECTOME** | 144 |

| SIX | **THE MAN OF A TRILLION WORLDS** | 174 |

| SEVEN | **THE SEARCH FOR INTELLIGENT LIFE ON EARTH** | 198 |

| EIGHT | **THE SACRIFICE OF CASSINI** | 226 |

| NINE | **MAGIC WITHOUT LIES** | 252 |

| TEN | **A TALE OF TWO ATOMS** | 278 |

| ELEVEN | **THE FLEETING GRACE OF THE HABITABLE ZONE** | 308 |

| TWELVE | **COMING OF AGE IN THE ANTHROPOCENE** | 332 |

| THIRTEEN | **A POSSIBLE WORLD** | 348 |

ACKNOWLEDGMENTS	372
FURTHER READING	376
ILLUSTRATIONS CREDITS	377
INDEX	379

PAGE 1: Artist's vision of a possible world, over 500 light-years away. Kepler-186f was the first validated Earthlike exoplanet, discovered in 2014. **PAGES 2-3:** The Milky Way's Carina Nebula, a stellar nursery 7,500 light-years away. **OPPOSITE:** A Victorian art form made possible by the microscope. This one includes diatoms (microscopic algae with silicon dioxide skeletons) and butterfly scales.

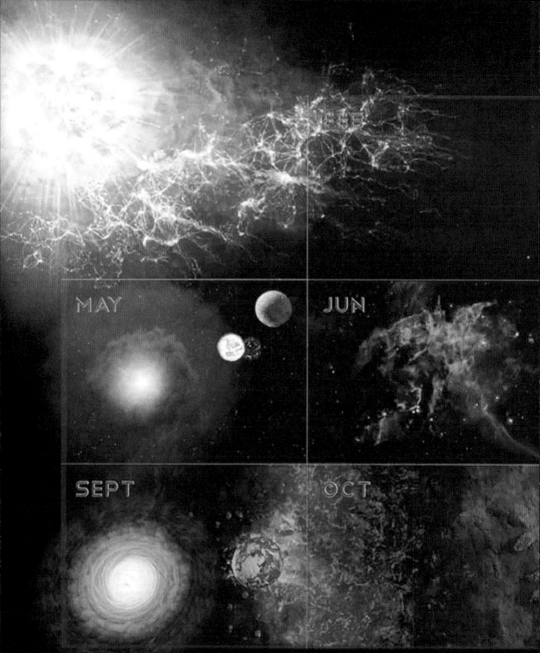

| THE COSMIC CALENDAR |

1 YEAR = 13.82 billion years • **1 MONTH** = 1.136 billion years • **1 WEEK** = 265 million years
1 DAY = 37.86 million years • **1 HOUR** = 1.578 million years • **1 MINUTE** = 26,294 years
1 SECOND = 438.23 years

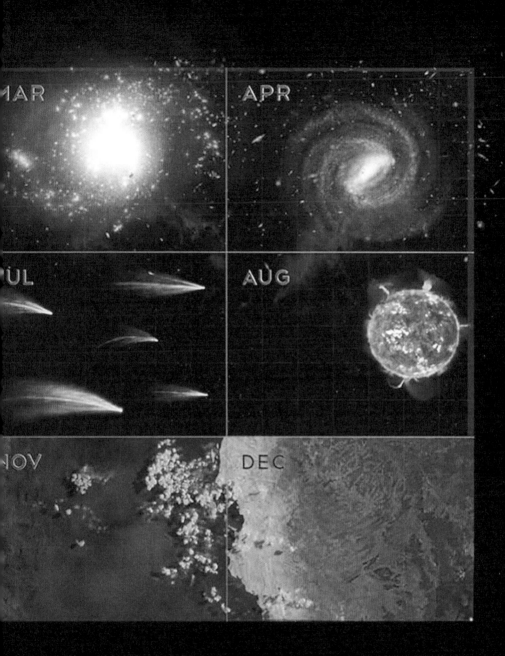

The whole sweep of time, from the big bang to this very moment, at a glance: the highlights of cosmic evolution compressed into a single calendar year. That tiny glint in the lower right-hand corner represents all of human existence.

WORLD'S FAIR 2039

Imagine a 2039 World's Fair, symbol of optimism and the wonders of a future world. Visitors pour in, awed by the five pavilions surrounding a vast elliptical reflecting pool.

WORLD'S FAIR 2039

In the fair's Pavilion of Possible Worlds walk the spiral arms of our galaxy to encounter
other civilizations of the Milky Way and assess their chances of survival.

*I was a child in a time of hope. I wanted to be a scientist from
my earliest school days. The crystallizing moment came
when I first caught on that the stars are mighty suns, when it
first dawned on me how staggeringly far away they must be
to appear as mere points of light in the sky. I'm not sure
I even knew the meaning of the word "science" then, but
I wanted somehow to immerse myself in all that grandeur.
I was gripped by the splendor of the Universe, transfixed
by the prospect of understanding how things really work,
of helping to uncover deep mysteries, of exploring new
worlds—maybe even literally. It has been my good fortune to
have had that dream in part fulfilled. For me,
the romance of science remains as appealing and new as it
was on that day, more than half a century ago, when
I was shown the wonders of the 1939 World's Fair.*
—CARL SAGAN,
THE DEMON-HAUNTED WORLD

A contemporary poster highlights the Trylon and Perisphere,
iconic symbols of the 1939 New York World's Fair.

On a rainy night in Queens, the future became a place, one you could visit. A downpour at sunset in Flushing Meadows couldn't discourage the 200,000 people who had gathered there for the opening ceremony of the 1939 New York World's Fair, whose theme was the "World of Tomorrow." Before it closed in the fall of 1940, 45 million visitors would travel to this art deco land of promises.

One of them was a five-year-old boy whose parents were so poor that they had brought their own brown-bag lunch. The 20 cents for a dish of chocolate ice cream topped with fluffy whipped cream was out of their reach, as were the blue and orange Bakelite flashlights and key rings that the boy craved. The apple from home would have to do for dessert. Despite his tantrums, the child came away empty- handed—but with the coordinates for his life trajectory set. At the playground in the Hall of Electrical Living, he was allowed to operate an infrared musical light beam, which enchanted him. He had fallen in love with the place called the future, and grasped that the only way to get there was science. Dreams are maps.

The aspirations of this possible world were as egalitarian as they were scientific. In fact, one of its model communities was

Futurama, the 1939 World's Fair's city of 1960, presaged tiered modern highways and garden-topped skyscrapers.

known as "Democracity." There were no slums—but there was a television set, a word processor, and a robot. It was there, for the first time, people saw these things that would change their lives.

But on this last night of April, they had come to hear the greatest scientific genius since Isaac Newton say a few words. Albert Einstein was the opening act for a dramatic production number that would choreograph forces of nature as if they were the synchronized swimmers in the water ballet at the fair's Aquacade. Einstein was to give brief opening remarks and flip the switch that would illuminate the fair. The spectacle promised to be the largest flash of man-made light in technical history, visible for a radius of 40 miles. A wow—but not as mind-blowing as the source of this sudden, unprecedented brilliance.

Across the East River in Manhattan, Professor W. H. Barton, Jr., of the Hayden Planetarium of the American Museum of Natural History was calibrating instruments that would grab mysterious thunderbolts from unknown parts of the universe and turn them into light, seizing power from the cosmos just as Prometheus stole fire from the gods.

A few decades earlier, a scientist named Victor Hess had discovered that the universe was reaching out to touch our world many times a day. Streaks of radiation in the form of charged particles were striking Earth. A single proton could contain the energy of a baseball pitched at 60 miles an hour. They came to be called cosmic rays. Three oversize Geiger counters were installed at the Hayden Planetarium to capture 10 cosmic rays for the momentous opening of the World's Fair.

Once ensnared by the Geiger counters, their energy was to be magnified through vacuum tubes and then transmitted across a network of wires to Queens, where Einstein and the crowd were waiting. The cosmic rays would supply the energy that would turn night into day, flooding with blinding light a new world made possible by science.

But first, it fell to Einstein to explain cosmic rays to the public. He was instructed to keep it to 700 words at most. Initially he refused. Impossible, he thought. Cosmic rays were a mystery to Einstein and his contemporaries, and to the scientific community when I began writing this book. But such is the relentless probing of science that, as I was completing the final draft of this book, cosmic rays were revealed to be from distant galaxies, generated by some of the most violent processes in the universe.

Einstein thought that 700 words couldn't possibly be enough to explain the complexity of this mysterious phenomenon. But above all, he was a true believer in the scientist's duty to communicate with the public. And so he agreed to give the talk.

Imagine that last night of April 1939, an evening more freighted with cinematic foreshadowing than many a movie. The world was mere months away from the German invasion of Poland, the start of the Second World War, the most catastrophic global bloodletting in human history. A five-year-old Carl Sagan couldn't have a fancy dessert and the World's Fair souvenirs he coveted because his parents and the rest of humanity still hadn't crawled out of the impoverishment of the worst economic depression that ever was. In Germany, where hyperinflation in the 1930s meant a wheelbarrow was required to carry enough paper money to purchase a loaf of bread, the desperate population turned to a demagogue. And yet, on a planet that was about to murder 60 million of its own, and to impose unimaginable suffering on tens of millions more, a world with some of the dimmest prospects in human history, people came together in massive numbers to celebrate, even worship . . . *the future.*

As the sun was setting, Einstein stepped up to the microphone. He had just turned 60 the month before and had already enjoyed decades of the rarest form of iconic celebrity, a renown based on his discoveries of new physical realities on the grandest possible scale.

For 2,400 years, since the time of the Greek genius Democritus, scientists had theorized about the existence of invisible units of matter called "atoms," but no one had been able to demonstrate that they were real. When Einstein was 25, he provided the first definitive evidence for atoms, and their collectives, molecules. He even measured their sizes. He challenged the dominant wave theory of light and proposed that light traveled as packets of particles called photons. He provided the foundation for quantum mechanics. He expanded classical physics by discovering the energy inherent in particles at rest.

And he realized that gravity bends light. The formula he devised to express this idea is the equation that we both already know because it is the most famous scientific/mathematical statement of all. He took Newton's law of universal gravitation to a new level when he understood it as a property of spacetime. This was the gateway to modern astrophysics and to exploring the darkest places of the universe, where light is imprisoned by gravity.

Einstein began to speak. Those who stood there in the rain that night to hear him were only a fraction of those in the United States and around the planet who listened to the event on radio. He told the crowd about Victor Hess, the Austrian physicist who had discovered cosmic rays by making a series of perilous high-altitude hot-air balloon trips between 1911 and 1913. Einstein used up some of his meager 700-word allotment to remind the world of Hess's status as an immigrant, "who incidentally, like so many others has recently had to seek refuge in this hospitable country." He went on to explain what scientists knew about the cosmic rays, and concluded by speculating that they could provide the key to the "innermost structure of matter."

An announcer's voice boomed across the Queens night: "We will now call on these interplanetary messengers to reveal the World of Tomorrow; the first ray that we will catch is still five million miles away, traveling toward us at the rate of 186,000 miles per second." A roll call began as each cosmic ray arrived and registered on one of the Geiger counters. But when they got to the 10th and Einstein flicked the switch, it was simply too much for the wiring system; some of the lights blew. Still, it was magnificent. The way to the future was open.

The next day, the *New York Times* reported that due to the heaviness of Einstein's accent and the dueling acoustics of the

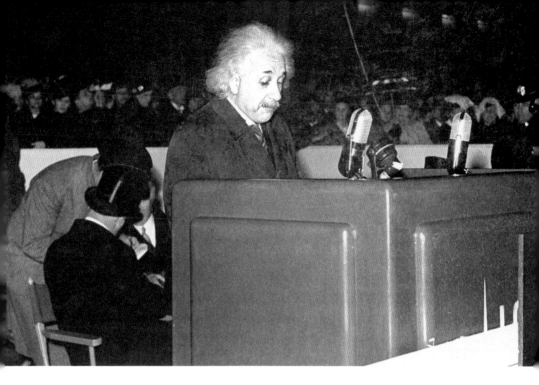

The most respected mind on the planet opens the
1939 New York World's Fair with a challenge to science.

amplifiers, those attending heard not much more than the words that began his speech: "If science, like art, is to perform its mission truly and fully, its achievements must enter not only superficially but with their inner meaning into the consciousness of the people."

This always has been and always will be, the dream of *Cosmos*. When I stumbled upon Einstein's rarely quoted words of that night during some random late-night wandering on YouTube, I found the credo for 40 years of my life's work. Einstein was urging us to tear down the walls around science that have excluded and intimidated so many of us—to translate scientific insights from the technical jargon of its priesthood into the spoken language shared by us all, so that we may take these insights to heart and be changed by a personal encounter with the wonders they reveal.

Carl Sagan and I fell in love in 1977 during our collaboration on NASA's Voyager interstellar message. Carl was by that time a celebrated astrophysicist, communicator, and a principal investigator on the

NASA's 1977 Voyagers 1 and 2 carry a complex interstellar message deep into the Milky Way galaxy and five billion years into the future. The etchings on the cover are scientific hieroglyphs indicating our cosmic address and instructions for playing the record.

Voyagers' planned mission of exploration. We had already collaborated on a television project. It was never produced, but that experience of thinking together moved Carl to ask me to be the creative director of the message that would become known as the golden record.

It was Carl's vision that once Voyager 1 completed its epochal reconnaissance of what was then thought of as the outer solar system, and sent back its final image of Neptune, it should turn its camera homeward to document our world. For years, he mounted a one-man campaign within NASA and was met with strenuous objections. What possible scientific value could such a picture have? But Carl was convinced of the potentially transformative impact of that image. He would not take no for an answer. By the time Voyager 1 was high above the plane of our solar system, NASA gave in. The family album photos of the worlds of our solar system were taken, including one of an Earth so small, you had to strain to find it.

The "pale blue dot" image and Carl's prose meditation on it have been beloved the world over ever since. It exemplifies just the kind of breakthrough that I think of as a fulfillment of Einstein's hope for science. We have gotten clever enough to dispatch a spacecraft four billion miles away and command it to send us back an image of Earth. Seeing our world as a single pixel in the immense darkness is in itself a statement about our true circumstances in the cosmos, and one that every single human can grasp instantly. No advanced degree required. In that photo, the *inner meaning* of four centuries of astronomical research is suddenly available to all of us at a glance. It is scientific data and art equally, because it has the power to reach into our souls and alter our consciousness. It is like a great book or movie, or any major work of art. It can pierce our denial and allow us to feel something of reality—even a reality that some of us have long resisted.

A world that tiny cannot possibly be the center of a cosmos of all that is, let alone the sole focus of its creator. The pale blue dot is a silent rebuke to the fundamentalist, the nationalist, the militarist, the polluter—to anyone who does not put above all other things the protection of our little planet and the life that it sustains in the vast cold darkness. There is no running away from the inner meaning of this scientific achievement.

We didn't know that particular Einstein quote when Carl and I began writing the original *Cosmos* in 1980 with astronomer Steven Soter. We just felt a kind of evangelical urgency to share the awesome power of science, to convey the spiritual uplift of the universe it reveals, and to amplify the alarms that Carl, Steve, and other scientists were sounding about our impact on the planet. *Cosmos* gave voice to those forebodings, but it was also suffused with hope, with a sense of human self-esteem derived, in part, from our successes in finding our way in the universe, and from the courage of those scientists who dared to uncover and express forbidden truths.

The original award-winning *Cosmos* television series and book of 1980 was embraced by hundreds of millions of people around our world. According to the Library of Congress, it is one of only "88 books that shaped America," included in the same category as *Common Sense, The Federalist, Moby-Dick, Leaves of Grass, Invisible Man,* and *Silent Spring.*

And so it was with a fair degree of fear that I set out with Steve, a dozen years after Carl's death, to undertake another 13 hours of the series, *Cosmos: A SpaceTime Odyssey.* My waking nightmare throughout the six years it took to write and produce was that my personal limitations would reflect poorly on Carl, whom I love and admire infinitely.

This, my third series of voyages on the Ship of the Imagination, marks my 40th year of writing *Cosmos.* The Ship and the Cosmic Calendar are not the only artifacts from previous flights. Some tropes, anecdotes, and teaching tools, in my view, have unrivaled explanatory power, and so I bring them along on this journey, too. Inevitably, there will be some repetitions and overlap from concepts Carl and I expressed previously, but they are now more urgent than before.

I am blessed once again to have brilliant collaborators, and I am still worried about not measuring up. Despite this, the times impel me forward.

We all feel the chill our present casts on our future. Some part of us knows that we must awaken to action or doom our children to dangers and hardships we ourselves have never had to face. How do we rouse ourselves and keep from sleepwalking into a climate or a nuclear catastrophe that may not be reversed before it has destroyed our civilization and countless other species? How do we learn to value those things we cannot live without—air, water, the sustaining fabric of life on Earth, the future—more than we prize money and short-term convenience? Nothing less than a global spiritual awakening can transform us into who we must become.

Science, like love, is a means to that transcendence, to that soaring experience of the oneness of being fully alive. The scientific approach to nature and my understanding of love are the same: Love asks us to get beyond the infantile projections of our personal

Ann Druyan and Carl Sagan in 1980, during the production of *Cosmos: A Personal Voyage* in Los Angeles

hopes and fears, to embrace the other's reality. This kind of unflinching love never stops daring to go deeper, to reach higher.

This is precisely the way that science loves nature. This lack of a final destination, an absolute truth, is what makes science such a worthy methodology for sacred searching. It is a never ending lesson in humility. The vastness of the universe—and love, the thing that makes the vastness bearable—is out of reach to the arrogant. This cosmos only fully admits those who listen carefully for the inner voice reminding us to remember we might be wrong. What's real must matter more to us than what we wish to believe. But how do we tell the difference?

I know a way to part the curtains of darkness that prevent us from having a complete experience of nature. Here it is, the basic rules of the road for science: Test ideas by experiment and observation. Build on those ideas that pass the test. Reject the ones that fail. Follow the evidence wherever it leads. And *question everything,* including authority. Do these things and the cosmos is yours.

If the series of pilgrimages toward understanding our actual circumstances in the universe, the origin of life, and the laws of nature are not spiritual quests, then I don't know what could be.

I am not a scientist, just a hunter-gatherer of stories. The ones I treasure most are those about the searchers who have helped us find our way in the great dark ocean, and the islands of light they left to us.

Here are stories of searchers who dared to venture into the bottomless ocean of the cosmos. Let's travel together to the worlds they discovered—the lost worlds, the worlds that still flourish, and the worlds yet to come.

In the pages that follow, I want to tell you the story about the unknown genius who sent a letter 50 years into the future that guided the successful Apollo mission to the moon. And another about the scientist who made contact with an ancient life-form which, like us, uses symbolic language to communicate. These beings who reflexively make mathematical calculations informed by physics and astronomy live a commitment to a consensual democracy that puts ours to shame.

I want to take you to the worlds that science has made it possible for us to imagine, bring back to life, and even visit: one where it rains diamonds, and the ancient city at the bottom of the sea where life on Earth may have begun. I want you to witness what is perhaps the most intimate stellar relationship in the cosmos, two stars locked in perpetual embrace, joined by a bridge of fire eight million miles long.

Let's eavesdrop together on the hidden worldwide terrestrial network that is an ancient collaboration among the kingdoms of life. I want to tell you about the little-known scientist who provided the key to a long-lost world. This same man also exposed a logical hole in reality more than 200 years ago, one that still remains unexplained, despite Einstein's best efforts.

Most heart-wrenching to me is the passion of the man who chose a slow horrible death at the hands of one of the most terrifying murderers in history. He might have saved himself by telling a scientific lie. But he just couldn't. His disciples willingly followed him into martyrdom to protect what must have been nothing more than an abstraction to them—the generations to come. *Us.*

Which brings us to the possible world that excites me the most—the future we can still have on this one. The misuse of science endangers our civilization, but science also has redemptive powers. It can cleanse a planetary atmosphere overburdened with carbon dioxide. It can set life free to neutralize the toxins that we have scattered so carelessly. In a society that aspires to become a democracy, a conscious and motivated public can will this possible world into existence.

These are stories that make me more optimistic about our future. Through them I have come to feel more intensely the romance of science and the wonder of being alive right now, at these particular coordinates in spacetime, less alone, more at home, here in the cosmos.

—ANN DRUYAN

CHAPTER ONE

LADDER TO THE STARS

Not I, but the world says it, all is one.
—HERACLITUS, CIRCA 500 B.C.E.

In this great future, you can't forget your past.
—BOB MARLEY, "NO WOMAN NO CRY"

For 99% of the time since our species came to be,
we were hunters and foragers . . . We were bounded only by
the Earth and the ocean and the sky . . .
. . . We, who cannot even put our own planetary home
in order . . . are we to venture out into space, move worlds,
re-engineer planets, spread to neighboring star systems?
. . . By the time we're ready to settle even the nearest other
planetary systems, we will have changed. The simple passage
of so many generations will have changed us. Necessity will
have changed us. We're an adaptable species.
. . . For all our failings, despite our limitations and fallibility,
we humans are capable of greatness . . . How far will
our nomadic species have wandered by the end
of the next century? And the next millennium?
—CARL SAGAN, *PALE BLUE DOT*

The stunning sweep of Saturn's rings—gravity's rainbow. NASA's Cassini spacecraft provides perspective for the pale blue dot, Earth, nearly 900 million miles in the distance.

We are very young, newcomers to the vastness. We cling to our shore on the cosmic ocean like the toddlers we are, making the occasional foray away from our mother before remembering our fear and scurrying back to her protection.

Half a century ago we humans paid a series of brief episodic visits to the moon. Our voyages of exploration have been conducted by robots ever since. In 1977, we sent Voyager 1, our boldest robotic emissary, farther away from Earth than anything we have ever touched, beyond the reach of the winds from our star, into the interstellar deep.

But our sun is just the closest star. At the 38,000 miles an hour that Voyager 1 is traveling, it would take the spacecraft almost 80,000 years to get to the next nearest star, Proxima Centauri. That's only a trip from one star to another in the Milky Way galaxy, a gravitational collective of hundreds of billions of stars. And our Milky Way galaxy is only one of perhaps a *trillion galaxies—two trillion* if we count all the dwarf galaxies that have since merged into the larger galaxies such as our own. These observations present us with a cosmos of billions of trillions of stars and likely a thousand times as many possible worlds.

One of the biggest stars in the Milky Way, Antares, shines brightly over Chile's Atacama Desert despite its location more than 600 light-years from Earth.

And that's just the part of the universe we can see. Most of the cosmos is hidden from us by curtains of time and distance. The early faster-than-light expansion of the fabric of spacetime sent huge volumes of the universe beyond the reach of our most powerful telescopes. And there is the possibility that our entire universe, a place of staggering immensity to us, might just be one tiny particle in a multiverse beyond our ken or imagining. No wonder we feel afraid and cling to delusions of our centrality, to our cherished status of being the Creator's only children. In the face of this overwhelming reality, how can tiny beings who regularly get lost on a dot come to feel at home in the universe?

Ever since we've been human we've been telling ourselves stories to help us cope with our fear of the darkness. "Darkness" is a quality, not a quantity. Night in a child's bedroom is a cosmos all its own. Our story-driven species finds its way by parsing the darkness into narratives. Before there was science, we had no way to test our stories against reality. We were adrift on the ocean of spacetime with no idea of *where* or *when* we were, until generations of searchers began to establish our coordinates.

Our latest understanding of how old the universe is comes from the European Space Agency's Planck satellite, which scanned the whole sky for more than a year, meticulously measuring the light that was first emitted when the universe was newborn, a mere 380,000 years after the big bang. The Planck mission revealed a cosmos that was actually 13.82 billion years old—a hundred million years older than scientists previously thought.

This is one of the things I love about science. When the evidence for a slightly older universe was discovered, there were no scientists who sought to suppress it. As soon as the new data were verified, this revision in our understanding was embraced by the whole scientific community. That permanently revolutionary attitude, that openness to change, at the heart of science is what makes it so effective.

THE SCIENTIFIC STORY OF TIME begins so long ago, we need to break it down into human terms. The Cosmic Calendar translates all of time, that 13.82 billion years of the scientific version of the story, into something we can all relate to, a single Earth year. Time begins in the upper left-hand corner with the big bang on January 1 and ends at midnight on December 31, in the lower right-hand corner. On this scale, every month represents a little more than a billion years. Every day represents 38 million years. Every hour, almost two million years. A single cosmic minute is 26,000 years. A second of the cosmic year takes 440 years, not much more time than has elapsed since Galileo's first look through a telescope.

And that's why the Cosmic Calendar is so meaningful to me. For the first nine billion years of time, there was no planet Earth. It's not until the cosmic year is two-thirds over, not until late summer, on August 31, that our tiny world coalesces out of the disk of gas and dust surrounding our star. Nothing of ours even exists for most of the history of the universe. I find that a profound source of humility.

Our planet took quite a beating for much of its first billion years. In the beginning, it was all part of the collisions between the new worlds that swept their orbits clean of most debris. Later it was likely the solar system–wide chaos caused by massive Jupiter and Saturn drifting into other orbital lanes and gravitationally luring asteroids from their orbits into collisions with the planets and moons.

This Late Heavy Bombardment, as it's known, wasn't even over before life got started at the bottom of the sea. This is encouraging news for those of us who hope to find life elsewhere in the universe. The story of our star and its worlds is probably a common process throughout the cosmos. The bodies that bombarded Earth could have been a routine delivery service for the necessary ingredients for life, and even the heat required to get life cooking.

Every living thing on Earth is thought to descend from a single origin. We think it began in the deep ocean darkness on September 2, in a lost city of rocky towers on the ocean floor, a story told in much greater detail later on in our voyage. Within this first life was

ABOVE: Low tide in Australia's Shark Bay reveals microbe colonies similar to those alive more than three billion years ago. **OPPOSITE:** A 160-million-year-old fossil found in China in 2011 suggests the first placental animal looked like a shrew.

a copying mechanism that could make more life. It was a molecule, a collection of atoms, shaped like a twisted ladder—DNA. One of its great strengths was its imperfection. Sometimes it made copying errors or was damaged by those incoming cosmic rays. All of it was random, but some of these mutations led to more successful lifeforms—what we call *evolution by natural selection*. The ladder grew, adding more and more rungs.

It took another three billion years for life to evolve from one-celled organisms to the complexity of plants we can see with the naked eye. But there were no eyes to see. However, even back then there was consciousness. Arguably, the one-celled organism that knows "you I eat, me I don't" is already evincing a degree of awareness.

THE STORY OF HOW LIFE became human is on that same continuum. But there was a dramatic new development during the last week of the cosmic year. If the Cosmic Calendar had holidays, surely December 26 would be one of them. For it was some time on this day, about 200 million years ago, that the mammals appeared.

The first true mammals were tiny shrewlike creatures. When I say "tiny," I mean really small—not much bigger than a paper clip. They only ventured out at night because their predators, dinosaurs and others, ruled the day. Back in the Triassic, the odds must have seemed stacked against these tiny creatures, in favor of the monstrously powerful dinosaurs. But the meek did inherit the Earth.

The mammals possessed a new component in their brains: the neocortex. Like them, it was small at first, but it contained an awesome potential for growth and development—including the capacity for social organization in larger groups. The mammals brought another innovation. They suckled their young. They nurtured them. Mother's Day on the Cosmic Calendar falls on December 26.

Evolution by natural selection means that those living things that can better adapt to their environment are more likely to survive and leave offspring. Intelligence—that is, if you use it—can be a huge selective advantage. By folding into different layers, the neocortex added more surface area for information processing. The lobes of the brain became more furrowed, allowing still more area for computing power.

The brain continued to evolve, changing shape, growing larger and getting more folds and creases. At around 7 p.m. on December 31, we had an evolutionary parting of the ways with our closest relatives, the bonobos and chimpanzees. They would evolve into forest creatures that groomed each other, grieved for lost friends and kin, used reeds as tools to lure ants for a meal, taught their young to do the same, and paused

together to admire the sunset. But little is known about what they were like at the time of our last common ancestor.

Today, we share the vast majority of our genes with them, about 99 percent. So, what makes us so different from chimpanzees? Why, of all the five billion species that have ever lived on Earth, did we alone evolve into the civilization-making, world-altering, spacefaring life-form we are today? Not so long ago we were mystified by fire. Somehow we transformed ourselves into beings who communicate at the speed of light. Who see into particles, atoms, and cells. Who look back to the beginning of time and find the light of distant galaxies across billions of light-years all the way to the edge of forever.

It may come down to nothing more than this: Around seven million years ago something happened on a scale infinitesimally small that led to a change that would affect this whole planet and ultimately touch others. The largest human cell, an egg, is barely visible to the human eye. The smallest in volume, a sperm cell, is just too small to see. But inscribed within the nucleus of most every cell is a coded message consisting of three billion base pairs, or rungs, in the twisted ladder of the double helix.

The fate of this planet was changed forever by an event in *a single rung,* involving just 13 atoms. How small is 13 atoms? It's a quadrillionth the size of a grain of salt. A mutation *one-quadrillionth the size of a grain of salt* occurred in the DNA of one of our ancestors several million years ago and that's part of why you're who you are, reading these words at this moment.

Every source of self-esteem—everything we've learned, and built—is the result of a change in a base pair of a single gene, just a single rung on a ladder three billion rungs long. That single rung programmed the neocortex to grow larger still and fold more deeply. Maybe it was a random zap from a cosmic ray, or a simple error in transmission from one cell to another. Whatever it was, it led to a change in our species that would ultimately affect every other species of life on Earth. It happened after dinnertime on New Year's Eve on this Cosmic Calendar of ours.

To think that, for good or evil, our ability to feel loyalty and concern for increasingly larger groups, our obsession with certain belief systems, our capacity to imagine the future, our power to transform the world and to search the cosmos for answers—the very name we gave to our own species, *Homo sapiens,* Latin for "wise man"—all of it might not come down to anything much more than this: a single rung on our microscopic ladder to the stars.

For most of the last hour on the Cosmic Calendar—for more than 59 of its 60 remaining minutes—our ancestors were proto-humans who evolved into hunters and gatherers, living in small bands, *"bounded only by the earth and the ocean and the sky."*

When people just shrug and say "chalk it up to human nature," it puzzles me. They're usually talking about our greed, our arrogance and violence. But we've been human for half a million years or more. For most of that time we weren't that way at all. How do we know? From the accounts of explorers and anthropologists encountering surviving hunter-gatherer societies across four centuries. There are, of course, exceptions. Scarcity has always brought out the worst in us. But the overwhelming consensus paints a picture of humans that lived in relative harmony with each other and the environment.

We shared the little we had because we knew that our survival depended on the group. We didn't prize wealth beyond our needs because it would just weigh us down as we wandered. We began to differ from our nonhuman primate ancestors with their alpha males bullying their way to dominance. The surviving evidence contains instances of gender equality and painstaking efforts to share resources equitably. Most of these societies acted as if they knew how much they needed each other.

The most prized virtue among our hunter-gatherer ancestors was humility. It was as if our ancestors recognized that the hunter who got too full of himself posed a danger to the group. If he seemed too boastful when he brought home his prey for them to eat, they would claim that the meat was tough and didn't taste good. If that didn't remind him of how he should act, they would do the one thing he feared most—they would shun him. No matter what he did, they would act as if he wasn't there at all.

(Sometimes when an individual is raised to impossible heights of celebrity and then disgraced and banished from public life, I wonder if these events are not ritualized echoes of something deep within us from our distant past.)

And where was God? Everywhere. In the rocks and the rivers, in the trees, in the birds and every living thing. And that was human nature for half a million years.

AT 11:52 P.M. ON NEW YEAR'S EVE on the Cosmic Calendar, or a couple of hundred thousand years ago, Africa was home to all the world's *Homo sapiens*—all 10,000 of them. When I learn that a species' population is down to 10,000, I worry about them. If you were an extraterrestrial visiting Earth on a survey mission back then, you might have thought we were an endangered species. Now, we number in the billions. What happened?

Our ancestors made a giant leap forward in a place called Blombos Cave, and perhaps, in many others that we've yet to discover. Located at the southern tip of Africa, along the coast on the Indian Ocean, Blombos Cave is our oldest surviving chemistry lab and the earliest evidence for one of our species' greatest adaptive advantages: the ability to take what's available in our environment and reshape it for new purposes.

Beneath the lofty natural ceiling of the cave are seashells used as mixing pots, an assembly line of lance heads, ocher-processing kits, engraved bones, meticulously assembled beads of uniform size strung together, tortoise and ostrich eggshells, and refined

The first work of art? The earliest artifact of human culture yet discovered, this ocher block from South Africa's Blombos Cave was crafted some 70,000 years ago.

bone and stone tools. What were these first chemists like? Us. No traces of our ancestors' bones have yet been found in Blombos Cave. Just seven human teeth. We can tell from them that these people were anatomically just like us. And not *just* anatomically.

Seventy sea snail shells of similar size and color, all pierced in the same place, attest to bead production by Blombos jewelers. And they did something else that gives me the chills. They were conducting chemistry experiments with a mineral rich in iron: ocher. Using abalone shells as test tubes, they mixed the ocher with the dust of animal bones and charcoal. And then they formed it into an elongated brick. The ocher itself may have been used to decorate objects or humans with bits of red color, but it may also have had other applications—to preserve animal hides or as a medicine, or as a way to sharpen their tools, or maybe as an insect repellent.

Here comes the part that, as far as we know, was something completely new on the planet. They engraved the ocher with a geometric design. Art. Not to be eaten. Not to provide shelter or to catch food or attract a mate. But to symbolize something. Or just to be. The distinct crosshatched design looks a little bit like a ladder, or . . . a double helix. Whatever it was supposed to convey, it's the earliest remnant we have of human culture. We had found a way to leave something distinctly human behind. A means to communicate, however enigmatically, to you and me a hundred thousand years away in the future. A great power was first discovered here in Blombos Cave.

Over the tens of thousands of years that followed, some of our ancestors moved out of Africa to explore and settle the planet, leaving evidence of their desire to be remembered. In one particularly memorable testament to human ingenuity in the Cave of the Spider, in what is now Valencia, Spain, a human figure dares to climb a rope, or ladder, using a smoke pot to raid a beehive for

A cave painting near Valencia, Spain, from around 5000 B.C.E. depicts
a human figure using a smoke pot to chase away bees and steal their honey.
The artist used a hole in the wall for the hive.

honey. In the literature, the human is always assumed to be a man, but I wonder if that's just an artifact from the days of our species-wide assumption that the term "man" subsumed us all. I think the honey thief looks more like a woman. There's nothing visible in that cave painting to contradict me.

Eight thousand years after it was painted, the bees still flee the smoke, enduring proof of an early human victory over our greatest nemesis—time. But as old as this image is, it still dates back to less than 20 seconds ago on the Cosmic Calendar.

JUST A FEW THOUSAND YEARS BEFORE, people all over the world discovered another great power. Instead of hunting and foraging for food or following the migratory herds, our ancestors learned how to grow food in the earth and domesticate the wild animals. This changed everything. It moved our ancestors to do something else they had never done before. They settled down and moved indoors. They invented new tools—technology—to plant and pull food out of the earth. Our relationship to nature, and to each other, would never be the same.

The agricultural revolution—the domestication of plants and animals—is the mother of all revolutions because all others trace back to it. Its consequences reach far beyond even our own moment in time. And, like most revolutions, this one brought change that was both great and horrifying. The word "home" must have taken on a new meaning. Where it had once meant wherever we wandered on Earth, it now came to mean a specific place on the planet. And over time those settlements grew larger, until, at about 20 cosmic seconds to midnight, another leap.

Welcome to one of the mothers of all cities, Çatalhöyük, a community on the Anatolian plain that is now part of Turkey. I'm imagining it's 9,000 years ago and everyone has settled in for the

Female figurines, some standing and some seated like this one, have been found among the ruins of Çatalhöyük. Some archaeologists have interpreted them as fertility goddesses, but others believe they honored female elders within the community.

An artist's depiction of Çatalhöyük, one of the first proto-cities, about 9,000 years ago, before the street and the front door were invented.

evening. Tonight, roughly the same number of people who once populated all of Africa are living together in a proto-city like this one. Çatalhöyük consisted of attached dwellings covering 33 acres. Things sure have changed in the 90,000 years since humans assembled a chemistry set at Blombos Cave.

The city was so new back then, they hadn't invented the street yet—or the window. So the only way you could get into your apartment was to walk over your neighbors' rooftops. A ladder was propped against the skylight opening of your apartment.

Çatalhöyük lacked something much more significant than streets and windows. There was no palace here. The bitter price of inequality that the invention of agriculture cost human society had yet to be paid. Here, there was no dominance of the few over the many. There was no one percent attaining lavish wealth while most everyone else merely subsisted or failed to subsist. The ethos of sharing was still alive and well. There is evidence of violence against women and children, but the weakest ate the same food that the strongest ate. Scientific analyses of the nutrition of the women, men, and children who lived here show a remarkable similarity. And everyone lived in the same kind of home. But, man, it was anything but drab. Dominating the room was a giant head of an auroch with massive pointed horns, mounted on the richly painted wall. The walls were lavishly festooned with the teeth, bones, and skins of other animals.

The apartments at Çatalhöyük have a distinctly modern look. The floor plan is highly utilitarian and modular, uniform from dwelling to dwelling, with cubicles for work, dining, entertaining, and sleep. Bare wood beams support the ceiling. It was home for an extended family of seven to 10 people.

The ocher that our ancestors picked up in Africa about a hundred thousand years before was now the medium of choice for the interior decorators of Çatalhöyük. Murals abound of aurochs, leopards, a running man, vultures pecking the flesh from headless corpses, hunters taunting a deer. And they didn't just use it to depict animals. It played an important ceremonial role in the way they honored their loved ones after death.

A procession, bearing a corpse, would leave Çatalhöyük for a wide-open space on the Anatolian plain. A high platform awaited them. They would leave the corpse on the platform to be consumed by birds of prey and the elements. One person would remain to stand guard and assure that the bones would not be taken. Vultures circled the platform, a storm moved in. Time passed. The procession returned when nothing was left but the skeleton. Now, it was time to decorate it with red ocher and fold it into a fetal position before burying it beneath the living room floor of their apartment. From time to time, perhaps in the context of ritual, they would open the tombs beneath them and remove the skull of a loved one to keep with them where they lived. I wonder if they were more at peace with their dead than we are with ours.

And the red ocher had yet another profound application. They used it to create two new art forms—history and cartography. An artist drew the contours of the rounded rooftops, all connected into a single organism in relation to the nearby volcano. For the first time ever, humans created a two-dimensional reflection of the reality of their location in space and time. "This is where my home is in relation to the volcano." And with a few magical strokes depicting wisps of smoke, the artist sent a message across 9,000 years: "I was here when the volcano reawakened."

THE EXPERIMENT AT ÇATALHÖYÜK and other proto-cities was successful and within a few thousand years there were cities everywhere. When people from different cultures congregate in a single place, ideas are exchanged and new possibilities arise. The city is a kind of brain—an incubator of new ideas.

In the city of Amsterdam, in the 17th century, citizens of the old and new worlds mingled as they never had before. This cross-pollination produced a golden age of science and art. In Italy, Giordano Bruno and Galileo had announced the existence of other worlds. For this heresy they had been made to suffer cruelly. But a mere 50 years later in Holland, the astronomer Christiaan Huygens, who held the same belief, was showered with honors.

Light was a motif of the age, the symbolic enlightenment of freedom of thought and religion, the light of exploration as our planet's humans began their brutal stumbling toward the recognition that we inhabit a single organism, the light that made glorious the paintings of the time, particularly the work of Vermeer, and light as an object of scientific inquiry.

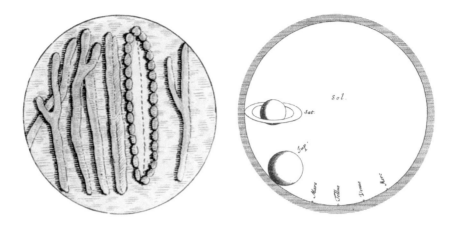

LEFT: First to view life under a microscope, Antoni van Leeuwenhoek drew the life-forms he saw, calling them "animalcules." **RIGHT:** In his 1698 *Cosmotheoros,* Christiaan Huygens depicted *Sol,* the sun, in the center, with planets circling it.

In the Amsterdam of that time, there lived three men whose passion for light inspired them to invent and perfect devices that could make light do seemingly impossible things. They found a way to concentrate or disperse rays of light with just a curved piece of glass—the lens. A textile merchant's gadget for examining the quality of finely stitched tapestry became a window into hidden worlds.

Antoni van Leeuwenhoek used a single lens to reveal the cosmos of the microbial world. He examined spit and sperm and pond water with it and discovered whole communities of living things that no one had ever dreamt existed.

His friend Christiaan Huygens used two lenses to bring the stars, planets, and moons closer. Huygens became the first to see that Saturn's rings did not touch the planet and to understand their nature. He discovered Saturn's moon Titan, the second largest moon in our solar system. He invented the pendulum clock and so much else, including the motion picture projector and animated cartoon. We'll spend an all-nighter with him, later on in our travels.

Huygens recognized that the stars were other suns, orbited by their own systems of planets and moons. He imagined a universe filled with an infinite number of worlds, many graced by life. But why was there no hint of those other worlds and their living creatures in the sacred books? Why would God leave that out? God had been very clear on that point. He made no mention of having any other children besides us.

Whatever disquiet this contradiction may have stirred in the hearts and minds of the leaders of the Enlightenment, there was one man who dared to address it head-on. He was another wizard of light. When his late father's dried fruit importing company failed, he made his living grinding the lenses for finding hidden worlds, both great and small.

Baruch Spinoza, born in 1632, had been a member of the Jewish congregation of Amsterdam through his teenage years. But in his early 20s, he began to speak publicly of a new kind of god. Spinoza's god was not an angry and disappointed tyrant, obsessed with what rituals you performed, what you ate, and who you loved. Spinoza's god was the physical laws of the universe. His god took no interest in your sins and his Torah was the book of nature.

Spinoza's fellow congregants at the synagogue in Amsterdam were understandably unnerved by what they viewed as his impiety. The Jews of Amsterdam were mostly refugees from the vicious Inquisitions in Spain and Portugal, where so many of them had been tortured, forced to convert or sit by helplessly as their loved ones were murdered. Amsterdam had offered the Jews a refuge and they must have seen Spinoza's radical ideas as a threat to their hard-won security in Holland. They excommunicated the young rebel and decreed, as our hunter-gatherer ancestors might have done for a very different cause, that he must be forever shunned.

Their decree of July 1656 was an inversion of the prayer in Deuteronomy 6:4, 6-7 that commanded them and their ancestors to love the lord with everything they had. I learned it as a child and remember it still.

Hear, O Israel: The LORD our God is one LORD:
. . . .
And these words, which I command thee this day, shall be in thine heart:
And thou shalt teach them diligently unto thy children, and shalt talk of them when thou sittest in thine house, and when thou walkest by the way, and when thou liest down, and when thou risest up.

The condemnation by the rabbis of the Jewish community of Amsterdam used a variation on that same trope to express their rage at Spinoza's "evil opinions" and "abominable heresies": "Cursed be he by day and cursed be he by night; cursed be he when he lies down and cursed be he when he rises up. Cursed be he when he goes out and cursed be he when he comes in."

We can understand the anxieties of the Jewish community. They had seen their world turn into a nightmare in Spain and Portugal and reasonably craved tranquility and acceptance above all else. But, still, there is irony here. The Torah prayer instructed us to think of God in every ordinary act we performed every day. And isn't that what Spinoza did when he came to see God everywhere, in everything—in all of nature, no matter what else he happened to be doing?

And this is why Spinoza felt a particular distaste for miracles. He devotes the sixth chapter of his *Theological-Political Treatise,* published in 1670, to an exhaustive exploration of why he could not bear their purported significance. Do not look for God in miracles, Spinoza was saying. Miracles are violations of the laws of nature. If God is the author of natural law, should not God be best apprehended in those laws? Miracles were misinterpretations of natural events. Earthquakes, floods, droughts were not to be taken personally. God was not a projection of human hopes and fears but the creative force behind the existence of the universe, a force best encountered through the study of nature's laws.

For thousands of years, since soon after the invention of agriculture, our sense of the sacred had been rootless in nature. We were taught that we had been created separately from the fabric of life. And God asked us to deny and subdue our natural selves, which were largely sinful in his view. To worship Spinoza's god was to study and revere the laws of nature.

Spinoza accepted the punishment and rejection of the Dutch Jewish community with equanimity. Then, as now, there were those who were threatened by this view of God. Spinoza was attacked by a knife-wielding assailant who only succeeded in slashing his cloak before fleeing. Spinoza never had it mended, wearing the shredded cape as a badge of honor. He moved away, finally settling near The Hague, where he continued grinding lenses for microscopes and telescopes.

There was something even more daring in his *Theological-Political Treatise* than his rejection of miracles. Spinoza wrote that the Bible was not dictated by God but written by human beings. To Spinoza, an official state religion was more than spiritual coercion. Spinoza regarded the supernatural events central to the major religious traditions as nothing more than organized superstition. He believed that this kind of magical thinking posed a danger to the citizens of a free society.

No one had ever said these things aloud before. Spinoza knew that he was going too far even for free-thinking Holland. The *Theological-Political Treatise* introduced the ideas at the heart of the American and many another revolution, including the fundamental need of a democratic society to separate itself from any church. It bore no author's name, no true city of origin, and a fictitious publisher. Despite this, word of Spinoza's authorship spread throughout Europe, making him the most notorious figure on the continent. He died in 1677 at 44, possibly from inhaling all those fine particles of glass dust during his years of grinding lenses.

In November 1920, another man with a passion for light made a pilgrimage to the humble workroom near The Hague that had been preserved as a testament to the vast influence of Spinoza's philosophy. This scientist, world-famous for finding a new law of nature, was often asked if he believed in God. Albert Einstein would answer, "I believe in Spinoza's God, who reveals himself in the harmony of all that exists."

OUR UNDERSTANDING OF NATURE'S LAWS has advanced far beyond Spinoza's wildest dreams. But how can we repair our dysfunctional relationship with nature itself? Let me tell you another story, a parable of one of life's most enduring collaborations. We'll need to walk back to the afternoon of December 29 on the Cosmic Calendar.

In that long ago time, there were two kingdoms. An alliance was formed between them, one that would bring them both riches beyond measure. It was a beautiful relationship for nearly a hundred million years—and then a new kind of being evolved in one of the kingdoms. Its descendants plundered the riches and violated the alliance. In their arrogance they became a mortal danger to both kingdoms . . . and to themselves.

This parable is true. It's the story of two of the half dozen realms of life on Earth—the plant and animal kingdoms.

It's not easy being green. Sex is challenging when you're stuck in one place. There's no dating. You just sit there and cast your seed to the winds. Literally. You just wait for the wind to blow. If you get lucky, some of your pollen will be carried away and land on the female sexual reproductive part of another plant—its pistil, a part of its flower.

The plants played this hit-or-miss game of chance for a couple of hundred million years—until insects evolved to play Cupid. The result was one of the great coevolution marriages in the history of life. The insect would visit a flower for a dinner of protein-rich pollen. Inevitably some of the pollen would stick to the body of the insect.

When it was ready for its next meal, the insect would visit another flower, inadvertently bringing along the leftovers on its body. That pollen fertilized the next flower, allowing it to reproduce.

It was a win-win deal for the flowers and the insects, causing a series of evolutionary developments. A plant arose that produced sugary nectar in addition to pollen. Now, the insects came not just for their meal of pollen but also for dessert. The insects got chubbier, evolved furry bodies and even little pouches on their legs to snag more pollen on their daily rounds of the flowers—bees.

This was a bonus for yet another species of the animal kingdom. Us. Our ancestors loved honey, as the woman/man with the smoke pot in the Spanish cave and numerous other ancient images attest. They feasted on it and even figured out how to get high on it by fermenting it into a drink called mead.

The birds and the bats wanted in on the pollination business, but they never achieved the same degree of success as the insects and most especially the bees. We have a lot of reasons to be grateful to bees—beauty, for instance. Plants, in their competition with each other for the reproductive services of the bees, evolved other strategies besides nectar. Fragrance and color.

Bees have three photoreceptors, just as our eyes do, only theirs are different. Ours perceive red, blue, and green; theirs see

ABOVE: Golden grains of pollen dapple a carpenter bee's body.
OPPOSITE: A bee's-eye view of a bergamot blossom, thanks to ultraviolet-induced visible fluorescence photography

ultraviolet, blue, and green. They perceive red in the reddish wavelengths of orange and yellow.

We are indebted to the bees for something even more vital to our survival than beauty. Every third bite of food you take, and this is even true for those of us who are carnivores, was made possible by these little guys. And they didn't just increase the quantity of available food. We owe them much of the biodiversity that has made our food supply so dependable.

And now we come to the sad part of the parable, when a newer member of the animal kingdom messes with that ancient alliance through a lack of awareness and thoughtless acts of greed and short-term thinking. I think you know where this is headed and whom the culprit will turn out to be.

OUR HUNTER-GATHERER LIFESTYLE had half a million years to evolve in a balanced equilibrium with nature. Yes, there were extinctions due to overhunting, but our ancestors never caused a catastrophe on a global scale. The invention of agriculture some 10,000 or 12,000 years ago changed us. In some sense, we've been living with a bad case of postagricultural stress syndrome ever since. We haven't had enough time yet to evolve strategies to live in harmony with nature and with each other. The blessing and the curse that stemmed from the agricultural revolution and our abilities to enhance and enlarge our food supply, which resulted in a burgeoning human population, have brought us to the crisis we now face.

Somewhere, I imagine there's a memorial to all the broken branches on the tree of life. It's a place I call the Halls of Extinction. You must cross a lifeless wasteland to find it, an imposing edifice of austere and tragic form, windowless and bereft of landscaping to soften its testament to finality. An eerie beam of light shines down through its oculus on the sand-strewn floor of the granite circular central chamber. Six grand entrances lead to separate hallways, each filled with dioramas of the life-forms that perished in the six mass extinction events so catastrophic that life itself on this world was endangered.

Until just a few years ago there were only five named mass extinction events, and so only five of these six hallways were named, their titles engraved over the arches—Ordovician, Devonian, Permian, Triassic, and Cretaceous—honoring the cataclysmic chemical, geological, and astronomical events that caused so much death. Now the sixth hallway is named, but it is different. It has our name on it: Anthropocene. "Anthropo" derives from the Greek for "human," *cene,* the Greek suffix for "recent." We are now officially living in the age of human-caused mass extinction.

LET'S NOT GO DOWN THAT HALLWAY NOW. We'll save it for another time. We're just setting out on this voyage of discovery and we humans have beaten the odds many times before. Why, just recently we accomplished something that Einstein himself deemed impossible. He erred because he underestimated our potential. We should not do the same.

It was Einstein who first saw the cosmos as an ocean made out of space and time. He realized that matter could send ripples across spacetime. In 1916, Einstein imagined that catastrophic explosions of matter in the far reaches of the universe should create something much bigger than ripples—great waves—gravitational waves.

Now, here is that rare instance where even Einstein's imagination failed a challenge. He stated flatly that it would never be possible to design and execute an experiment to prove the existence of gravitational waves. Why not? Try to imagine measuring the width of a human hair all the way from a distant galaxy. Einstein reasoned that the gravitational waves would be too faint to detect across the vast distances of the cosmos. By the time they crossed this largest of oceans, they would just be too feeble for us to perceive.

For another hundred years, theoretical and experimental physicists would struggle to find direct evidence that would verify their existence. How small was the thing they hunted? Smaller than an atom, smaller than a single particle; in fact, one ten-thousandth the diameter of a single proton. That would allow us to trace it back to its source—the collision of two black holes a billion light-years away.

In 1967, scientists and engineers began the project that would come to be known as the Laser Interferometer Gravitational-Wave Observatory, or LIGO. All they needed was a massive event to disturb spacetime—say, two colliding black holes—and a pair of detectors so sensitive that they could register the impact more than a billion light-years away. When the black holes collided, they would set off a spacetime tsunami that stretched space in all directions. Time itself slowed down—before speeding up and slowing down again.

Why did each detector have to be two and a half miles long? Because to hear something so faint, you need really big ears. And why two detectors? Because that was the way you could distinguish the gravitational wave from mere noise. The second detector was needed to provide the confirmation. By having two separate detectors a continent apart in Livingston, Louisiana, and Hanford, Washington, scientists could calculate the tiny gap in the arrival time of the signal. That would allow us to trace it back to its source— the collision of two black holes a billion light-years away.

Just like a great wave on the sea, gravitational waves dissipate as they travel. By the time Einstein had his revolutionary idea a century ago, this gravitational wave was still about a hundred light-years from Earth, gently washing over yellow dwarf star HD 37124, and its planets and moons, in our own Milky Way galaxy. Wonder if anybody was there to detect it on that world?

An artist's conception of two black holes about to merge. In 2017 LIGO observatories detected a gravitational wave caused by such a collision that occurred 1.1 billion years ago. It resulted in a single black hole 20 times the mass of the sun.

By the time the gravitational wave reached the LIGO detectors, it was but a tiny wisp of its once mighty self. Nothing more than a chirp, but enough to prove the existence of gravitational waves, to provide the first direct evidence for black holes and to win the scientists who led the project the 2017 Nobel Prize in physics.

There is something about a 50-year-long project and the multigenerational nature of these most ambitious scientific endeavors that remind me of the building of the soaring cathedrals of our past. They exemplify an expression of selflessness in the larger service of the human enterprise that gives me hope.

The Breakthrough Starshot project envisions ultralight nanocraft riding light at speeds of more than 100 million miles an hour. With this technology, a flyby mission could reach Proxima Centauri, our nearest neighboring star system, in only about 20 years.

AS I WRITE, SCIENTISTS and engineers are working on Breakthrough Starshot, humanity's first reconnaissance mission to the nearest star. They do so without the likely prospect of being alive when it is completed.

About 20 years from now an armada of a thousand ships will depart Earth. These interstellar craft, powered by the laser light captured in their sails, weigh but a gram. Each is no larger than a pea, and yet every one of them is equipped with all that NASA's Voyagers, our first interstellar spacecraft, have—and much more.

Inside each nanocraft is everything necessary to perform the preliminary reconnaissance of the worlds of another star, and return that visual and scientific information back to Earth.

Voyager 1 has been traveling at 38,000 miles an hour for more than 40 years. This is an impressive speed to us, and the ship is still running on a single gravitational assist that came from rounding massive Jupiter in the first years of its odyssey. But on the scale of even just a single galaxy, it's like running a race in a dream. Fast, yet far too slow to get anywhere.

The Starshot nanocraft will overtake Voyager in only *four days*. Astonishing, yes, but Starshot is still traveling at only 20 percent of the speed of light. The stars are very far apart. The nearest one, Proxima Centauri, is four light-years away. That's a 20-year-long, one-way trip.

In the Proxima Centauri system, we know there is a world in the habitable zone, where water might flow, and life might flourish. There may be more worlds in this system that we have yet to discover. Our robot emissaries will send back travelers' tales from this new world(s). Their data will race back to us on radio waves at the speed of light. They will take four years to reach us. What revelations will they send home 40-something years from now?

Some of you will be there to read these new pages in the book of nature.

From Blombos Cave to riding the light to the stars in just a few minutes on the Cosmic Calendar. Yes, we are at a dangerously critical branch point in our species' history. But it's not too late. We humans have proved we can exceed the most extravagant hopes of our greatest minds. The past and future possible worlds we are about to visit and the heroic searchers whose stories we are about to tell attest to our great powers to survive our technological adolescence, protect our little home, and secure safe passage across the great ocean of spacetime, no longer *bounded by the earth, the ocean, or the sky*.

CHAPTER TWO

OH, MIGHTY KING

Minds are not conquered by force,
but by love and high-mindedness.
—BARUCH SPINOZA, *THE ETHICS*, 1677

Do not hold grain waiting for higher prices
when people are hungry.
—ATTRIBUTED TO ZOROASTER

The entrance of Pir-e Sabz, a sacred Zoroastrian grotto in today's central Iran. Legend has it that Nikbanu, daughter of the last Sassanian king, took refuge here. Condensation inside the cave, imagined to be her tears of sorrow, earned the shrine its other name: Chak Chak, meaning "drip, drip."

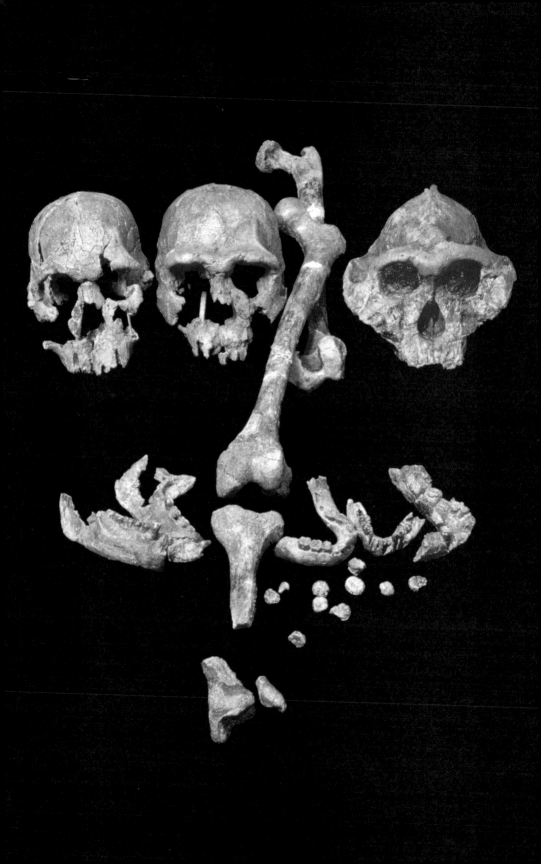

Here we are, some 10,000 years after the invention of agriculture, awakening to the cosmos and taking our first baby steps to explore it, at the very same moment that our short-term thinking and our greed threaten to bring our civilization down. We know we have to change if we don't want this to happen, but is that possible? Are we, as a species, capable of transforming ourselves? Or is there something inside us that impels us to self-destruction?

Carl Sagan and I were haunted by this question. We made a pact that we would follow the evidence wherever it might lead. Years of research and thinking about this matter became our book *Shadows of Forgotten Ancestors,* from which portions of this chapter have been adapted. If anything, the question that inspired us then feels more urgent than ever.

This question might be less of a mystery if human memory could reach all the way back to the beginning of life. But we have awakened to our distant past so recently. We have only just begun, in earnest, to try to reconstruct what may have happened to our species before our conscious memories kicked in—and even those events long before our existence as a species that may have resulted in congenital deficits.

Three skulls bear testament to an era when three different kinds of human families lived in the same time and place: from left, *Homo habilis, Homo erectus,* and *Australopithecus robustus.* Found in Kenya by Richard Leakey's expedition teams, all lived about 1.5 million years ago.

Wonderwerk Cave, South Africa, one of the earliest hearths. Our ancestors gathered here around their campfires as long as a million years ago, inventing the social structures that we still recognize in ourselves today.

I think of us humans as a family of amnesia victims who kept making up stories about our past until we found a means to reconstruct it—the sciences. Still, we sift through the earth to find the bits of flint and animal bone that are the few surviving artifacts of our childhood.

IF THERE ARE places on Earth that are sacred to our species, surely Wonderwerk Cave, in the Kurumanheuwels of the Northern Cape Province of South Africa, must be one of them. Wonderwerk is the earliest site we know of where fire was tamed for human needs. A million years ago, our ancestors gathered there and became among the first to kindle the hearth of human culture.

It's a cave that has the grand contours of a ballroom. Even the tallest among us can stand up in it and walk more than 400 feet into its deepest recess. Scientists from many disciplines worship here in their own way, practicing the arcane rituals of their creed, scanning the cave with lasers, scrutinizing each micron of pollen and sediment with optically stimulated luminescence and cosmogenic isotope dating techniques. All in an effort to piece together the lost history of this ancient place and, ultimately, to discover who we once were.

The scientific study of the way microscopic pieces of ash curl this way or that can help us differentiate between which fires were wild and those that were deliberately set and tended to grow more intense. The remnants of the fires deep in this cave, those that went cold many hundreds of thousands of years ago, tell us that our ancestors made these fires for warmth and for cooking.

Every one of us alive today is a member of the genus *Homo*. We are *Homo sapiens*—the so-called "wise men." Our forebears, the ones who gathered in Wonderwerk Cave, were *Homo erectus*—"man who stood up." They were not yet "us," but we carry them within us. We don't know much about them. We think they took care of each other when they became old or ill. We know they were skilled toolmakers.

Visit all the worlds of the sun—every comet, asteroid, moon, and planet—there is only one world where you will be able to build a fire. *Ours.* And that became possible only when there was sufficient oxygen in the atmosphere—just for the last 400 million years, or the last 10 days of the cosmic year. At Wonderwerk Cave, our ancestors tamed the power of fire and were handsomely rewarded for their ingenuity. It was around fires such as ones kindled there that we began to cook our food, which tenderized it, giving our bodies far more energy than that expended on the endless chewing of the uncooked, and therefore much tougher, raw meat. The fire warmed us and frightened away the predators that terrorized us. We gathered around the fire as a group at night, eating together and telling each other the stories that created a shared, learned identity with our kin and bound our children to our elders.

THE DOMESTICATION OF FIRE can be considered distinctly human among animals. (Plants have actually evolved survival strategies that exploit wildfires to vanquish competitors, but they cannot start them or put them out.) The recognition of fire's central role in human consciousness and culture reaches its apogee in the spiritual beliefs and practices of one of the oldest living religions.

Around the time of the ancient Hebrew prophet Abraham, there was another prophet in the land of Persia, in what is now Iran. As with Abraham, the year of his birth remains a mystery, with informed guesses placing these two patriarchs around four millennia ago. Zoroaster was his name, and fire was his avatar. Every Zoroastrian temple was consecrated to fire. Tending an eternal flame through the centuries was one of the few ritual obligations of the Zoroastrians. Fire symbolized both the purity of their god and the light of the illuminated mind.

Zoroaster's god, Ahura Mazda, didn't ask much—he didn't want ritual sacrifices, he didn't want money—all he asked of human beings was to keep that flame burning bright, to think good thoughts, speak good words, and perform good deeds. But for some reason, most people couldn't fulfill these simple requests. Often they had bad thoughts and said bad things. And some of them committed crimes that were evil. *Why?*

We still don't have a comprehensive answer to this question. One of the earliest attempts to answer it was formulated by the Zoroastrians. All the bad things in the world, the crimes committed by humans, as well as the catastrophes of natural disasters and disease, were caused by Ahura Mazda's polar opposite, the original evil twin, Angra Mainyu, and his unceasing mischief. Ahura Mazda

Angra Mainyu, archetype for evil among the Zoroastrians, savages a bull in this image based on a bas-relief from ancient Persepolis.

looked to human beings to help him defeat Angra Mainyu. Any person, by their actions, could tip the scales of the whole future of the universe in either the direction of good or evil.

There is a depiction of Angra Mainyu in the muscular, still vivid bas-relief at Persepolis, the magnificent complex built by the Persian emperors of the sixth century B.C.E. when theirs was the only superpower on Earth. Angra Mainyu has short, stubby horns, a long pointy tail, and cloven hoofs for feet. Sound familiar? Our own conception of the devil is a distant echo of Angra Mainyu. Zoroastrianism was the dominant religion from Greece to India for a thousand years. No wonder it was so influential on the religions that came after.

Ahura Mazda was a god who liked dogs, not cats. In fact, if a Zoroastrian accidentally killed a dog, the only way to atone for this crime was to kill ten thousand cats. Angra Mainyu, on the other hand, was into cats. Is the fact that cats are associated with witches, the devil's handmaidens, an artifact of this preference?

IN THE PRESCIENTIFIC WORLD, when evil reared its ugly head, what better way to understand it than the unceasing malevolence of Angra Mainyu.

Imagine you're an ancient Persian minding your own business, when the beloved family dog, a saluki, suddenly changes from the loyal family protector you have loved for years into a seething monster. His expression becomes unmistakably malevolent. He growls viciously and bares his canines, as bits of foam begin to form at the corners of his mouth and drip from his exposed vampiric incisors. He suddenly rises from his sitting position and moves deliberately toward your youngest, a seven-month-old daughter, cooing in her basket. In a horrifying flash, you realize your dog is about to lunge at your baby. How else to explain this horrifying metamorphosis as anything other than demonic possession?

But this is not a story of good and evil, of the struggle between a god and a demon. It's actually just a story of a predator and its prey. In this case, the predator is microscopic. Disease microbes are diabolically clever hunters—they can bring down their hosts after exploiting them as delivery systems for the disease they carry. Because of a chance encounter with a rabid bat sometime between three weeks and several months back, that poor, unlucky dog, through no fault of his own, now finds himself the main character in a zombie horror story.

Once they've broken into the bloodstream, a pack of bullet-shaped viruses race to his brain, where they will attack his limbic system. These rabies viruses, or lyssaviruses, named for the ancient

Greek spirit of madness and rage, are masters at manipulating the circuitry of anger. The dog regresses into the snarling wolf from which he evolved. A battle ensues—squadrons of lyssaviruses besiege the nerve cells, invading them and hijacking the machinery of the nervous system. By attacking the nerve cells, the rabies virus is converting the poor animal into a heartless monster without loyalties or love for anyone. Rabid animals can be fearless.

A squadron of viruses peel off and head down to the nerves in the dog's throat. Now that the limbic system has been conquered, another detachment of rabies viruses is dispatched to kick saliva production way up. Their assignment is to paralyze the dog's ability to swallow. This maximizes the chances for the infected saliva to leave the dog and invade the next target. Torrents of saliva flow from the dog's mouth onto his chest and the floor, improving the virus's prospects for new victims to invade.

How can a virus coordinate such a sophisticated series of tactical assaults? How can a virus know which part of another creature's brain is the seat of anger? We ourselves didn't figure that out until very recently. This is the power of evolution by natural selection. Given enough time, a random mutation, no matter how highly specialized—say, a virus's ability to paralyze a victim's throat—will take hold. If it enhances the virus's chance of survival, it will be passed on. In the case of the rabies lyssavirus, all it needs in every generation is a victim to carry the disease, keeping that wicked flame alive.

From its uncanny knowledge of the neuroscience of its prey to the order and precision of its plan of attack, the rabies virus is a master manipulator. Its invasion and enslavement of its victim conjures up the meticulously conceptualized war plan of one of history's most celebrated generals. What an ingenious strategist the rabies virus is.

We are at the mercy of unseen forces: viruses, microbes, hormones, our very own DNA. Our ancestors seized upon the only explanation at their disposal for the suddenly demonic behavior of

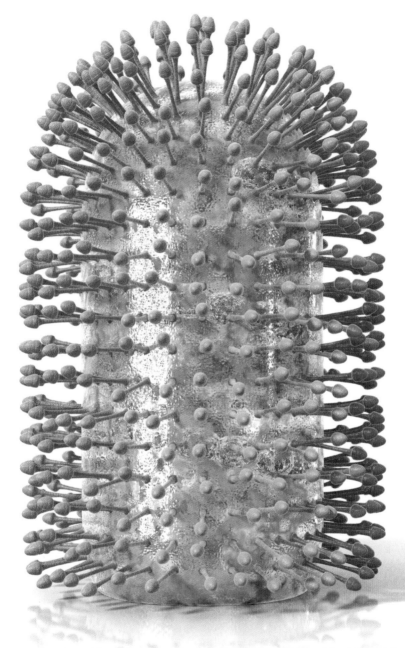

The bullet-shaped lyssavirus, or rabies virus, uses glycoprotein spikes—the pink protrusions shown in this computer model—to latch on to cells to subvert and destroy the personality of its unfortunate host.

a beloved dog or a child who was so normal until she reached her 20s and suddenly started acting strangely at the behest of creatures only she could see. What else could it be but the devil's curse?

NOW THAT WE ARE BEGINNING to understand the processes of these biological mechanisms once hidden from us, can we still hold on to our ideas of evil? Yes, the deeds themselves may be evil, but those impelled by unseen forces to commit them may be as innocent as that poor dog. We can only hope to understand what's really happening when we stop offering Ahura Mazda and Angra Mainyu, or any of their counterparts, as an explanation of why we and our world are the way they are. And yet so much of popular culture is dominated by depictions of the physical personifications of evil and the supernatural avatars of good that almost inevitably triumph, after spending a suitable amount of screen time on the ropes.

Become an extraterrestrial or an archaeologist of the distant future trying to gain insight into our civilization. The rate of scientific and technological development in the 21st century was unprecedented. Humans were extending their senses across the universe in space and time as never before. They were opening up new nanoverses long hidden in the deepest recesses of matter. And they had learned to create seamless three-dimensional experiences of reality that would otherwise be foreclosed to them. And did they use these newly acquired powers to take them on voyages of discovery to the worlds revealed by science or to deepen the public's understanding of nature? Not that much. Mostly they were used to construct giant menacing robots in massively destructive battles to the death—ritualized reenactments of the gladiatorial contests between Ahura Mazda and Angra Mainyu entailing the wholesale destruction of cities and countless lives, for which our appetites are apparently bottomless.

And all the while they were building a sixth wing on the Ha of Extinction. In a rare instance of self-awareness, they named it for themselves—the Anthropocene. Its corridors rapidly lengthened with the tableaux of destroyed species and habitats, until we humans were shocked back to our senses by . . . what?

IS WHAT'S WRITTEN IN EVERY CELL OF OURS, four billion years of life's scripture, is that what's calling the shots? Is existence just a battle between the genetic instructions of competing organisms— with all us plants and animals little more, or maybe nothing more, than their pawns? Is that all history and life adds up to? Can it never be anything more than that? Is DNA destiny? We are still grappling with aspects of this question. Our knowledge of ourselves and the much larger nature of which we are a part is nowhere close to complete.

Carl and I were struck by the power of a particular chemical to trigger a specific ritual on the part of another life-form. A dying honeybee releases a special chemical called oleic acid. The odor of this "death pheromone" alerts the hive mates that whichever bee is wearing that scent must be carted outside by pallbearers. It amazed us that even a healthy bee dabbed with a smidgen of oleic acid will be carried off as a corpse, no matter how vigorously it protests. This is true even for the queen bee, who plays such a critical role in the hive.

We were shaken by this information. What did it say about our own rituals? Do the bees grasp the danger of infection that the deceased poses to the hive? Do bees have a concept of death?

In the many tens of millions of years of their collective experience no bee has ever given off oleic acid except in the last throes of death. There has been no need for a nuanced response to oleic acid until the last 10th of a second on the Cosmic Calendar. The instant

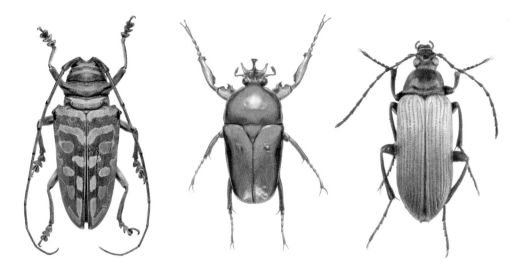

funeral behavior of the bee's response to a whiff of oleic acid is perfectly suited to bee needs.

We can find similarly straightforward behaviors, unsupervised by any apparent central executive order, in a lot of animals. When an egg rolls out of the nest, a mother goose nudges it back in—a behavior with obvious value for the maintenance of goose genes. In fact, she will roll back anything vaguely egglike placed near the nest. Her behavior makes us ask: Does she understand what she is doing?

What about the moth that keeps flying into a window, attracted by a light on the other side? Attraction to light is an inborn behavior, shaped over millions of years. Transparent window glass only entered the scene about a thousand years ago, so no internal programming has evolved in the moth on how to avoid it.

Does a beetle have a mind? Did the eons of evolution that shaped and decorated so many different kinds of beetles like a master jeweler utterly fail to sharpen a beetle's decision-making capabilities, its consciousness and emotions? Or is a beetle just a robot whose DNA chips rob it of any potential for originality or spontaneity or improvisation? Are we?

In every one of these cases, it seems that the DNA coding is driving the animals' actions. Put that way, we might even agree to the proposition that bees and beetles—even geese—are mindless

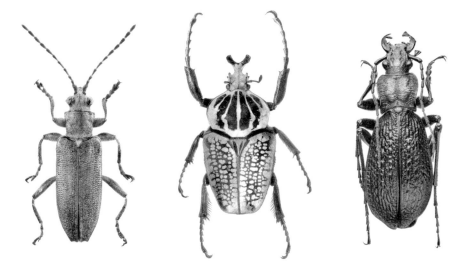

Six of the world's 350,000 species of beetles. Natural selection is a peerless artist. **LEFT TO RIGHT:** African longhorn *(Sternotomis bohemani)*, Neptunides flower *(Neptunides stanleyi)*, male darkling *(Proctenius chamaeleon)*, reed *(Donacia vulgaris)*, goliath *(Goliathus meleagris)*, and blue ground *(Carabus intricatus)*.

machines. But what about us, the animals called *Homo sapiens*?

That's the sort of question pondered by a young French soldier on a chilly evening in November 1619 as he was spending the night in an overheated room in a town in Bavaria. He prepared for bed, extinguished his lantern, lay down—but he couldn't sleep. He was captivated by thoughts that shook him and wouldn't let go. Years later, as he recounted those moments, he claimed that he was visited by a holy spirit who revealed to him a new way of thinking. As he grasped the idea, he sought ways to share it with others.

That young man was René Descartes. *"Cogito, ergo sum*—I think, therefore I am," is his most famous statement. The idea that struck Descartes that night has come to characterize modern civilization. He was instructed, so he said, to unite philosophy with science. To know what is real, one must subject one's ideas to the rigorous, error-correcting mechanism of science, seeking verification that can be expressed mathematically.

At the very heart of Descartes's vision was the distinguishing feature of the modern world: *doubt*. Just think how radical this idea must have been in the early 17th century. Galileo had just been tried, convicted, and imprisoned for his mathematically verifiable observation that Earth revolved around the sun! For a thousand years, the church had successfully controlled public discourse. There was no debate about the literal truth of the Old and New Testaments. Faith was not up for question; there was no room for doubt. But for Descartes, doubt was the starting point of knowledge.

Descartes was no atheist—in public, at least. He repeatedly affirmed the existence of God, and believed that only humans have immortal souls. When he looked at the bee, the moth, and the beetle, all he saw were little machines. This was an age when clocks were still remarkable—on the cutting edge of technology. Descartes viewed insects and other creatures as equally elegant, as efficient as clockwork, but soulless and mechanical nevertheless.

But today, we can take Descartes's principle of doubt and push the boundaries even further. Let's go ahead and ask whether other animals think. Are they making decisions? What might they say if they could? The mother goose may roll a ball back into the nest alongside her eggs. But as soon as her goslings hatch, she is uniquely attached to them. Their particular scent, the sound of their peeps, the way they look—only that combination of qualities can evoke her maternal concerns. She would never confuse them with an alien object, or even with another mother's goslings—what exquisite intelligence! But we, who call ourselves "wise," can't necessarily tell two broods of goslings apart!

Back to the beetle. That's quite a repertoire of abilities packed into so small a creature. It has the full panoply of sensory and reproductive abilities. It can walk, run, and even take to the air. It responds to its environment: Move toward it, and it rears up or dashes off in the opposite direction. As tiny as it is, it has internal capabilities and specialized organs for achieving all these actions.

Many scientists get nervous if you start talking about the consciousness of an insect. And there's good reason for that. Our species has a tendency to project, to anthropomorphize other species. But we may have overcompensated. I have the eerie feeling that the partition separating robotic programming from consciousness in that beetle may be more porous than we imagine. The beetle decides what to eat, who to run away from, who to find sexually attractive. Doesn't that mean that on the inside, within its tiny brain, it has some awareness?

That question has great implications—far beyond the fate of that little beetle. If, after carefully weighing such matters, we still see the insect as robotlike, programmed by its DNA to perform every one of its life-and-death functions, how sure are we that this judgment does not apply to us as well? And if we are willing to view human actions as DNA driven, programmed into our very natures, where does that leave the question of free will? How can we even talk about good and evil? Are we any better off than the Zoroastrians, who believed that Ahura Mazda and Angra Mainyu, forces beyond their control, controlled human behavior for better or worse? Is there any hope that we can choose our actions and shape our destiny—driven not by genetics but by our higher ideals?

I KNOW A STORY THAT GIVES ME HOPE. It's the saga of a life that embodies the most extreme polarity of human behavior. From this distance in time, it's hard to know how much of it is true. The myths of competing religions swirl around this man's life, obscuring it and making it hard to find its truth. I do know that whether it's true or not, generations have tried to suppress his story, to erase this man's life, and all that he wrote and built, from history. Despite this, the light of his memory still burns. And, then again, whether history or myth, if dreams *are* maps . . .

About 200 years after the life of Zoroaster, in the fourth century B.C.E., a young man came out of an obscure backwater called Macedonia and in less than a decade carved out an empire that stretched from the Adriatic to beyond the Indus River in India. Along the way, Alexander the Great crushed the seemingly invincible Persian army, and somehow, his devouring of the Achaemenid Empire, the largest the world had ever known, left him lusting for more worlds to conquer. He wanted India, too.

But after biting off a piece of the northwestern portion and what is today Pakistan, Alexander's men rebelled in 324 B.C.E. Their appetite for empire was unequal to Alexander's and they were homesick, so they packed up and left. In the aftermath of their departure, a Hindu warrior named Chandragupta decided he would try his own hand at empire building. In a mere three years he had founded the Mauryan Empire that grew to encompass most of the widest upper part of India and what is now Pakistan.

Seleucus I Nicator, a member of Alexander's inner circle, thought he might succeed where his late commander had failed. He and his army crossed the Indus River to attack Chandragupta's forces, but Seleucus's Indian campaign was a miserable failure. It didn't take long for him to realize that a marriage that would ally Chandragupta's family with his own was a far more sensible option. This relationship, cemented by gifts of hundreds of elephants and all manner of aphrodisiacs, was to endure for generations as an open channel between India and Greece.

Chandragupta proved to be an excellent administrator, building infrastructure that included large-scale networks of irrigation and modern roads, reinforced by metal, built to last, and to unify his empire for trade and war. Chandragupta was succeeded by his son, Bindusara, whose life seemed to have not much more distinction than as a generational link between two giants.

Some accounts claim that Bindusara's son, Asoka, born in about 304 B.C.E., was disfigured by a childhood disease. As a result, his skin was rough and pockmarked. This was said to have repelled Bindusara, who exiled his little son far from the court. Perhaps, this story was offered as a psychological rationale for the monstrous crimes that Asoka was later to commit.

As Bindusara lay dying, a struggle for the throne began among the sons of his many wives. History accuses Asoka of murdering between one and as many as 99 of his own brothers to attain the throne. Even if we give Asoka the benefit of the doubt and assume that he was guilty of a single fratricide, that one murder is said to have been accomplished with maximum cruelty: Asoka trapped his brother in a blazing fire pit.

This theme became part of Asoka's imperial brand: Annihilating one's enemies is insufficient if they don't suffer unimaginable horrors in the process. It begins with the legend of Asoka storming into the room where his father lay dying. Bindusara's will designated another successor, likely the son whom Asoka deceived into a fiery death. Dressed in the finery that only an emperor was entitled to wear, the hated son stood before his dying father, and declared contemptuously, "I am your successor now!"

According to some accounts, Bindusara is said to have turned red with rage and collapsed back on his pillow, dead. Imagine Asoka smiling with pleasure at making his own father's last moments as miserable as possible, for that is the heartless young emperor on whom all the legends, and even history, can agree.

After a couple of years, no other pretenders to the throne survived. Strangely, Asoka's wrath now turned to the many luscious fruit trees that surrounded his palace. He decreed that every one of them be cut down. When his ministers balked at his command, counseling further thought, Asoka went into one of those rages for which he was becoming famous. Fine, he bellowed to his cowering ministers, "I have an idea, let's cut off your heads instead." Armed guards dragged them away to be decapitated. But Asoka was just getting started.

Asoka had an even more magnificent palace constructed, one with five immense wings. Upon its completion, elegant invitations began to go out to the most prominent citizens in Asoka's empire, which was now most of the subcontinent, except for the southernmost tip and two small nibbles out of the east coast. We can only

imagine the delight and the thrilling surge of self-importance experienced by the invitees. How awestruck they must have felt by the opulence of the new palace, how privileged to be among the first to see its interior.

In the grand central atrium, each potentate was greeted by a host who escorted him to one of the five corridors. It was then, when there was no possible hope of escape, that they learned that each wing was devoted to what was, in Asoka's view, one of the five most excruciating ways to die. Over time, word got out and the palace came to be known as Asoka's Hell. By this means, Asoka eliminated any potential rivals and made an indelible impression on the popular imagination. His fiendishness knew no bounds.

But somehow, Asoka's terror memo failed to reach the people of Kalinga, the thriving region on the northeast coast of India that had no king. Kalinga was known as an open cultural center, possibly the closest thing to a democratic society at the time. It had its own harbor to trade freely and little need for the yoke of an empire run by a sadist.

They had thus far managed to avoid being gobbled up by Asoka's empire. Eight years into his reign, Asoka decided to move against Kalinga, whose people knew that no peace could be made with such a madman. The courageous resistance Asoka encountered at Kalinga would lead to his most heinous atrocity.

Asoka and his army besieged Kalinga for a year before they breached its ramparts and stormed the starved and weakened city. Asoka's men torched the homes as brutal hand-to-hand combat ensued. They slew the defenseless, committing every kind of barbarism. When it was over, a hundred thousand citizens and soldiers had perished. Some 150,000 of the rebellious Kalingas were deported, dispersed as a way to rid Asoka's empire of a concentrated independent-minded population.

A Tibetan Buddhist representation of Asoka depicts him after his conversion, his gestures and dress influenced by the Buddha's own. Contemporary representations of Asoka from India do not survive because of the hatred he inspired.

Now came Asoka's reward: a leisurely stroll through the battle-field, so thick with dead, there was hardly a place for him and his guards to step. Death for as far as the eye could see. Asoka savored his triumph among the corpses.

In the distance, a figure in rags dared to walk toward the victors. Seeing this, the generals tensed, putting their hands on their swords. As the stranger approached, they could see he was carrying something small in his arms. The man seemed strangely fearless, not the least bit intimidated by the monster despot. The guards made ready to kill the man, but Asoka ordered them to stand down. His curiosity was aroused by the man's courage and he assumed he had nothing to fear from this scrawny beggar. As the beggar drew closer to Asoka he offered the emperor what was in his arms—the lifeless body of a baby, a casualty of Asoka's triumph. The beggar held up the dead infant for Asoka to see closely. He looked the murderer right in the eye and spoke these words: "Oh, mighty king, you, who are so powerful you can take hundreds of thousands of lives at your whim. Show me how powerful you really are—give back but one life—to this dead child." Asoka looked at the tiny corpse and all the joy of his victory curdled into something com-pletely different. The intoxicating power that had been like a drug for him turned to something else.

Who was this fearless beggar who dared to confront Asoka with his crimes? His exact identity is lost to us, but we do know that he was a disciple of Buddha, then a little-known philosopher, who had lived almost 200 years before. Buddha preached nonviolence, aware-ness, and compassion. His followers renounced wealth to wander the earth spreading Buddha's teachings by their example. This monk on the battlefield is believed to have been one of them. And with his courage and wisdom, he found the heart in a heartless man.

The haughty triumph drained from Asoka's face as his gaze turned to the field of dead bodies—which now filled him with revulsion and remorse. Asoka erected a pillar, one of many, on the site of his gravest crime. It was topped with four lions facing in the

To convey his revolutionary ideas throughout his vast empire, Asoka had teachings carved into rocks and pillars. Some 150 have been discovered, including this fragment, which shows an edict carved in Brahmi, an early and influential Indian writing system.

cardinal directions, and engraved in Brahmi. On it was one of the first edicts of Asoka: "All are my children. I desire for my own children their welfare and happiness, and this I desire for all."

In Asoka's 13th edict, he wrote of his stricken conscience: "Directly after Kalinga had been annexed began His Sacred Majesty's zealous protection of the Law of Piety, his love of that Law, and his inculcation of that Law. Thence arises the remorse of His Sacred Majesty for having conquered the Kalingas, because the conquest of a country previously unconquered involves the slaughter, death, and carrying away captive of the people. That is a matter of profound sorrow and regret to His Sacred Majesty."

But it wasn't just that he was sorry for committing his many crimes. A new kind of leader emerged, one the world had never seen before.

Asoka signed peace treaties with the small neighboring countries that had once trembled at the mention of his name. He would govern India for another 30 years and he used that time to build schools, universities, hospitals, and even hospices. He introduced the education of women and saw no reason that they could not be ordained as monks. He instituted free health care for all, and made sure that the medicines of the time were available to everyone. Asoka mandated wells be dug to bring water to the villages and towns. He planted trees and built shelters along the roads of India so that the traveler would always feel welcome, and animals would have the mercy of shade. He decreed that all religions be honored equally. He ordered judicial review of those wrongfully imprisoned or harshly treated, and he abolished the death penalty.

Asoka's empathy extended beyond his own species to all life. He banned the rituals of animal sacrifice and all hunting for sport. He established veterinary hospitals throughout India, and counseled his citizens to be kind to animals. It wasn't that Asoka was violating the laws of kin selection, that evolutionary strategy that says we are, above and beyond, concerned with the survival of those who share the greatest number of our genes. It was that his definition of who was kin to him had expanded to include everyone.

And Asoka had another idea that was thousands of years ahead of its time. Asoka didn't think that just because you were the son of a king, you should be one, too. He believed that the nation should be governed by the most enlightened person, not the heir to the throne.

This is not to say that he never did anything violent or cruel again in his life. There are accounts that toward the end of his

Atop the pillars conveying his edicts, Asoka often placed four lions standing on a wheel with 24 spokes, a symbol of Buddhism later chosen as the centerpiece of the flag of the independent nation of India.

One of four sacred caves carved into the granite hills in northeastern India, Lomas Rishi's elegant entryway leads into an austere interior with remarkable acoustics. It was visited by Asoka in the third century B.C.E.

36-year reign he may have lapsed into episodes of mayhem, murderous rages like the ones of his youth. But the evidence suggests that his pathfinding acts of enlightened governance continued.

AFTER ASOKA'S DEATH OF OLD AGE, the Mauryan dynasty lasted only another 50 years. The temples and palaces of Asoka's reign—and most of the pillars he erected throughout India—were destroyed by generations of religious fanatics, outraged by what they considered to be his godlessness. For them, holiness required the strictest maintenance of the dominance hierarchy. But despite his detractors' best efforts, his legacy lives on, thanks to the rediscovery of his edicts in the 18th and 19th centuries. When the modern nation of India was founded in the 20th century, it took the lions of Asoka as its emblem.

Asoka is credited for making Buddhism one of the world's most influential religious philosophies. A couple of hundred years before the birth of Jesus, Asoka's edicts were carved in stone in Jesus' language, Aramaic, and other languages. These were Rosetta stones for teaching compassion, mercy, humility, and the love of peace. We know that his emissaries traveled to Alexandria and other cities in the Middle East, accomplishing, perhaps, an even greater influence for their teacher.

The Lomas Rishi Cave in the hills of Barabar, India, is one of the few temples of Asoka that survives. Apart from a few inscriptions, the temple is shockingly plain inside. But it does have one distinctive feature: an exceptionally resonant and long-lasting echo. The sound waves ricochet off the highly polished walls of the cave, becoming fainter and fainter until they're completely absorbed by their surfaces—and there's no sound left at all. Silence.

But Asoka's dream seems different to me. Its echo grows louder and louder with time.

CHAPTER THREE

LOST CITY OF LIFE

There is, one knows not what sweet mystery
about this sea, whose gently awful stirrings seem
to speak of some hidden soul beneath . . . And meet
it is, that over these sea-pastures, wide-rolling
watery prairies and Potters' Fields of all four
continents, the waves should rise and fall,
and ebb and flow unceasingly; for here, millions
of mixed shades and shadows, drowned dreams,
somnambulisms, reveries; all that we call lives
and souls, lie dreaming, dreaming, still; tossing
like slumberers in their beds; the ever-rolling
waves but made so by their restlessness.
—HERMAN MELVILLE, *MOBY-DICK*

The sea's mystery takes shape in "Memory,"
an 1870 painting by American artist Elihu Vedder.

When our Milky Way galaxy was young—just a few billion years old—it was far more fertile than it is today. Back then, about seven billion years ago, it birthed 30 times as many stars as it does now: a firestorm of star creation.

Our own star was a child of the galaxy's later years, and that may be one of the reasons we exist. After the older, more massive stars died out, there was time—another five billion years—for those dead stars to bequeath their heavier elements to us. These elements enriched and nurtured the formation of the planets and moons of our solar system. And we, ourselves, are made of that starstuff.

Blazing pink clouds of hydrogen gas swaddled the newborn stars. Gravity's embrace transformed them. Bright blue clusters of slightly older sibling stars, and amorphous collections of gas and dust, joined the pink clouds to become the galaxy we call home today.

The universe makes galaxies. Galaxies make stars.

One of those stars becomes a supernova, sending shock waves of matter to disturb the cloud of gas and dust. This nebula begins to condense and spin, quickly flattening into a disk. The bulge at

Combining data from three telescopes, astronomers captured NGC 602, a young star cluster some 200,000 light-years away in the Small Magellanic Cloud (SMC), a dwarf galaxy orbiting our own Milky Way. Since this region of the SMC contains fewer metals and less gas, dust, and stars, it could serve as a model of star birth in the early universe.

its center brightens suddenly into the blinding light of a fusion reactor. Our sun is born.

Sparkling green jets begin to shoot out of our star and rain down on the surrounding disk like emerald glitter. Our star is endowing its surrounding worlds with precious minerals—sparkling diamonds and green olivine, a major character in our story.

The disk continues to spin and articulate into concentric rings. One ring starts to clump, growing larger and larger, until it becomes a spherical world. This is Jupiter, the firstborn of the planets of the sun.

Stars make planets, moons, and comets.

Now, other worlds begin to coalesce and collide like a demolition derby out of the clumping gas and dust. Planets form, and collide with the debris in their way, snowballing into larger worlds and sweeping clean their orbits around the sun. These future planets and moons are awash with organic molecules—the chemical building blocks of life. This is their inheritance from the deaths of other stars.

DOES THE COSMOS GIVE RISE TO LIFE as naturally as it makes stars and worlds? Dive with me like a torpedo, deeper and deeper into the past and down through iron-rich, bloodred waters to the bottom of the sea.

Long, long ago, more than four billion years ago, when our world was young, there was a city of towers that soared between 50 and 100 feet high, their foundations anchored deep in the ocean floor. It took tens of thousands of years to build this city. But there was no life on this world back then. So, who built these submarine skyscrapers? Nature did. She made them with carbon dioxide and calcium carbonate: the same mineral she uses to make seashells and pearls.

A found lost city of life? Towers of porous limestone, called tufa, rise above the California landscape. Less than a thousand years old, they were daylighted when the surrounding lake was drained.

Our restless Mother Earth cracked open. Cold seawater poured down into the hot, rocky mantle, getting richer in organic molecules and minerals, including that green jewel called olivine. This mix of water and minerals got so hot, it shot out with great force. The mixture became trapped in the pores of the carbonate rocks that would later become the towers. These pores were incubators, safe places where the organic molecules could become more concentrated. This is the way that we think the rocks built life's first home. It was the beginning, at least in our little part of the cosmos, of an enduring collaboration between the minerals of Earth—the rocks—and life.

When water and carbon dioxide were converted into the organic molecules that fueled the origin of life, they cranked out hydrogen and methane. The process left evidence in the form of snaky cracks in the rocks called serpentinization. Scientists who search for life on other worlds used to say "follow the water" because water is the most basic requirement of life. Now, they also say "follow the rocks" because serpentinization is so closely associated with the processes that make life possible.

But how did it start? Does science offer a vision of the origin of life that equals the drama and beauty of Michelangelo's hand of God reaching out to Adam? Organic molecules, the building blocks of life, collected in the microscopic pores in the mortar of these underwater towers. The molecules, like everything, including you and me, were made of atoms. Darting among the scattered organic molecules were glowing dots of energy called protons.

Energy was needed to turn these inanimate molecules into something alive. It came from the reaction that resulted when the alkaline water entrapped within the towers met the acidic water of the ocean. This is thought to have powered the first self-replicating molecules, the precursors of modern RNA and DNA molecules. Other tiny molecules collected to line the inner wall of the pores. These forerunners of what we call lipids formed the first cell membranes.

Over time, these hydrothermal towers with their countless pores began to dissolve and fall away. But the complex molecules inside them—Earth's earliest cells—remained intact. They evolved into microbes that could reproduce.

This version of events is the most plausible scientific creation myth we have today for the origin of life. It's a hypothesis that required the reunification of four long-separated scientific fields— biology, chemistry, physics, and geology.

SOME SCIENTISTS THINK LIFE first took hold in the rocks. But from day one, life was an escape artist, always wanting to break free to conquer new worlds. Even the great big ocean couldn't contain it.

The planet on which these first forms of life emerged looked nothing like it does today. Ocean covered most of Earth's surface, its waters red with iron. The sky was a hazy yellow-orange rather than blue. And the moon had not yet spun away from Earth to its current orbit. The atmosphere was a hydrocarbon smog. There was no oxygen to breathe and nothing to breathe it. The land was a series of lifeless, purple volcanic calderas that would blow their tops from time to time. Life would eventually remake the world, the sea, and the sky. But life doesn't always act in its own best interest. There came a day of reckoning, when life nearly destroyed itself.

To witness one of the most catastrophic epochs in the history of Earth, let's go back to the Cosmic Calendar. Nothing much really happened in our neck of the universe until about three billion years after the beginning of time. It wasn't until March 15 that our Milky Way galaxy began to form and not till the last day of August, six billion years later, that our sun burst into stardom. Soon after that, Jupiter and the other planets, including our own, began to coalesce. A mere three weeks later, on September 21, we think life began in those little nooks and crannies at the bottom of the sea. As another three weeks of cosmic time passed, more volcanic mountains pushed up and out of the sea and their eruptions began to form landmasses.

We've only recently begun to appreciate how powerfully life has shaped the planet. When we think about the ways life has changed Earth, the first things that come to mind are the green expanses of forests and the sprawling cities. But life began transforming the planet long before there were any such things. A billion years after that tiny spark ignited at the bottom of the sea, life had become a global phenomenon thanks to a champion that to this day has never been vanquished—the cyanobacteria.

In business for 2.7 billion years, cyanobacteria, also known as blue-green algae, can make a living anywhere. Freshwater, salt water, hot springs, salt mines—makes no difference, it's all home to them. They're alchemists. They can do something we, with all our science and technology, still don't know how to do. They can turn sunlight into sugar, creating their own food by photosynthesis.

Over the next 400 million years, the cyanobacteria—taking in carbon dioxide and giving back oxygen—turned the sky from yellow to blue. The cyanobacteria didn't just change the sky and the sea; they reached into the very rocks themselves and changed them, too. Oxygen is corrosive. The oxygen released by the cyanobacteria rusted the land and worked its magic on the minerals. Of the 5,000 kinds of minerals on Earth, some 3,500 of them arose as a result of the oxygen made by life.

Earth was once the planet of the cyanobacteria. These tiny one-celled organisms didn't look like much, but they were the dominant life-form on this planet, wreaking havoc wherever they went, changing the landscape, the water, and the skies. This was 2.3 billion years ago, or late October on the Cosmic Calendar.

The cyanobacteria shared the planet with other beings: the anaerobes, life-forms that had come of age before the cyanobacteria had begun to pollute Earth with oxygen. For the anaerobes, oxygen was poison, but the cyanobacteria wouldn't stop loading up the atmosphere with the stuff. This was disastrous for the anaerobes, and nearly all the other life on Earth. The cyanobacteria brought on an Oxygen Apocalypse. The lone survivors among the anaerobes were those who sought refuge at the bottom of the sea, deep in the sediment where the oxygen could not reach them.

Remember those serpentinized rocks at the bottom of the sea that were cranking out hydrogen and methane. Methane is a

Yellowstone's Grand Prismatic Spring is lifeless at the center, rendering the 150°F waters a deep cerulean blue. Microbial mats frame the mineral-rich hot spring with intense yellow and orange hues.

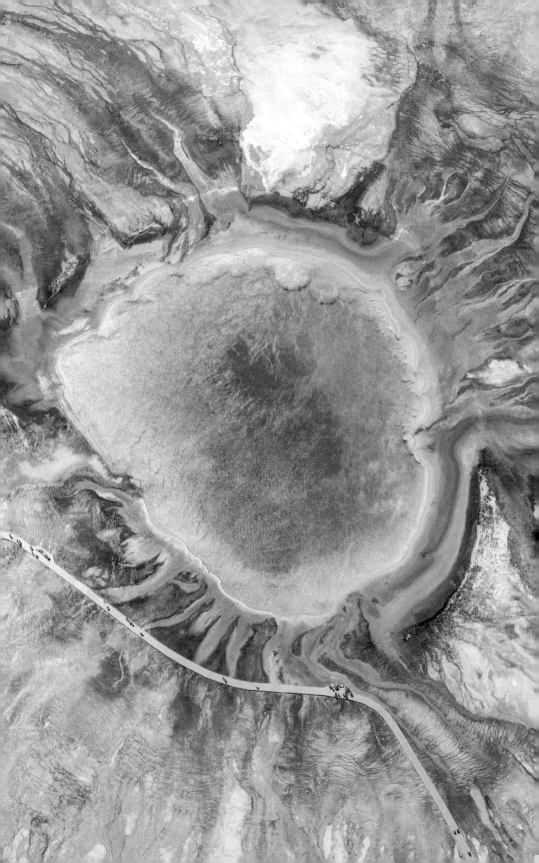

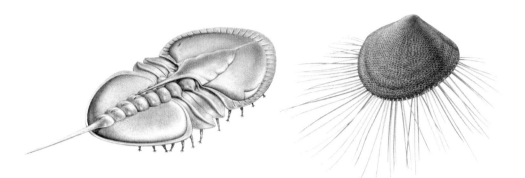

powerful greenhouse gas, and back then it was the main thing keeping the planet warm. But once again, the oxygen produced by life shook things up. It gobbled up the methane, but it excreted carbon dioxide, a much less potent greenhouse gas—meaning it was not as efficient at trapping heat in Earth's atmosphere. Earth grew colder and the green life on the land began to die.

The polar ice caps advanced and spread to envelop the whole planet until Earth was a snowball, completely encased in snow and ice. The cyanobacteria had gone a little too far. The dominant life-form on the planet came close to total self-annihilation. A sobering thought for any beings who happen to occupy that ecological niche today.

THAT FIRST GLOBAL WINTER HAPPENED about 2.2 billion years ago. It lasted for about a couple of hundred million years—or from November 2 to November 6 on the Cosmic Calendar—until massive volcanic eruptions blasted through the ice and lava began to flow across the surface. Life, the escape artist, busted out of the icy death grip that entombed the planet. The ice pack retreated back to the poles.

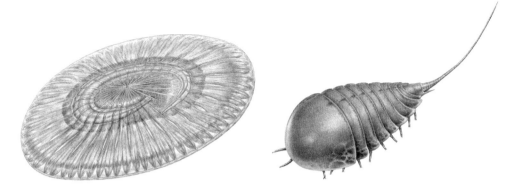

Life-forms abound among the Burgess Shale fossils of the Canadian Rockies, all emerging some 500 million years ago during the Cambrian explosion. **LEFT TO RIGHT:** a trilobite *(Pagetia bootes)*, a brachiopod *(Micromitra burgessensis)*, a soft-bodied animal *(Eldonia ludwigii)*, and an arthropod *(Molaria spinifera)*.

The corpses of dead cyanobacteria left behind a planet-wide reservoir of carbon dioxide. Erupting volcanoes pumped the carbon dioxide into the atmosphere, warming the planet and melting the ice. Over the next billion years, life and the rocks continued their elaborate dance, taking the planet through cycles of freezing and thawing.

Then, 540 million years ago—December 17 on the Cosmic Calendar—something wonderful happened. By then, our planet had blue sky and oceans with two large continents and various island chains. Life, which, until now, had been all about microbes and simple multicellular creatures, suddenly took off in what we now call the Cambrian explosion. Life grew legs, eyes, gills, teeth—and rapidly began to evolve into forms of stunning diversity. Legions of Cambrian critters—armored trilobites, shell-like creatures with gills called Vetulicolia; spiny, headless worms named *Hallucigenia;* and more—proliferated across the planet.

We don't yet know what it was that allowed life to diversify so dramatically, but we have some plausible theories. It could have been all those calcium minerals in the seawater that came from the volcanoes. Life grew a backbone and put on a shell. It had found a way to collaborate with the rocks to make its own armor. Now life could grow larger and venture forth into untenanted territories—the land.

Or maybe life diversified thanks to the protective canopy built by the cyanobacteria. Their oxygenation of the atmosphere created the ozone layer, which made it possible for life to break out of the safety of the oceans and inhabit the land without being assaulted by the sun's deadly ultraviolet rays. For billions of years, all life could do was ooze. Now, life began to swim, run, jump, and fly.

Or perhaps a kind of evolutionary arms race broke out between competing life-forms. One species, say, an anomalocaris, a giant shrimplike creature, grew a shell and longer pincers to lift and turn its trilobite prey over, to get at the part of it that was vulnerable. This might have worked extremely well until trilobites evolved a winning defensive strategy—a flexible, segmented shell that enabled the trilobite to defend itself by rolling into an armored ball. The trilobite survives the attack and gets to leave more offspring. The anomalocaris goes away hungry before fading out to extinction.

Or, could viruses have triggered the Cambrian explosion of new life-forms? We tend to think of them as life's nemesis, but they aren't all bad. Viruses have a tendency to be sloppy. Might they have acted as couriers, leaving bits of DNA behind as they traveled from host to host? Some hosts were changed by the cast-off DNA in ways that worked better with their environments.

The unprecedented diversity of life that begins in the Cambrian period could have been the result of all of the above. Or it could have been caused by factors we have yet to understand. Whatever the cause, life had gotten so good at wriggling out of every confine that no prison on Earth could hold it. And there would come a day, hundreds of millions of years after the Cambrian explosion, when life would even escape from Earth. Life will not be penned in.

RETRACING LIFE'S ODYSSEY BACK to the very beginning required a new kind of science, one that reunited the disciplines. The man who founded this new scientific approach also happened to be an escape artist himself. He fled history's most implacable killers, jesting at his tormentors every step of the way.

Victor Moritz Goldschmidt was so brilliant, he was offered a position at the University of Oslo without ever taking a test or earning a degree. That was in 1909, when he was only 21. Three years later, he was awarded Norway's greatest scientific honor, the Fridtjof Nansen Prize.

Goldschmidt was one of the first scientists to see Earth as a single system. He knew that in order to get the whole picture, you couldn't just know physics, chemistry, or geology—you had to know them all. This was in the early days of the study of the elements, before the discovery of those unstable elements that lie beyond uranium on the periodic chart, called transuranic.

In the 19th century, chemists made great progress in our understanding of the nature and properties of chemical substances. Chemists by this time were mostly convinced that elements—the most basic kind of chemical—are made of indivisible atoms. Different atoms have different chemical properties, and when they react and combine with other atoms to form molecules, all the amazing variety of substances in the world—air, water, metals, minerals, proteins—are created. Some of these molecules, like water, are quite simple. Others, like the protein molecules that build life, are staggeringly complex, sometimes comprising millions of atoms. But every material thing in the cosmos is ultimately assembled from just a few dozen fundamental elements combined in different ways and numbers.

In the 1860s, the Russian chemist Dmitri Mendeleev, among others, began looking for patterns among the elements. Mendeleev

Dmitri Mendeleev continued refining the periodic table of elements throughout his lifetime, starting with these notes in February 1869. He gave scientists a framework for understanding matter with astonishing predictive powers.

discovered that when he organized the elements based on increasing atomic weight, they seemed to fall into natural groups of eight, based on their chemical properties (reactivity, flammability, toxicity, and so on). Organizing these groups into a table revealed gaps in the various rows of elements. Mendeleev surmised that these gaps represented as yet undiscovered elements, and he correctly predicted the chemical properties of several of them before they were eventually discovered.

Goldschmidt applied this new knowledge to create his own version of the periodic table, one that is still in use today. But in Goldschmidt's mind, his new periodic chart was not merely something to replace an outdated bit of classroom or laboratory wall decoration. With it he could see how crystals and complex minerals could be formed from more basic elements. His new, enhanced periodic chart illuminated how those elements formed some of the most majestic geological structures on Earth—the Himalaya, the White Cliffs of Dover, the Grand Canyon. Goldschmidt was discovering the fundamentals of geochemistry and helping us understand how matter evolves into mountains.

In 1929, he made a fateful decision to accept an appointment at the University of Göttingen, in Germany, where an institute had been built just for him. His colleagues thought that these were his happiest years, until 1933, when Adolf Hitler came to power.

Goldschmidt was Jewish, but not religious. Hitler changed all that for him. He now began to publicly identify himself with the local Jewish community. Hitler made it compulsory for everyone to list any Jewish ancestors going back several generations. There were those who tried to conceal a grandfather who might land them in a concentration camp. But Goldschmidt proudly declared on his forms that ALL his ancestors were Jewish. Hitler and Hermann Göring, founder of the Gestapo, were not amused. They personally sent a letter to Goldschmidt in 1935 telling him he was summarily dismissed from his university position. He fled back to Norway with only the clothes on his back.

Olivine, a mineral thought to be crucial to the origin and chemical evolution of life

Goldschmidt concentrated his research on olivine, that green jewel of a mineral left over from the formation of the solar system. Fascinated by its power to withstand even the highest temperatures, Goldschmidt was the first to speculate that olivine may have played a role in setting the stage for the origin of life. As he studied the olivine, which when polished and mounted in a piece of jewelry is known as peridot, Goldschmidt pioneered new applications for it. First, he used it to line furnaces and kilns, but later generations would see its heat resistance as ideal for nuclear reactors and rockets.

At the same time, Goldschmidt wondered about the presence of olivine throughout the cosmos. This was the beginning of a field called cosmochemistry. But there was another, more traditional form of chemistry that had much greater urgency for him. On the eve of the Nazi invasion of Norway, Goldschmidt suited up in protective garb to make himself some cyanide capsules. He took to concealing them on his person so that he could kill himself instantly if/when the Gestapo came for him. When a fellow scientist asked if he could get one, too, Goldschmidt answered, "This poison is for chemistry professors only. You, as a physicist, will have to use a rope."

And they did come for him. In the middle of a night in 1942, the SS pounded on his door. Goldschmidt kept the cyanide in his pocket. He was sent to the Berg concentration camp before they were ready to deport him to Auschwitz, a place, he told friends with his deadpan humor, that "had not been highly recommended."

He was waiting on a pier, pale and gaunt, one of a thousand Jews to be deported, when a detachment of Nazi soldiers came to single him out. As they approached, he surreptitiously played with the little blue capsule in his pocket. But he decided to take his chances, knowing that there would be other opportunities to swallow the capsule.

Goldschmidt was too important a scientist for the Nazis to exterminate. He would be permitted to live outside the camp if he would put his science in the service of the Reich. Goldschmidt seized the opportunity to use the one advantage he had over his captors—his knowledge of science. He toyed with his captors, sending them on scientific wild goose chases. He dispatched whole detachments to search for nonexistent minerals and deceived them into believing these were resources that would be critical to the war effort. His ruse could have been discovered at any moment—and that would have meant certain death.

By the end of 1942, the Norwegian resistance knew that Goldschmidt was in grave danger. They arranged for him to escape at night across the Swedish frontier. Goldschmidt spent the rest of the war in Sweden, and then England, contributing his knowledge to the Allies. Always in frail health, he never recovered from the hardships of the war. Victor Goldschmidt died in 1947. But during that last period of his life, he wrote a paper on the complex organic molecules that he thought might have led to the origin of life on Earth. The ideas in that paper remain central to our understanding of how life came to be. Goldschmidt never knew that the generations of geochemists who came after him would consider him the founder of that field.

Among his last wishes was a simple request: He wanted to be cremated, and to have his ashes encased in an urn made of the thing that he believed was the stuff of life—his beloved olivine.

THE UNIVERSE MAKES GALAXIES. Galaxies make stars. Stars make worlds. Are there other lost cities of life in the cosmos? "In dreams begin responsibilities" is a phrase that comes down to us via Ireland, the poet W. B. Yeats, and the short story writer Delmore Schwartz. It's a phrase that has echoed in my head for most of my life, and seems especially applicable to our dreams of exploring the possible worlds of the Milky Way.

There are dues to be paid for cosmic citizenship. As a space-faring species, we have to worry about contaminating the worlds we visit, and about bringing back alien stowaways that might pose a danger to our home world.

In 1958, in the immediate aftermath of Sputnik, Carl Sagan and Nobel laureate Joshua Lederberg began arguing for a stringent set of protocols for planetary protection to become part of international law. It was largely motivated by their wish to avoid the terrestrial contamination of these worlds, so that they could provide answers to questions regarding the origin of life. But Sagan and Lederberg were also thinking about the tragic history of the European conquest of other continents. Other scientists felt such an overwhelming imperative to explore, they downplayed the basis for concern. Eventually, a consensus evolved supporting Lederberg and Sagan. But when NASA began to codify planetary protection conventions in 2005, they came up with a formula that emphasized missions rather than worlds. The categories were defined solely by how a mission might interfere with research on how life began rather than the preservation of the beings of that world—and ours.

NASA designates five such major categories, with additional modifying subcategories. Earth's moon is considered to be so lifeless that it is deemed a place "not of direct interest for understanding the process of chemical evolution or the origin of life." For this reason it's considered eligible for any kind of mission from Category 1, be it a flyby, orbiter, or lander.

A Category 2 mission is for those worlds that may have "significant interest" on the life question, but the nature of the mission has a relatively small chance of contaminating its target world, so they too can be visited by any type of mission. Venus, famously inhospitable to our kind of life, falls into this division.

The restricted Cat-5 designation is a recognition of life's genius for escape. It applies to sample return missions from those worlds where life may have gotten started—those worlds that may have, or *once may have* had, lost cities of life lying at the bottom of their seas.

Mars is a special case. It has various subdivisions of its lofty Category 5 status, and NASA decrees for such worlds that "spacecraft going to target bodies with the potential to support Earth life must undergo stringent cleaning and sterilization processes, and greater operating restrictions." But in some sense, our robot emissaries themselves—our landers and rovers—are a manifestation of life's relentless imperative to seek out and take new territory.

After conducting a multiyear reconnaissance of Jupiter, NASA will send the Juno spacecraft to its death in the Jovian atmosphere. Juno will begin to glow from the friction before bursting into a fireball and sinking into the oblivion of the deeper cloud layers below. NASA is not commanding Juno to self-destruct because they are worried about Jupiter. There's hardly any chance that one of our spacecraft could compromise future investigations of the giant gas planet. Any rogue microbe from Earth would catch a downdraft and sink down, where it would be broiled by the scathing temperatures. That's why Jupiter's only a Category 2 world. But one of Jupiter's 79 (and counting) moons is a restricted Cat-5, and NASA cannot take the chance that Juno might inadvertently crash into it: Europa is the second of only three restricted Cat-5 worlds in the solar system.

Like Earth, Jupiter has a magnetic field, which becomes visible to us if we look at it in radio waves. Jupiter's magnetic field is much stronger than Earth's, and a million times greater in volume than ours. It's a gigantic trap for the charged particles that make up the solar wind. On Jupiter as it is on Earth, the magnetic field channels the charged particles from the sun to the north and south poles,

where they fuel the eerie, neon, swirling aurorae. Jupiter's solar winds are also being channeled to the surface of Europa, where they spiral over unique terrain that looks as if it's been gored by a tiger.

Jupiter dominates the sky. Imagine what it's like for little Europa and its sister moons to live so close to the king of the planets. Massive Jupiter holds Europa in a gravitational embrace so powerful that in four billion years, the moon has never been able to turn its face away from the planet. Jupiter's grip on Europa is so fierce that it tears the moon's skin apart. The *lineae,* those broad wounds in its surface, are some 12 miles wide and 900 miles long. They move perceptibly, rising and falling. We can almost hear the seismic grinding.

This gravitational torment is called tidal flexing—and Jupiter's not the only culprit. Europa's sister moons pull on it, too. The thickest layers of Europa's surface rise as much as 100 feet every three and a half days, the time it takes for Europa to complete an orbit of Jupiter. Europa is half a billion miles from the sun's warmth, five times farther away than Earth is. But this tidal flexing keeps Europa toasty inside. And that's one of the reasons the moon is a restricted Cat-5 world. Beneath its chaotic surface, there's an ocean 10 times deeper than the deepest sea on Earth.

Imagine being able to dive into one of the lineae to reach Europa's subsurface ocean and see if anyone is swimming there. Such a mission is within our grasp and scientists are proposing it to NASA. Imagine the spacecraft descending rapidly, diving for miles past the icy blue walls of a narrow crevasse to splash down on the great ocean and send images and other data back home to us on Earth.

The tormented surface of Europa, a moon of Jupiter, as seen by NASA's Galileo spacecraft. Enhanced color highlights in red the *lineae*—cracks and ridges—on its surface, which mask a vast ocean below.

AND WHAT OF THAT THIRD restricted Category 5 world in our solar system?

It's not Saturn. Any Earth life passing through Saturn's cloud belts wouldn't have a chance—the uppermost clouds are made mostly of ammonia ice, so this world is a Category 2. Below them are bands of water vapor. Saturn's interior is hot; it generates more than twice as much heat as it gets from the distant sun.

Saturn's moon Titan is another Category 2 world. Just as with Saturn, the possibility of us interfering with the life that might be there is too remote. Of course, there's always the chance that Titan life is stranger than our ability to imagine. Even if that's the case, there is little likelihood that any form of Earth life could harm it.

But another of Saturn's 62 moons is our restricted Cat-5 world. And it's not like any moon we've ever seen: Its entire southern hemisphere is hemorrhaging a curtain of blue matter, creating Saturn's outermost ring. It was discovered by the first person ever to see into the deeper waters of the cosmic ocean.

William Herschel, born in 1738, was a German-born musician and astronomer who emigrated to England. William discovered the planet Uranus in 1781 and proposed it be named "George," after his sovereign, King George III. That didn't catch on, but the king was so delighted by the tribute, he financed the building of the largest telescope on Earth for Herschel at Slough, within sight of Windsor Castle.

Herschel's younger sister, Caroline, waited fretfully at home in Hanover until William, who was to remain the central figure in her life, sent for her to join him in Bath. At first they worked together as musicians, but they achieved greater renown as astronomers. Caroline was the first woman ever to be paid by the British government for holding an official position. And the first woman anywhere to earn a salary for being a scientist. Caroline was just four feet three. When she was 10 years old, she was stricken with typhus—she lost some vision in her left eye and stopped growing. And yet, she defied the limitations of her time . . . to a point.

Caroline made a number of important astronomical discoveries. She published her work in the *Catalogue of Nebulae and Clusters of Stars*—but, under her brother William's name. It *was* 1802, after all. William's son, her nephew, John, would grow up to enlarge Caroline's catalogue. It was later renamed the *New General Catalogue*. Many astronomical bodies are still designated by their NGC number today.

William discovered a new moon of Saturn, and he called it Saturn II. (Naming worlds was not one of his talents.) He gave his son, John, the privilege of naming this new world and John decided to call it Enceladus, after the giant in Greek mythology who was the son of Gaia (Earth) and Uranus (Sky). Enceladus fought the goddess Athena in an epic struggle for control of the universe. Enceladus, our third Cat-5 world, is one of the most highly reflective worlds in the solar system. The surface is composed almost entirely of freshwater ice. It's largely smooth and dotted with the rare crater here and there. We know this about Enceladus thanks to NASA's Voyager 2.

You don't have to be an astrobiologist to know at first glance that life is everywhere on Earth. As we have learned, it has changed virtually every square inch of the place. Earth's restricted Cat-5 status would be obvious to any life-respecting, spacefaring civilization. But Enceladus keeps its secrets hidden deep inside.

South of Enceladus's equator, we begin to see the tops of blue towers of ice and water vapor hundreds of miles high. Imagine a robotic craft from Earth flying right through the curtain of geysers, and taking us along via camera. Those geysers of ice and water vapor are shooting out of Enceladus at 1,300 miles an hour. The water jets are so highly pressurized they've fractured the crust and arc miles into space. They're this moon's contribution to the outermost, so-called E ring of Saturn. But there's a lot more in them— nitrogen, ammonia, and methane. And where there's methane, there may be olivine.

Enceladus has been at this for at least a hundred million years. It could keep cranking out water for another nine billion years. Where's all that water coming from?

Glow from *Cosmos*'s Ship of the Imagination illuminates mineral towers that could exist at the bottom of the ocean on Enceladus, a moon of Saturn.

Enceladus's rocky core is surrounded by a blue global ocean, which, in turn, is surrounded by an icy crust. In the southern hemisphere the crust is thinnest, only a couple of miles thick. That's why it's the best possible place to gain access to the moon's underground ocean. That global ocean, the crazy curtain of geysers, the weird snow at the surface—it's all real. We have multiple observations from the Cassini mission telling us that this is what awaits us on Enceladus.

But what would we find if we dove straight into the heart of this planet? Scientists think that a spacecraft visiting Enceladus would descend through hot fog until it arrived at a pitch-dark crevasse filled with steam generated by Enceladus's internal heat. When water is exposed to the vacuum of space, it turns to steam. As our spacecraft plunged deeper, we'd arrive at the subsurface ocean, which would likely have a grand vaulted ceiling of ice. The surface of the ocean might have a scummy layer of red and green organic matter.

That scum is the stuff of life—organic molecules. And what could be waiting for us farther down below? Enceladus's ocean is about 10 times deeper than the oceans of Earth. If we could look at the water under a powerful microscope, we might see tiny molecules of organic carbon and hydrogen. If such molecules are common, it would be very promising for life. Perhaps we'd find that Enceladus has its own city of life at the bottom of its sea. If it exists at all, its pillars might be taller than ours because the gravity on Enceladus is so much weaker than it is on Earth. But the currents are strong and they would likely topple them. Might there be serpentinized rock and Victor Goldschmidt's olivine? Might the rocks have made a place for life? But even if that were the case, would life have had enough time to take hold?

We humans think we're the story. That we're the be-all and end-all of the cosmos. And yet, for all we know, we're just the by-product of geochemical forces—ones that are unfolding throughout the universe. Galaxies make stars, stars make worlds, and it may be that planets and moons make life.

Does that make life less wondrous—or more?

CHAPTER FOUR

VAVILOV

Here the most beautiful girls fight
For the honor of marrying executioners.
Here they torture the righteous at night
And wear down the untamable with hunger.
—ANNA AKHMATOVA
(translated by Judith Hemschemeyer)

Philosophy will have conscience of tomorrow,
commitment to the future, knowledge of hope,
or it will have no more knowledge.
—ERNST BLOCH,
THE PRINCIPLE OF HOPE

Dewdrops bejewel newborn sprouts of wheat.

Many a mighty civilization has been brought to its knees by famine. The Maya, the Egyptians of the Old Kingdom, the 13th-century Anasazi people of the American Southwest—all over this planet, from Kinshasa to Beijing and everywhere in between—to be human has been to know the torment of hunger.

For the first couple of hundred thousand years that we were human, we were wanderers living beneath the stars. We depended on the wild plants we gathered and the animals we hunted until about 10,000 or 12,000 years ago, when our ancestors realized that hidden inside the plants they foraged was the means to make another plant—a seed. That discovery led to the single most fateful choice our species ever made. We could continue to wander in small bands, following the wild herds, and living off the forest, or we could domesticate some of the animals, such as the pigs that roamed the forest with us, feasting on what we ourselves could not digest. We could settle down to grow and raise our food—small crops of wheat and barley, lentils, peas, and flax. This required sacrifice, and intense work over long periods for rewards that would not come until much later. We were starting to live in the future.

An Egyptian wall painting from the New Kingdom, circa 1539 to circa 1075 B.C.E., shows, bottom to top, the sowing, harvest, and threshing of wheat; it adorned the tomb of Unsu, the pharaoh's grain accountant.

Of course, the choice between wandering and settling down wasn't made in an instant. It unfolded across generations. We feel so far removed from our hunter-gatherer past, but in the great sweep of cosmic time, it was less than half a minute ago on the Cosmic Calendar. Our ancestors began to domesticate animals and plants less than 25 seconds ago on the Cosmic Calendar, or around 10,000 years ago. This shift in food production profoundly altered our relationship to the rest of nature. We had always seen ourselves as members of the same family as the bird, the lion, and the tree. Now, we began to see ourselves as created separately from the rest of life on Earth.

For the first time, the wanderers were settling down, domesticating animals, and storing large quantities of food that made it possible for them to spend their time in pursuits other than the relentless search for nourishment. They could dare to touch a more distant future. They began building things to last for more than a single season. And they built some things so well, they still stand, nearly 10,000 years later.

THE TOWER OF JERICHO is the oldest stairway in the world. How old? It was already 5,000 years old before the first Egyptian pyramid was built. It is so ancient that the earth has had enough time to slowly and imperceptibly, over the millennia, swallow it whole. What was once the uppermost step, the 22nd, the place to stand for the optimal view of the Jordan River and surrounding areas, is now deep below ground level.

Was it a watchtower for protecting the city from invaders? Or just a way to get closer to the stars? It took 11,000 human workdays to build, something that could only be possible with the food surpluses that agriculture provided. To climb it is to follow in the footsteps of 300 generations. Isn't it astonishing that people who had barely ceased wandering were able to create something of such awesome permanence in human terms? The builders, sometimes referred to as part of the Sultanian period, remain a mystery to us.

Just as the citizens of Çatalhöyük did, those who built the Tower of Jericho buried their dead beneath the living room floor for easy access, and festooned the skulls of their dead with plaster to reconstruct their faces, embedding them with unseeing seashell eyes and jack-o'-lantern pebble teeth. What were they thinking? Were the skulls objects of veneration, or art, or were they pieces of evidence of something new: property claims? Were the masks a way of proving "My ancestors died here protecting this land; it's mine"? The idea that these skulls may have been the first proof of ownership underscores the visceral nature of real estate from the very beginning, even when it must have seemed that the planet held limitless tracts of unclaimed land.

Jericho and Çatalhöyük thrived at about the same time in human history. But the evidence suggests that life in Jericho posed dangers not yet known in Çatalhöyük. Living in close quarters with larger populations spurred epidemics. And with the harvest and the wall came the shackle. Our new way of life intensified class warfare and sexism. The enslaved and the powerless suffered inferior nutrition. Forensic examinations of their bones and teeth bear witness to the rise of inequality. The rich and varied hunter-gatherer diet of plants, insects, birds, and other animals was largely replaced by a few carbohydrate crops.

And when the rains didn't come, or the locusts swept through, or a fungus afflicted the grain, there was hunger on a massive scale—famine. Sometimes the famine was caused by an event halfway around the world and far beyond the ken of its victims. On February 19 in the year 1600 at 5 p.m., the Huaynaputina volcano erupted in southern Peru. It propelled boulders, gases, and dust sky-high, forming a massive, elongated plume, the largest explosion in South America in recorded history. The plume blasted through Earth's atmosphere: the troposphere, the stratosphere. It didn't start to fall back Earthward until it reached the dark blue,

The Russian people made desperate by the famine caused by the Huaynaputina
volcano eruption a half world away in Peru, in 1600, as depicted in this 1836
illustration for Nikolay Karamzin's famous 12-volume history of Russia

almost black mesosphere. This nasty mixture of sulfuric acid and
volcanic ash blocked the sun's rays from reaching Earth. Winter
was coming—*volcanic winter.*

For the people of Russia, it brought the most brutal winter
weather in six centuries. For the next two years, even the summer
temperatures fell below freezing at night. Two million people, a
third of Russia's population, would die from the resulting famine.
Shivering workers, rags tied around their faces, dug mass graves for
the piles of corpses. It led to the downfall of the tsar, Boris Godunov.
And all because of a volcano that erupted 8,000 miles away in Peru.
The idea that our planet is a single organism has the ring of hollow
sentimentality for many people. But it's just a scientific fact.

In the 18th century, famines caused by drought, and British colonial mismanagement in India, killed 10 million people. In China, during the famines of the 19th century, over 100 million people perished. (A number as hard for us to grasp as the distance to the nearest galaxy.) The Great Hunger in Ireland, also caused by British colonial mismanagement, starved a million to death, and forced another two million to flee the country in search of a living. The Brazilian drought and pestilence of 1877 was comparable. In a single province, more than half died of starvation and the opportunistic infections that attack the malnourished. The dead remain uncounted from the famines that wracked Ethiopia, Rwanda, and the Sahel in Africa in the 20th century.

For a couple of thousand years, ever since records were kept, somewhere on Earth, people in great numbers have starved. The success of the modern scientific revolution with its astonishing powers of discovery and technological advancement raised the possibility that human existence could be perfected. Could agriculture become a science, with a predictive theory of crossbreeding as reliable as Newtonian gravity? One that could consistently produce breeds that could stand up to drought and disease?

FOR MILLENNIA, FARMERS AND HERDERS had recognized the advantages of preferentially selecting the hardiest specimens for crossbreeding to produce a more successful offspring. This was known as artificial selection. But the mechanism of how these traits were passed on to succeeding generations remained a complete mystery. This was still true even after Charles Darwin demystified how all life evolved by means of natural selection.

In 1859, as Darwin enlightened and enraged the world by publishing his book *On the Origin of Species,* an abbot at the rural St. Thomas Abbey monastery in what is now Brno, in the Czech

Republic, was trying to become a science professor. Gregor Mendel flunked the qualifying exam both times. The only career path open to him was to become a substitute teacher. So in his spare time, he took up the study of pea plants. He bred tens of thousands of them, carefully scrutinizing their height, and the shape and color of their pods, seeds, and flowers. As his garden flourished, the abbot faithfully sketched and recorded the progress of every pea plant. Mendel was searching for a predictive theory of breeding that could tell in advance exactly what one would get by crossing a tall plant with a short one, or a green pea with a yellow one.

Mendel found that when he crossed a green pea plant with a yellow one he would get a yellow pea every time. We didn't have a word for the power of the yellow over the green, until Mendel coined it. He called that quality "dominant." And to his delight, he found that he could predict what would happen in the next generation of peas after that. If the first three pea pods had yellow peas, he knew before he popped open the fourth pea pod, that it would be green.

One in four pea plants would be green. Mendel named the hidden trait that popped up in the next crop "recessive." There were things hidden inside the plants—he called them "factors"—that caused particular characteristics. And they operated by a law that Mendel could describe with a simple equation, just as Newton had described gravity. There were laws governing the way life's message was passed on from generation to generation. The substitute teacher had invented a whole new field of science. But nobody noticed for another 35 years.

Mendel published just one paper documenting his experiments in his lifetime, and died without ever knowing that the world would come to see him as a giant in the history of science. His work was rediscovered in 1900, and he had no more vigorous proponent than the British zoologist William Bateson, who with his colleagues used Mendel's equation to develop new breeds of plants and animals. Mendel's factors came to be called by a new name: genes. And Bateson named this new field of science genetics.

Gregor Mendel, a failed substitute teacher, cracked the hidden code of inheritance by studying pea plants.

Bateson believed that science and freedom were indivisible, and that's how he ran his laboratory at the John Innes Horticultural Institution at Merton, in South London, collaborating mostly with female scientists from Newnham College at Cambridge University. Among those women was a young man, a visiting botanist from Russia who dreamed of a possible world where, through science, no one would ever perish from hunger, and famine would be no more.

NIKOLAY IVANOVICH VAVILOV was born in 1887 to parents who had already won their struggle to escape poverty. His father had become a prosperous textile merchant with an elegant town house in Moscow, comfortably insulated from the droughts and famines that continued to sweep through Russia. But as a precocious four-year-old, Nikolay may have witnessed ghastly events through his family's town house windows. These tableaus of widespread desperation may have scarred his young soul and sealed his fate.

Winter came early in 1891, killing the crops. Wealthy Russian merchants continued to export grain at a profit, even as millions went hungry. Tsar Alexander III was slow to respond. All he had to offer his starving subjects was "famine bread"—a miserable mixture of moss, weeds, bark, and husks. Nikolay may have looked out from his window on a Moscow square as the tsar's troops doled out loaves to the freezing citizens, fighting desperately among each other over the inedible rations. Half a million Russians perished that winter, most of them from opportunistic diseases like cholera that find easy victims in those weak from hunger. All the while the aristocracy and the wealthy remained untouched. They feasted on fresh strawberries from the south of France, and clotted cream from England. Many historians believe that this famine was the spark that ignited the long fuse leading to the Russian Revolution 26 years later.

Nikolay had three siblings, all scientifically inclined. His brother, Sergei, would become an eminent physicist, Alexandra, a doctor, and Lydia would study microbiology before succumbing to smallpox. An anecdote from their adolescence contrasts the brothers' different approaches to tyranny. Their father had become enraged at the boys for some teenage infraction. He dramatically removed his belt and summoned the boys upstairs for a beating. Sergei deftly stuffed a small decorative pillow into the seat of his pants on his way up the stairs. Nikolay listened to his brother's feigned cries before bounding over to the open third-story window. When his father approached, he screamed, "Come any closer and I'll jump!"

By 1911, as Nikolay was entering adulthood, Russia was the largest grain exporter on Earth despite the fact that its farming methods were antiquated. Debates raged about how to modernize the country's agriculture. The Petrovsky Agricultural Academy was the only place in Russia where scientists could hope to modernize food production through the new science of genetics. Vavilov, now on his way to becoming a botanist, respected the personal experience of the farmer and the knowledge passed down through the generations. He wanted to arm the peasant with the predictive powers of science. The peasant couldn't foretell which traits would dominate, or which would be recessive. The farmer played a game of agricultural roulette, and was therefore about as successful as the average gambler.

Mendel's equations had made it possible for him to know the odds, to know what number the ball would land on. The moment Mendel expressed his ideas mathematically, agriculture became a science. Vavilov believed passionately that a scientific approach offered the only hope to efficiently feed the world. Some of his fellow students at the Petrovsky Agricultural Academy would recall years later that he would get so carried away during their lunchtime debates, he would eat dessert first, or endearingly grab his pet lizard as it emerged from his breast pocket and began inching up his neck. Vavilov would gently wrap the lizard in his handkerchief and return him to his pocket, without missing a beat.

IN THIS PERIOD OF VAVILOV'S formation as a scientist, some faculty still adhered to the ideas of the heroic warrior and pioneering 18th-century biologist Jean-Baptiste Lamarck. History can be so cruel in who and how it chooses to remember. Poor Lamarck is far better known for the thing he got wrong than for all the important contributions he made to biology and his remarkable heroism while still a teenager.

When Lamarck's father died in 1760, he purchased a horse and raced across France to join the army in their fight against the

Prussians in what is now Germany. He made a name for himself by displaying extraordinary courage on the battlefield only to sustain a career-ending injury during horseplay with a comrade. While recuperating in Monaco, he happened to pick up a book on botany. There, he found his true passion.

Lamarck was one of the first to believe that life evolved in accordance with natural laws that were knowable. He named and classified thousands of plants and animals, adding them to the scientific book of life. He ended the ancient misconception that insects and spiders were members of the same family and coined the term "invertebrates." A true Hall of Famer in the history of science, Lamarck's contribution formed a vital bridge between the mystics who came before him and the scientific demystifiers of nature who would come after. There are elements of his insights that are gaining new respect, yet to remember him at all is to conjure up a name synonymous with a famously wrong idea—that plants and animals could acquire characteristics during the course of their lifetime and then pass them on to their offspring. In this view, giraffes stretch their necks to reach higher up in the trees, and so the next generation "inherits" longer necks.

Lamarck, Darwin, and Mendel laid the foundation for the discovery of genes, the hidden means of transmitting life's messages and mistakes. Vavilov dreamed of building on their research to shape the future of essential food plants such as wheat, rice, peanuts, and potatoes. He, Bateson, and others worked feverishly to apply this new knowledge to solving problems that had afflicted our species since Jericho. They were founding the scientific field of genetics.

When the First World War broke out in 1914, Vavilov and his bride, Katya Sakharova, returned to Russia. Their marriage was already unraveling when Vavilov was dispatched to the Persian front to solve a mystery. Soldiers were acting strangely, reeling from dizziness, their heads too clouded to think clearly. Vavilov deduced that their symptoms were caused by a fungus on the wheat used to make their bread. With the mystery solved, he was free to take samples of the local plants as bullets whizzed past him. As the Turkish forces moved in with light artillery, Vavilov placed the plant samples in neat squares of delicate wax paper, carefully folding them and placing them in his breast pocket. They were among the first items in what would become the largest botanical collection on Earth. This steely, purposeful calm in the face of mortal danger proved to be a lifelong trait. It made Vavilov seem superhuman when others were panicking all around him.

In 1918, Katya gave birth to a son, Oleg, but the marriage ended soon after. Vavilov wrote to a colleague a letter that made the true object of his ardor clear: "I really believe deeply in science; it is my life and the purpose of my life. I do not hesitate to give my life even for the smallest bit of science."

When Russian participation in the war morphed into the Russian Revolution in 1917, Vavilov enthusiastically put everything he had at its service. He saw the revolution as the chance to make it possible for everyone to have an education, not just the children of the rich. Now, anyone could become a scientist. Vavilov welcomed this newly liberated army of scientific talent, and some of them joined him in his research missions. He wanted to trace the lineage of modern food crops all the way back in time to when they had been wild and to the far-flung scrubby gardens where they were first deliberately planted.

In 1920, at the All-Russian Congress of Plant Breeders in Saratov, Vavilov established his scientific reputation when he proposed a new law of nature. In his paper, "The Law of Homologous Series in Hereditary Variability," he demonstrated that the same genes perform the same functions in different species of plants. When two completely different plant species have similarly shaped leaves, that shape is caused by the same shared gene from a common ancestor. In order to understand evolution, and to guide plant breeding scientifically, it was necessary to go to the oldest agricultural countries, where the common ancestors of the plants might still live.

Vavilov was among the first to grasp the critical importance of biodiversity. He knew that every seedling contained its species'

Still preserved at his institute today, specimens of *Aegilops ovata*, a wild relative of bread wheat, show how carefully Nikolay Vavilov and fellow botanists cataloged the seeds, stalks, and leaves of plants for posterity.

unique message. The contents differed, but they were all written in a mysterious language, one that would not be deciphered for decades. Vavilov wanted to preserve every phrase of life's ancient scripture—to ensure its safe passage to the future. To that end, Vavilov came up with an entirely new concept: a world seed bank that he hoped would be impervious to war and natural catastrophe. And there was a scientific underpinning to this humanitarian goal: If you could find the earliest living specimens of the plants we eat, you could parse its sentences and decipher life's language. You could know how it changed over time. This decryption would make it possible to write new messages—to grow food immune to disease, fungus, and insects, and resistant to drought.

So Vavilov became a hunter of plants. He traveled the world, identifying the first places on Earth to bear the seeds of many economically useful species and collecting samples for the seed bank. He traveled to the remote reaches of five continents, venturing to places no scientist dared go before him. He was suspicious of the prevalent theory that humans invented agriculture in the river deltas. It seemed unlikely to him that the first farmers would locate their fields at the crossroads of such heavy human traffic. He reasoned that remote mountain strongholds would be a much safer place to farm, far from the casual plundering of passersby.

As he conducted his research, he established 400 scientific institutes in the Soviet Union, where the children of peasants and laborers became scientists. Several of them would mature to become his closest scientific colleagues, even following him all the way to martyrdom.

In 1926, Vavilov traveled to Addis Ababa and waited there for permission to travel into the interior of Ethiopia. He was surprised to receive an invitation from the regent and future emperor, Ras Tafari—the man the world would come to know later as Haile Selassie. He wrote in his diary about their evening dining alone. They both knew French so no interpreter was needed. Selassie wanted to know everything about Russia and its revolution. Vavilov informed him of Lenin's death and Joseph Stalin's rise to power. He told him how Stalin's armed robbery of a bank in Tbilisi had raised three million dollars for the revolution, and made him a folk hero in Russia 20 years before. Ras Tafari gave Vavilov permission to venture freely throughout the country, where he discovered the mother plant of all coffee. And it was a good thing, too.

While camping on the bank of the Tekeze River, Vavilov wrote in his diary by a flickering lantern. It was his turn to stay awake all night on guard duty. Jacked up on caffeine, and cradling a rifle, Vavilov sat in the tent while his men slept soundly. He could hear the cries of leopards in the night, but that didn't faze him. Then, in the dimness, he noticed that the entire floor of the tent seemed to be moving. His men began to stir and scream. The floor was crawling with enormous black venomous spiders and scorpions!

Thinking fast, Vavilov moved his lantern outside the tent and the invaders followed the light.

The Breguet biplane that was carrying him across the Sahara crashed. When he and his pilot crawled away from the wreckage, they were immediately surrounded by a pride of hungry lions. They fended them off with debris from the crash until they could be rescued.

Without maps or roads, he was the first European in modern times to venture into the mountainous regions of Afghanistan, rife with tribal clashes and other dangers. In China, he found seeds from the poppy plant, camphor trees, and sugarcane. In Japan, tea, rice, and radishes. Many varieties of soybeans and rice from Korea. Oats from the mountains of Spain. Papayas, mangoes, oranges, and cacao from Brazil. Quinine from Java. And from Central and South America, amaranth, sweet potatoes, cashews, lima beans, and maize. Vavilov collected more than 250,000 varieties of seeds.

Vavilov was among the first to be awarded the newly minted Lenin Prize in 1926. That same year, he and Katya divorced, and he began the common law marriage with a colleague, Yelena Barulina, that would last for the rest of his life. His reputation as an explorer and daredevil was now almost as formidable as his scientific reputation, yet he remained humble. "Me, I'm nothing special," he would say. "It's my brother, Sergei, the physicist, who's the brilliant one."

But among those young people whom the revolution had rescued from the prison of class and a life of drudgery was the one who would destroy Vavilov and ruin Russian biology for four decades.

IN AUGUST 1927, a reporter from *Pravda,* the official newspaper of the Communist Party, wrote a fawning profile of a 29-year-old pea plant grower in Azerbaijan whose pea crop had withstood the

Nikolay Vavilov, intrepid collector of plant specimens from five continents

"No Room in Our Collective Farm for Priests or Kulaks" reads this 1930 Soviet poster, decreeing kulaks—affluent farmers—enemies of the proletariat.

Russian winter. He wasn't a scientist; he was a man of the fields. Born to a peasant family in Poltava, in the Ukraine, he hadn't even learned to read and write until he was 13. Trofim Denisovich Lysenko was a "barefoot scientist," the article said. He hadn't wasted his time attending university and "studying the hairy legs of flies" under a microscope.

Like any other blight that ravages every living thing in its path, his first appearance seemed small and harmless. But it was to become the first salvo in a war to the death against Vavilov and his quest to end hunger. Lysenko resurrected Lamarck's discarded idea that acquired characteristics pass on to the next generation. Genetics held the promise that generations of crossbreeding could lead to varieties of food crops that could survive the harsh winters and many of the other threats nature posed, but Lamarckism offered a far more instantaneous form of gratification. Soak the seeds of the peas or the wheat in ice-cold water and their offspring will resist the cold. This process, called vernalization, if real, would have been a panacea to the Soviet Union's chronic food insecurity. The promise of fresh green peas in the wintertime was irresistible to a country that was once again in the early throes of what would become one of the cruelest famines in history. But the antagonism toward science and the adoption of the agricultural scam of vernalization were two self-inflicted wounds, impairing the Soviet Union's ability to feed itself. The third would be the most devastating.

Almost seven decades before, the serfs, indentured farmers who did not even have the right to marry without their master's permission, had won their freedom from Tsar Alexander II. Their emancipation in 1861 created a relatively prosperous peasant class called kulaks. When the Russian Revolution began in 1917, the kulaks and their fellow citizens fought fiercely for five years to establish an independent Ukrainian People's Republic until they could fight no more and Ukraine was incorporated into the U.S.S.R. Such tendencies toward defiance could not be allowed to go unpunished, lest they spread.

Stalin bided his time before landing a death blow on the largest food-producing region in the Soviet Union. In 1929, he ordered that the kulaks be forced off their productive farms into industrial-style agricultural collectives. His stated goal was to modernize Soviet agriculture, but it brought about mass death and suffering in Ukraine. It is known as the Holodomor, meaning "killing through hunger." Stalin first eliminated the intellectuals and political activists in the area and then commanded that the kulaks be liquidated as a class, that their land, crops, and herds be confiscated.

For Lysenko, this massive tragedy was an opportunity. Here was his chance to begin whispering in Stalin's ear, Iago-like, of Vavilov's imagined disloyalty, of the danger posed by the scientific community, and his own cure for the U.S.S.R.'s famine. Lysenko's hunger for status and his willingness to deceive and flatter was a perfect fit with Stalin's paranoia.

All the while, Vavilov, clueless, was searching for the garden of Eden in Central Asia, because he had discovered that the first apples grew there. The Leningrad he returned to in 1932 was far from Eden. It was a different city, one in the grip of famine. The heady optimism of the revolution had been replaced with dread and despair. The pedestrians seemed haggard and threadbare. None of them seemed to notice that a dead man was lying on the sidewalk.

VAVILOV'S FATE WAS PROBABLY already being brooded about in the Kremlin, but it was sealed by one of those events that require countless trivial skeins of causality to weave together to create a single defining moment. A missed train connection, an extra moment lingering at a newsstand, a trip to the restroom. Little things like that.

Newly returned from one of his expeditions, Vavilov headed to the Kremlin for a debriefing. "Too little time, too much to do," was his mantra, and on this day he barreled down the corridors of the Kremlin, his briefcase overstuffed with papers and reports on agriculture in the nations he'd visited. Vavilov rounded the corner of a hallway at full speed precisely as another man came rushing around the same corner from the opposite direction. The collision was so intense it knocked each man to the floor. Vavilov's papers went flying out of his briefcase. The first thing he noticed was the naked fear in the other man's face. And this Vavilov recognized instantly as a sight no man could see and long survive. It was Stalin.

Vavilov couldn't know that the dictator was constantly afraid he would be assassinated. Stalin's first thought at the moment of impact was that, now, it was finally happening, it must be his turn at last for the violent end he had inflicted on countless others—the briefcase must contain a bomb. But, no, it was just that clumsy egghead, Vavilov—and now, he'd seen Stalin's fear. Vavilov's fate was sealed.

Vavilov's friends observed a change in his mood immediately after that fateful collision. And the pace of his efforts increased. With Lysenko and pseudoscience on the rise and the breadbasket of the Soviet Union destroyed, Vavilov worked with even greater urgency to develop that strain of wheat that could survive the Russian winter.

The different colored tags of the wheat and barley fields of the Pavlovsk Research Station fluttered in the wind like poppies as Vavilov carefully monitored each plant. His colleague Liliya Rodina took advantage of this rare moment of refuge from surveillance to plead with Vavilov to give up his experiments in genetics. She told her mentor that Lysenko took every opportunity to blame Vavilov for the famine.

Vavilov would have none of it. He told her that they must carry on with their work, no matter what might happen. They must hurry. They must work hard and keep accurate notes of their results, just like his hero, Michael Faraday. Vavilov told her that if he disappeared, she must take his place. The only thing that mattered was

Trofim Lysenko, right, measures wheat in a Soviet collective near Odessa, Ukraine, to bolster his pseudoscientific claims for vernalization: soaking seeds in ice water to harden their offspring to frigid winters.

getting the science right. It was the only hope of ending the famine—and the others to come.

"Comrade, they are going to arrest you!" she told him.

"Then we'd better work that much faster," was his reply.

Stalin appointed Lysenko to the top of the Soviet dominance hierarchy, awarding him membership on the Central Committee of the Communist Party, where he joined Stalin's staunchest and most deadly henchmen, Vyacheslav Molotov and Lavrenty Beria. Lysenko continued his whispering campaign against Vavilov. Vavilov's pretentious scientific nonsense was destroying Soviet agriculture and endangering Stalin's hold on power. The minutes of the committee meeting of the Soviet Institute for Plant Breeding, as unearthed from Vavilov's KGB file and translated by Mark Popovsky, are painful to read. They illustrate all too vividly how a person bound to the facts can never hope to best the rabble-rouser in the arena.

Vavilov

The committee had called for a report from Vavilov, outlining his research progress. Vavilov looked haggard and demoralized as he began his presentation. He had no encouraging headline for the hungry nation. Without a trace of hype or empty promise, he expressed his regret in a typically low-key but immaculately accurate report that the biochemists of his institute were still unable to distinguish the lentil from the pea by analyzing their proteins.

Imagine Lysenko's delight as the great scientist delivered himself to public slaughter. Lysenko didn't even get out of his seat to speak, only saying, "I reckon that anyone who tries them on their tongue can tell a lentil from a pea."

Vavilov stood at the lectern, unperturbed, still believing, as was true in science, that the best argument would inevitably triumph. "Comrade, we are unable to distinguish them chemically," he explained to Lysenko and the assembly.

Lysenko knew he had him now. It was time to go in for the kill. "What's the point of being able to distinguish them chemically," Lysenko now stood and turned theatrically to both far corners of the large auditorium, "if you can try them on your tongue?" It brought down the house.

The demagogue was reaping his harvest of resentment. Every minor official who'd ever felt intimidated by a scientist or baffled by the impenetrable jargon they used; every hungry, frightened man in the room could now feel superior to, and even laugh in the face of, the world-famous scientist and adventurer with nerves of steel.

Lysenko assumed that his work on Vavilov was now done. He asked Stalin to have Vavilov picked up so that he could be devoured by the police state. But Stalin feared that Vavilov's disappearance might not go unnoticed. The global scientific community admired him for his ideas and his courage. They had even been willing to move their International Genetics Congress to Moscow when Stalin wouldn't let Vavilov travel outside the country to participate in it. No, Vavilov wasn't quite ripe for the picking just yet. Lysenko would have to finish him off before Stalin would have him taken away. Lysenko chose to stage the coup de grâce at Vavilov's own Institute of Plant Industry in Leningrad, the place where his hundreds of thousands of seeds were stored.

THE AUDITORIUM OVERFLOWED THAT DAY in 1939 with Lysenko's supporters and Vavilov's dwindling but fiercely loyal defenders. Lysenko presented a fairy-tale scenario of how soaking seeds of all kinds in ice water would lead to a better-fed motherland. It was met with deafening applause from his sycophants. Vavilov waited until the accolades died down and then rose to his feet.

Vavilov boldly challenged Lysenko, asking him if that was all he had to present. Where was the science? The evidence? Should Lysenko's pronouncements be taken on faith like some kind of religion?

Lysenko asked Vavilov if he hadn't noticed how few supporters he had left. One can almost hear Lysenko bellow, "Vernalization is going to provide a HUGE winter harvest! Everyone says so!"

Vavilov knew he was sentencing himself to death, but someone had to make a public plea for returning Soviet agricultural policy to reality. He sought to reawaken the scientists to their sacred obligation to the people, even in the face of terrifying consequences for doing so. The minutes of the conference attest to his fearlessness in defense of science: "You can take me to the stake! You can set me on fire! But you can't make me give up my convictions!"

Vavilov prepared for the worst. He immediately began warning his colleagues that they must ask for transfers to other institutes to save themselves. They should feel free to denounce him. There were about a dozen who refused. Come what may, they would continue their work on the collection at the institute.

Months passed uneventfully. When the following year Vavilov

was given permission to take a research trip out of Leningrad, he might have wondered to himself if he had exaggerated the danger in his own mind.

The black car came for him at an experimental field station in western Ukraine on the evening of August 5, 1940. They were in a hurry to take him back to Moscow, where he was locked up in a cell in the innermost circle of hell in the Lubyanka prison of the NKVD secret police.

At first, Vavilov would admit no crime except a scientific difference of opinion, but Aleksandr Grigorievich Khvat, senior lieutenant of State Security, had plenty of experience softening up such stubborn subjects. He started interrogating Vavilov for 10, 12 hours at a time, usually rousing him out of his bed in the middle of the night. He must have been tortured because his legs were so swollen he was unable to walk. Vavilov would be dragged back to his cell and crawl to a place on the floor and just lie there, unable to move. It went on for 1,700 hours over 400 sessions—until Vavilov finally broke. He signed a confession. A year after his arrest, he was sentenced to be shot.

In fall 1941, Vavilov was on death row in Butyrka Prison in Moscow, where he languished in solitary confinement for months awaiting his execution. But that winter, when his cell door was finally thrown open and he was dragged away by the guards, to his surprise, he was not taken out to be shot. Instead, his guards were evacuating the prison because thousands of German troops and Panzer divisions were advancing on the city. Hitler had broken his nonaggression pact with Stalin, sending millions of German troops and thousands of tanks to invade Russia. When they arrived at the gates of Moscow, Vavilov and other prisoners were moved deeper into the interior.

The skies were thick with dark smoke. German planes flying in massive formations cast shadows over the city. Bombs exploded nonstop. But Moscow was nothing when compared to the siege of Leningrad. It was, by any metric, among the most ghastly of all battles for a city ever waged. Vavilov's Institute of Plant Industry, its windows boarded up against the assault, sat on St. Isaac's Square. Cold and dark inside, little curtains of plaster dust fell from the ceiling. It contained the world's genetic inheritance from the invention of agriculture—the seeds of the plants that had sustained humanity for 10,000 years. And Hitler, unlike Stalin, knew that it was priceless.

Vavilov's loyal colleagues gathered in a cellar storeroom. Georgi Kriyer, Alexander Stchukin, Dmitri Ivanov, Liliya Rodina, G. Kovalesky, Abraham Kameraz, A. Malygina, Olga Voskresenskaia, and Yelena Kilp shivered from cold as they tried to figure out what Vavilov would want them to do. They didn't even know if he was alive, but they resolved to do as he would have done. To keep on working, no matter what, like his hero Michael Faraday. They were terrified that if the siege lasted, their fellow citizens would get very hungry. The institute contained many tons of edible material. They knew they needed to figure out how to protect every last seed for the time when the world returned to its senses.

That Christmas Day in 1941, 4,000 people starved to death in Leningrad. The city had been under siege by Hitler's army for more than a hundred days. The temperature was minus 41°F, and the city's entire infrastructure had collapsed. It was only a matter of time, Hitler thought to himself. No city could endure such suffering for very long.

Hitler even had invitations printed and planned the menu for his victory celebration. He would hold it at the best hotel in Leningrad, the Astoria, instructing his bomber pilots to take special care not to damage it, lest they ruin his party. But that wasn't his only interest on St. Isaac's Square. While Stalin fretted over the safety of the artworks of the Hermitage Museum—devoting manpower and railroad trains to transporting its works by Michelangelo, Leonardo da Vinci, and Raphael to safer territory in Sverdlovsk—he never gave a single thought to Vavilov's seed bank. But Hitler had already taken the Louvre art museum of Paris. He wasn't lusting after more paintings, he coveted something much more precious—Vavilov's treasure.

As the months passed, the botanists grew thinner and blue with cold. They worked by candlelight around a large table, struggling to complete the sorting and cataloging of the seeds, nuts, and rice. They could see their own breath.

Hitler had established a special tactical unit of the SS, the Russland-Sammelcommando—the Russian Collector Commandos —to take control of the seed bank and retrieve its living riches for future use by the Third Reich. They waited at-the-ready like a pack of Dobermans straining to be unleashed on the institute. The botanists were now down to a ration of two slices of bread a day, but still they continued their work.

In a way, the German army at the gates of the city was not their worst problem. One day, rats brazenly leapt onto their worktables laden with trays of seeds. The botanists were startled for a moment before attacking the rats with metal rods. Yelena Kilp ran out of the room and returned with an automatic weapon and took aim. The once perfectly sorted seeds, nuts, and rice were completely scattered and mingled on the table. The botanists painstakingly began the re-sorting process. If only Vavilov were here. They felt so lost without him. *Dear comrades,* they told each other, *as painful as it is, we must accept that he is gone forever.*

But Vavilov was alive—barely. He had been moved to another prison in another city, Saratov. He had survived to another Christmas and was now a skeleton, afflicted with scurvy, sitting in his tiny cell, writing a letter to his persecutor with what seemed like his last ounce of strength. "I am 54, with a vast experience and knowledge in the field of plant breeding," he wrote. "I would be happy to devote myself entirely to the service of my country . . . I request and beg you to allow me to work in my special field, even at the lowest level."

But no answer ever came. The state had decided not to shoot him. They had a crueler fate in mind for the man who did more than any other to eliminate famine and hunger. He was deliberately and slowly starved to death.

Only the gleaming entryway appears against the icy blue Arctic landscape beneath the aurora borealis in this artist's conception of the Svalbard Global Seed Vault. Inside, nearly a million seeds are stored.

YET ANOTHER CHRISTMAS CAME IN 1943 and the members of the SS unit Russland-Sammelcommando still waited for their chance to raid the institute. They rested against the sandbags piled high and topped with artillery.

The people of Leningrad had starved through three Christmases under siege. One in three of them were now dead from starvation: 800,000 human beings. But still they managed to hold out against the relentless German assault. The meager rations of two slices of bread a day for the botanists had run out long before, and the protectors of Vavilov's treasure began to succumb to hunger. They died at their desks in the darkened, frigid institute amid the specimens of peanuts, groundnuts, oats, and peas that their sacred honor prevented them from consuming. All of them perished from hunger. And yet, not a grain of rice in the collection was unaccounted for.

And what of Vavilov's nemesis, Trofim Lysenko? He maintained his stranglehold on Soviet agriculture and biology for another two decades—until another famine gripped Russia in 1967 and three of Russia's most distinguished scientists publicly denounced him for his pseudoscience and his other crimes.

After Stalin's death, and the recognition of the damage that he and Lysenko had done to the Soviet Union, Vavilov could once again be talked about in public. The Institute of Plant Industry was renamed after him, and it still exists. But a recent national poll of Russia names Stalin as the most admired man of all, coming in just ahead of Vladimir Putin.

In 2008, the governments of Norway, Sweden, Finland, Denmark, and Iceland opened the Svalbard Global Seed Vault, the modern successor to Vavilov's collection. It lies beneath the ice on an abandoned coal-mining island between Norway and the North Pole. As of now, it protects nearly a million samples of seeds. In recent years, the Norwegian government has been forced to spend millions to upgrade and better insulate the underground vault because lately it has been endangered by the rapid melting of the permafrost due to climate change.

So, why didn't the botanists at the institute eat a single grain of rice? Why didn't they distribute the seeds and nuts and potatoes to the people of Leningrad who were dying of starvation every day for more than two years?

Did you eat today? If the answer is yes, then you probably ate something that descended from the seeds that the botanists died to protect.

If only our future was as real—and precious—to us, as it was to Vavilov and his botanists.

CHAPTER FIVE

THE COSMIC CONNECTOME

The Brain—is wider than the Sky—
For—put them side by side—
The one the other will contain
With ease—and You—beside—

The Brain is deeper than the sea—
For—hold them—Blue to Blue—
The one the other will absorb—
As Sponges—Buckets—do—

The Brain is just the weight of God—
For—Heft them—Pound for Pound—
And they will differ—if they do—
As Syllable from Sound—

—EMILY DICKINSON

Enhanced color tracks the white matter nerve fibers of the human brain, seen from above, which transmit nerve impulses within the brain and to the spinal cord—an image from the groundbreaking Human Connectome Project.

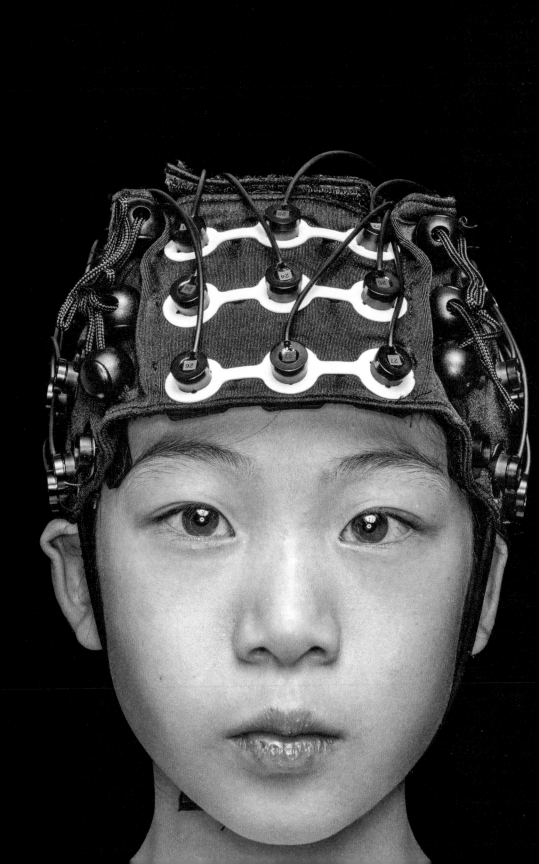

| s the universe knowable?

Are our brains capable of comprehending the cosmos in all its complexity and splendor? We don't yet know the answer to that question because the brain remains almost as much of a mystery as the universe itself. We think that the number of processing units in our brains is roughly equal to all the stars in a thousand galaxies—at least a hundred trillion. And it's possible that the real number of processing units is 10 times larger.

As I write this, my own processing units are in a panicky state of terror, as I wait in the neurology intensive care unit of Cedars-Sinai hospital in Los Angeles. One week earlier, my son, Sam, and I were working together with our colleagues in one of the editing suites in the television production offices of *Cosmos: Possible Worlds*. Sam stood up suddenly complaining of a severe headache and nausea. Something maternal and astute told me that this was not a reaction to lunch. I knew that I needed to get him to an emergency room immediately.

At Cedars-Sinai, the ER staff quickly recognized that his brain was hemorrhaging. Until that afternoon we had no idea that 27 years before he had been born with an AVM—an arteriovenous malformation, a cluster of blood vessels at the intersection where

A modern version of Hans Berger's electroencephalograph (EEG), for studying electrical activity inside the brain

an artery and vein in his brain connected. The AVM was bleeding and there was no place for the high volume of blood to go without putting increasing pressure on his brain and damaging it. Two drains were implanted in his brain to siphon off the blood. They were attached to a simple setup of weights and balances that reminded me of the ancient Greek engineer Archimedes. A three-foot ruler with a level in it, something from a hardware store, was used to make sure the drains could take advantage of gravity and fill them with the outward flow of blood from Sam's brain, day after day. A monitor beeped when the pressure in his brain became too great and the balance was quickly changed. But how to solve the problem? How to get rid of the AVM, which could rupture again at any time?

Enter Nestor Gonzalez, a soft-spoken interventional neuro-radiologist. He proposed first to perform an angiogram, a mapping of the veins and arteries of the affected area of Sam's brain. Somewhat risky, this would be the first step toward a more dangerous embolization, a slow and painstaking technique of sending a guide-wire through those byways to zap the AVM with a tiny droplet of glue or a coil, to keep it from ever bleeding again. It's a maddeningly delicate procedure requiring the most unforgiving precision, with the jeopardy being possible damage to Sam's brain or even the loss of his life, an unbearable thought. Sam looked into my eyes and asked me if I could survive his death. We've always tried to be honest with each other. I had to tell him I just didn't know.

The three of us talked several times in the days leading up to the procedure. Dr. Gonzalez asked Sam what he did for a living. When Sam replied that he was an associate producer on *Cosmos,* the quiet, placid Dr. Gonzalez seemed shaken. "Oh, forgive me. I didn't make the connection. Are you related to Carl Sagan?!?" he asked.

"I am his youngest son," Sam replied.

Dr. Gonzalez was visibly moved. "But that is why I am here!" he told us. "When you grow up in a poor country like Colombia and someone inspires you to pursue a life in science, as seeing Carl Sagan on TV did for me, medicine is the only avenue open to you."

It feels as if, in a completely *un*supernatural way, Carl has reached across the decades to help save our son's life. As I wait for news of the outcome I think of all the mothers and fathers who have faced this kind of anguish before me. And I remember the life of the man who first inspired *me* to love science.

People keep telling me that Sam's fate is in God's hands. They offer to pray. I thank each one of them sincerely, but I can't help but think that if this calamity had befallen Sam a century ago he would be dead. What has changed in that relatively brief amount of time? Not God, presumably. Only our knowledge of medical science and our technology to implement what we know. How did we get to the point of being able to visualize and even repair microscopic problems, hidden within the recesses of our deeply folded brains?

I THINK THE MOST SIGNIFICANT SINGLE LEAP we humans have made took place about 2,500 years ago, in a town of white-washed homes, contrasting exquisitely with the deep blue of the Aegean Sea. What was medicine then?

Imagine you're the loving parents of another precious child, a younger boy with a different sort of affliction. A large social gathering is in progress with many servants in attendance, providing refreshments to the elegant guests. A governess proudly escorts your son into the festivities. The boy is clever and given to moments of brilliance, which charm and impress your friends. When he's introduced to some of the more prominent guests, he displays poise and wit, disarming and delighting the adults, as you look on adoringly. Suddenly, the child appears distracted by something invisible in the middle distance. This thing that only he can see inspires a faraway smile of recognition. The storm is brewing inside his head. The boy swoons and collapses as his body goes rigid. A look of terror crosses your face as the guests move away from him in shock. You shake him and call his name to no avail.

The boy is now foaming at the mouth, biting his tongue as his body convulses. You dispatch a servant to fetch the physician as the guests make their awkward excuses and depart. The boy now lies very still. The seizure has passed. A grizzled, dirty physician enters the courtyard, his robes stained with the afternoon meal. He's followed by a retinue of enslaved attendants bearing a portable altar, incense burners, and a struggling goat. The "physician" doesn't even glance at the child, but instead starts barking orders at the slaves to set up the altar and make the goat ready for sacrifice. The goat is wild-eyed, wailing in fear. As you look on hopefully, the physician starts swinging the incense burner around the motion-less child, uttering incantations.

This was medicine 2,500 years ago in Greece. When the Greeks and people of other cultures performed their rituals, some of the afflicted recovered, due to the finite course of the illness, or to their own immune systems. But the patients and their loved ones believed that the gods had been appeased. Sometimes, though, the patient died. That just meant the gods were so angry, nothing could be done.

This way of thinking was a by-product of that great human strength, and weakness, called pattern recognition. In this case, *false* pattern recognition. The belief that epilepsy was caused by the anger of the gods was the confusion of correlation with causation, prompted by the wishful thinking that prevails when people feel powerless. That's not to say that the ancient Greeks didn't have remedies for some illnesses. There were plenty of plants and minerals in their medicine cabinets. But for a disease as mysterious as epilepsy, they could only light their incense and pray. They had yet to realize that it was related in any way to the brain—until Hippocrates.

So little is known of this great sea-changer. Was he the man born on the island of Kos in 460 B.C.E. or does his name stand for the collective genius of a whole school of medicine? All we know is that the writings ascribed to him in 400 B.C.E. are the first to

A figure, believed to be Hippocrates, examines a patient, in this bas-relief.

reject the notion that angry gods were the cause of disease and injury. "The physician must investigate the entire patient, his diet and his environment," wrote Hippocrates. "The best physician is the one who is able to *prevent* illness ... Nothing happens without a natural cause." For these insights alone, he could be called the father of medicine, but Hippocrates did so much more. He recognized the psychological plight of the ill, and the special ethical challenges that physicians confront. And he is credited with codifying an ethos for doctors. The oath ascribed to him in the third century B.C.E. is still taken today by those who would practice medicine.

And Hippocrates was one of the first to declare the brain to be the seat of consciousness. At that time, this was a revolutionary concept. Most believed we thought with our hearts. His recognition of the importance of the brain, combined with his understanding of the natural causes of disease, make his essay on epilepsy, titled "Sacred Disease," one of the most original, radical,

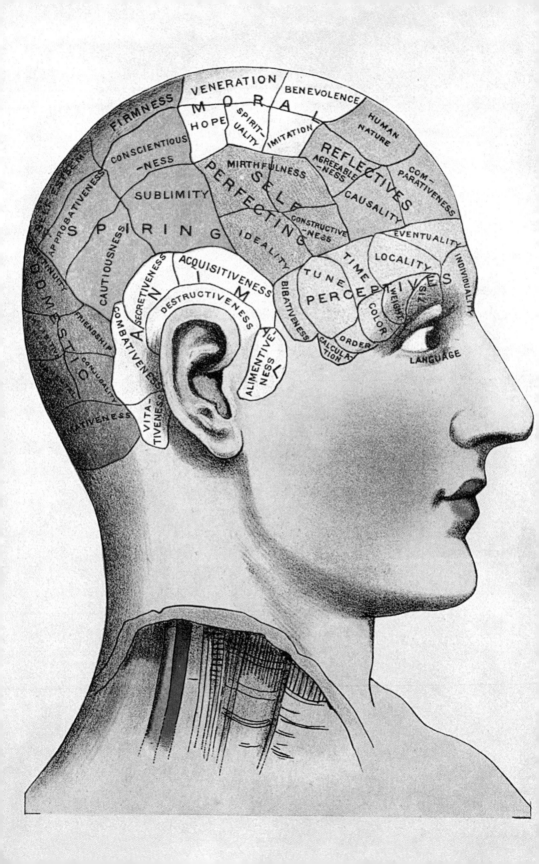

and prophetic statements in all literature. Hippocrates wrote that he and his contemporaries called epilepsy "the sacred disease" because they didn't understand its physical cause. But he predicted that we would understand it someday, and when that happened we would no longer think it divine. I first read a translation of Hippocrates when I was in college. That was when I fell in love with science.

That little boy in our story—representing all the real-life victims of epilepsy—was not cursed. The gods were not angry at him and his family. Epilepsy was caused by a physical malfunction inside the brain, but as long as we searched for its cause in the whim of the gods, we had no hope of helping the afflicted.

THOUSANDS OF YEARS PASSED after Hippocrates, and the brain remained a mystery. Between 420 B.C.E. and the 19th century, our understanding of the cosmos grew by leaps and bounds. We discovered the speed of light and the laws of gravity. We learned that our sun is part of a greater galaxy of stars. And yet, 2,300 years after Hippocrates, we still knew virtually nothing about the part of our own selves that made it possible to make these discoveries: our brains. It could be said that we actually knew less. The study of the brain had become stuck in a pseudoscientific dead end called phrenology, which held that from the shape of a person's skull, you could deduce their intelligence and character. A frenzy of head measuring ensued. According to phrenologists, signs that a person had a gift for languages resided above the cheekbone. Marital fidelity was indicated by the shape of the skull behind the ears. Not surprisingly, European phrenologists discovered that the

The pseudoscience of phrenology—proposed around 1800—held that the contours of a person's skull revealed their aptitudes and character. It was a transparent projection of the biases of the time.

shape of their particular heads represented the universal standard of cerebral excellence.

The first real scientific insight regarding the connection between the mind and the brain was made in France in 1861. Once again, epilepsy played a critical role.

In those days, the Bicêtre psychiatric hospital in Paris was considered state of the art. In the previous century, it had been the first to introduce humane practices in the treatment of the insane and the intellectually disabled. Among the doctors there, a gifted young surgeon named Paul Broca was especially admired for his enlightened treatment of patients. He believed passionately in the importance of free inquiry, breaking through the obstructions that false pattern recognition placed in the way of medical understanding.

Broca was particularly interested in a 51-year-old patient named Louis Leborgne. He had been speculating that specific regions of the brain might be responsible for the powers of speech and memory, and Leborgne presented an interesting case to study. Everyone called this patient "Tan" because that was the only syllable in his vocabulary. "Tan, tan, tan." He had been repeating that word since he had suffered an epileptic seizure at the age of 30. It was not his first—he had had seizures since childhood—but his family had him committed to Bicêtre when he lost all powers of speech except for that one word, "tan." Now poor Tan lay dying. His right side had become paralyzed and gangrene had set in. Broca visited him often, wanting to know all he could about this patient in expectation of an eventual postmortem.

When Tan closed his eyes and uttered one last feeble "tan" before dying, Broca donned his leather apron and rushed to perform the autopsy that he hoped would explain Tan's disability. He lifted Tan's brain out of his skull and was immediately struck by its asymmetry. The left hemisphere of Tan's brain looked as if it had been dented.

We do not know if Tan's epilepsy caused the damage to his brain, or if an unreported childhood injury caused his epilepsy and later

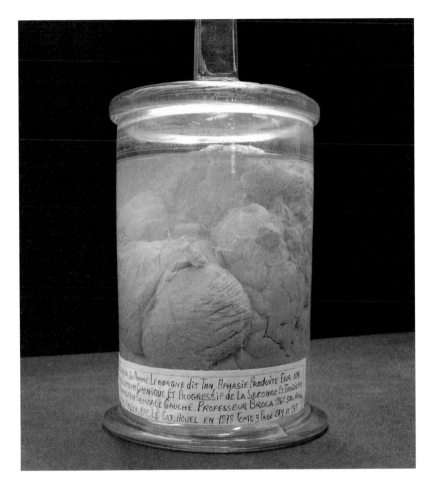

Paul Broca preserved the brain of Louis Leborgne, better known as Tan, whose disability provided clues to the language-forming region of the cerebral cortex.

loss of speech. But because of Tan's fate, Broca was able to do something that had never been done before. He correctly connected a part of the human brain, in this case the region that was damaged, to its specialized function: the ability to use language. His reward: that part of our anatomy has been known ever since as "Broca's area."

ON ONE OF THE MOST DELIGHTFUL DAYS of my life, I held Paul Broca's own brain, sloshing in a pool of preservative in a jar, where it had been kept since the summer of 1880. Almost a century later, Carl Sagan and I were in Paris, celebrating the first anniversary of the moment we had declared our love to each other. It was June 1 and our epic walk throughout the city is etched in hyper-vivid beauty in my own brain. Our foray took us to the Musée de l'Homme, where the director, Yves Coppens, welcomed us and showed us some of the fascinating hidden places in this museum dedicated to all things human.

He led us into a dark storage room lined with shelves laden with jars of oddities preserved in formaldehyde, ones no longer deemed appropriate for public display. It was there, on that day, that I learned the word "teratology," "the scientific study of congenital abnormalities and abnormal functions." Two-headed babies, shrunken heads, infants with facial deformities, anomalous body parts—and many brains. One of them was labeled "Broca." As Carl explained to me the meta-significance of holding Broca's own brain in my hands, a meditation on the meaning of science began to form in our minds.

In these sublime moments, of which there were many during our 20 years together, it felt as if we were two sides of a single brain. During these thrilling moments of oneness, Carl would dictate our thoughts into the small recording devices that he carried at all times. That particular inspiration in the Paris museum would form the title essay of the book *Broca's Brain*.

Broca was a visionary who advanced our knowledge of the brain. But, as Carl would point out, he was not free from the prejudices of his age. He believed that men were mentally superior to women, and white people superior to everyone else. As Carl would write, "His falling short of humanist ideals shows that even someone as committed to the free pursuit of knowledge as Broca could still be deceived by endemic bigotry."

Forty years later, I searched for Broca's brain for the third season of *Cosmos*. But it had vanished. Lost in the move of the collection to another museum, or, perhaps, no longer deemed a seemly exhibit for the public. Looking back, it's both gratifying and horrifying to realize how far we've come and how blind we remain.

BROCA ESTABLISHED FOR THE FIRST TIME that there were physical correlations between brain anatomy and function. But what of the crackling energy of consciousness? What of the stuff that dreams are made of? You can't put that in a jar.

When the ancient Egyptians looked up at night, they saw the underbody of Nut, goddess of the starry night. When they closed their eyes and began to dream, they believed they were transiting to the afterlife. So dreaming was ritualized into a form of worship, a means to learn what the future held, or to communicate with the gods during slumber. The faithful made pilgrimages to the temple to dream. To prepare themselves, they would withdraw to a place of isolation, and fast to cleanse mind and body. Using a stylus on a snow-white strip of linen, they would write a prayer to a particular god. The strip would be burned in the hope that its smoke would convey its contents to the underworld. Mystified by the boundary that separates our waking and sleeping lives, the ancient Egyptians believed that dreams had a material reality. How else to explain the stunning detail of a particularly vivid dream?

Thousands of years later, a scientist in 19th-century Italy also believed that conscious and unconscious thoughts actually do have a material reality, that dreams were physical phenomena that could be recorded. And he found a way to prove it in a place of broken minds and shattered dreams. The Manicomio di Collegno in Turin, Italy, was a majestic monastery when it was built in the 17th century, but by the time it became a psychiatric hospital in 1850, it had already lost much of its grandeur. It was there that Angelo Mosso conducted his experiments on dreams and thoughts.

Mosso, a child of the working class, had bootstrapped himself into becoming a scientist, working primarily in the fields of pharmacology and physiology. In a time when people were literally worked to death, without any recourse to legal protection, Mosso viewed science as a means to improve labor conditions. He designed and built an ergograph, or "fatigue recorder," to measure what the relentless stress of hard labor did to the human body and mind. Exhaustion, he believed, was a physical and emotional state, not a sign of weakness or a character flaw. It was your body's way of telling you to stop what you were doing to avoid injury. Mosso reasoned that fatigue had an evolutionary advantage, much like fear, and he wrote two influential, wide-ranging books with one-word titles on each subject: *Fatigue* and *Fear.*

Fatigue begins with Mosso's observations of the weariness of quail and other migratory birds arriving in Palo, Italy, after flying from Africa. One hundred fifty pages later, having explored overtiredness in many different species, he depicts the weariness of factory workers, revealing the hell of the industrial revolution and its toll on family life and physical safety.

In order to derive a truly quantifiable, scientific "law of exhaustion," Mosso designed an apparatus that could record the body's blood flow. To test it, he asked his assistant to disrobe and lie down on an exquisitely balanced table. He attached sensors to his assistant's big toe, hand, and heart. The sensors led back to a rotating drum, covered with graph paper and cranked like a music box. A stylus left a record of blood flow just as in a modern electrocardiogram, or EKG. Mosso had invented the sphygmomanometer, or blood pressure gauge.

If the pulsing of the heart could be recorded, what about the activity of the brain? Mosso wondered how he could transcribe the brain's delicate murmurings when it was housed in a protective

Angelo Mosso often used himself as subject of his experiments, developing instruments that sensed the flow of blood—precursors to today's electrocardiograph, or EKG.

skull. Was there any way to do that without harming the subject? Then a patient arrived at the hospital who helped Mosso answer these questions.

Giovanni Thron had fallen from a great height when he was only 18 months old. His skull had been so badly shattered some of it couldn't be put back together again. As a result of the blow, he began to have frequent and violent epileptic seizures. His parents, fearful, or perhaps unable to take it anymore, abandoned him at the Manicomio in Turin by the time he was five.

When Mosso met Giovanni six years later, he recognized that the catastrophic injury that had ruined Giovanni's life represented a rare medical opportunity. The boy wore a special leather cap that covered the missing part of his skull. Beneath that cap, Mosso found a doorway to the brain. He designed and built a machine so sensitive it could register the blood coursing through a brain. But Giovanni was so agitated during his waking hours,

Mosso could only study him while he slept. Mosso needed Giovanni to be perfectly still in order to record the faint signature of his thoughts.

"When I saw Giovanni in February 1877," Mosso wrote, "he had a large opening in the skull covered with skin. The terrible fall had forever arrested his intellectual development. It was a saddening circumstance, that in the midst of the ruin of his mind, one single, higher idea had remained, a remnant of his earlier life, a motto which he constantly repeated: 'I want to go to school.'"

As the boy slept, Mosso's assistant gingerly attached a sensor above the boy's right eye, where his brain was only covered by the thinnest of scar tissue.

"It was one of the most interesting sights to observe in the stillness of night," Mosso recorded, "by the light of a little lamp, what was going on in his brain, when there was no external cause to disturb this mysterious life of sleep. The brain-pulse remained for ten or twenty minutes quite regular and very weak . . . and then began suddenly, without any apparent cause, to swell and beat more vigorously. We scarcely dared breathe."

Mosso waited with apprehension to see if his instrument would record the pulses of the brain as well as his earlier invention had recorded the pulses of the heart. And then, at this point in his retelling of that night, Mosso the scientist and Mosso the poet become one. "Did dreams, perhaps, come to cheer the repose of the unhappy boy? Did the face of his mother and the recollections of his early childhood glow bright in his memory, lighting up the darkness of his intelligence, and making his brain pulsate with excitement? Or was it an unconscious agitation of matter, like the ebb and flow of an unknown and solitary sea?"

On that winter night, Mosso's instrument could not answer these questions, but it did register the signature of Giovanni's dream. Mosso had invented neuroimaging, and had shown that the brain has a night shift. Even in sleep it's abuzz with the processing of life's business, the plotting and casting of our dreams.

Three months after that night, Giovanni died of anemia. He was not yet 12.

ANGELO MOSSO'S PIONEERING breakthrough in the field of neuroscience inspired another man to take his work one giant step further. He wanted to demonstrate that psychic powers are real. It all happened because of a freak accident.

Hans Berger dreamed of becoming an astronomer, but he couldn't do the math, so in 1892, at the age of 19, he enlisted in the German army. While riding his horse a little too fast over a plateau into camp, Berger's horse stumbled and threw him into the path of a fast-moving heavy artillery wagon. Time seemed to slow for Berger as he realized he was about to be crushed to death. When time resumed its ordinary pace, Berger saw that the driver had stopped the wagon mere inches from where he lay. He was shaken by his brush with death, but something happened later that night that shocked him even more.

While his fellow soldiers caroused, Berger just sat on his bunk, still rattled. At first, he didn't even notice the boy who stood before him holding a telegram. Berger opened it, and what he read changed the course of his life. The telegram was from his father, a cold and distant man who had never sent him a telegram before. It said that Berger's older sister had become panic-stricken with the certainty that something terrible had happened to her little brother.

Was it possible, Berger wondered, that in the moment that he realized he was going to die, his brain had somehow telepathically delivered a message to his sister, the one closest to him? Berger resolved to find out. He buckled down and studied medicine, becoming a physician and a professor at the University of Jena. By day, he worked with his students and colleagues, who found him to be awkwardly formal, and scientifically unadventurous. But by night, he sneaked away to his secret laboratory in the Bavarian countryside to conduct experiments on the brain's activity. He was determined to prove that psychic energy was real, but he feared that if anyone were to discover his real scientific objective, he'd be laughed out of the profession.

He set up an experimental apparatus somewhat like Mosso's. Standing before a mirror, he stuck thin, silver needles into his own head. The needles were connected to wires that ran to a machine attached to a rotating drum. With the needles in place, he would pull a lever that sent a burst of electricity to the needles and wince with pain from the shock. The stylus was still resting on the paper wrapping the drum. It had not moved or made a mark. Seeing nothing, he became deflated—but soon he was at it again, always trying to perfect the instrument and make the measurements.

He kept this work secret for two decades. As the years passed, the apparatus became more efficient. He started using rubber suction cups instead of needles. Finally one day, he flicked a switch, sensed the apparatus humming, and looked over toward the rotating drum. There he saw it: The stylus was inscribing an oscillating wave. He smiled broadly, and the stylus's outline arced in response.

This was the first electroencephalograph, or EEG. Berger's electroencephalograph made it possible to interpret the electrochemical signals that the brain produces, and to diagnose many neurological diseases, including epilepsy. Berger never did find any evidence for psychic energy, or telepathic communication. He sank into a deep depression, and hanged himself in his secret laboratory in 1941.

The EEG is still in use today, although we now have far more accurate ways of seeing and recording what the brain does—and we are even beginning to decrypt the electrochemical language of thought.

EXACTLY 100 YEARS AFTER Angelo Mosso first recorded the electrical whispers of Giovanni's dream, in 1977, I recorded my own brain waves for a message to any beings in the Milky Way galaxy who might happen upon one of two derelict spacecraft at any time in the next five billion years. It came about when Carl Sagan asked me to be the creative director for an interstellar message of unprecedented complexity to be affixed to the side of NASA's Voyager 1 and 2 spacecraft. The Voyagers would undertake the first reconnaissance mission of the outer solar system before wandering through the galaxy for the next several billion years. One part of what came to be called the "golden record" consisted of music representing many human cultures, including Delta blues, Peruvian panpipes, Javanese gamelan, a Navajo night chant, Senegalese percussion, Japanese *shakuhachi,* a Georgian men's chorus, and much more. Another section of the record was devoted to different kinds of sounds: a newborn's first cry and her mother's soothing murmurs, the roar of an F-111 flyby, a cricket song, a kiss, and greetings in 59 different human languages and one whale language. We had no idea who would ever hear this recording or what it would mean to them, but we knew it was a sacred undertaking. Nothing we had built would ever travel so far and last so long. In 1977, with the Cold War raging, we looked upon our task as building an ark of human culture.

Carl and I fell in love that same spring while we were making the golden record. We had known each other for three years as platonic friends and co-workers, each committed to another person. In that other life I had asked Carl if it would be possible for our imagined extraterrestrials to decipher the signals from a recording of a meditation that registered my EEG, EKG, and REM (rapid eye movement) sleep. Carl replied, "Billions of years is a long time, Annie. Go do it."

The recording session at a New York hospital fell only two days after we had blurted out our feelings to each other in a long-distance phone call and decided to marry. My thought itinerary for the meditation included a broad narrative of the multibillion-year history of our planet. Toward the end of the hour, I permitted myself a

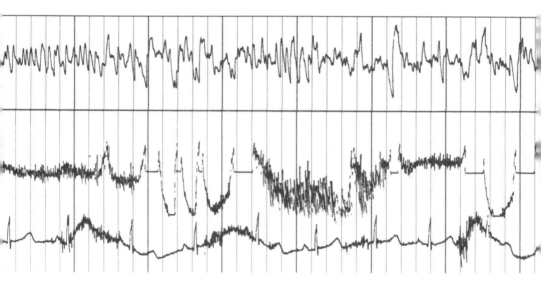

Ann Druyan's brain waves and heart sounds, recorded in June 1977 for the Voyager golden record. Might the extraterrestrials in another part of the Milky Way galaxy some five billion years from now be able to interpret the joy contained therein?

personal exploration of the love that I had discovered only hours before. My fresh joy at finding my heart's true home will endure on those records longer than Earth itself.

From horse-drawn carriage to interstellar craft in just a hundred years. From hand-delivered telegrams to sending our thoughts to each other at the speed of light, and our deepest feelings through the Milky Way to billions of years from now. How did we make that leap? And why us? Of all the billions of species that have ever lived on Earth, why us and no other? Primates who descended from the African savanna have sent their robot emissaries to explore the red deserts of Mars, and ring that world with satellites. We've only been at this for 60 years, not even a lifetime, and yet look at how far beyond our little planet our robots have ventured!

Every one of those odysseys of discovery began in our brains. It's easy to see why the seat of all these mythic achievements would itself seem beyond our ability to understand. It's hard to believe that our minds are made of the same matter as our stomachs and our feet.

CONSCIOUSNESS SEEMS SUPERNATURAL. Identity, awe, skepticism, imagination, love—how do you assemble transcendence from the periodic chart of the elements? What distant star had to explode to seed our world with inspiration?

If you want to know how matter was turned into consciousness, you have to go all the way back to the first one-celled organisms in the ocean. Now, I know what you're thinking: No way these little guys have brains. You're right. They don't. But this is the dawn of awareness. Microbes used their tiny flagella to swim toward the sunlight dappling the surface of the ocean, while others sought refuge in the deep. These one-celled microbes may not have known much, but they did know some things: "Go to the light . . . Oops, too much light. Find somewhere dark." You get the idea. We do not know for certain precisely when the first flagella evolved, but it was sometime during the autumn of the Cosmic Calendar year.

When you think about it, the defining quality of being alive is the ability to adapt to your environment. And you can't do that very well without being aware on some level. Over billions of years, these creatures became so much more than the sum of their parts.

At the bottom of the sea, off the coast of Chile and Peru, lives what is probably the largest living organism on Earth. Composed of millions of tendrils swaying in graceful underwater motion, it's a community of microbes the size of Greece. It may not look like much more than an undulating shag carpet, but there's something even more amazing about it than its immensity. The ancient ancestors of these colonies, preserved as fossils called stromatolites, consisted of cyanobacteria, microbes that could photosynthesize. This was an early step in the development of brains. When the microbes living at the center of this vast mat get hungry, they dispatch electrical messages on waves of potassium to their fellow citizens at the outer edge. These communiques travel via passages called ion channels. Waves of amber potassium shoot from the local microbes and are relayed by other microbes to the periphery. A message goes out saying, "Hey, guys, stop hogging all the food!" And the residents of the mat's outer edge respond by reducing their intake of nutrients. It's possible that the ancient ancestors evolved cells called neurons that specialized in this kind of messaging.

Neurons are the basic unit of nervous systems in almost every life-form in the animal kingdom—including us. And they vary very little in nature, if at all, from species to species, but they vary dramatically in number. In fact, we now think that epilepsy may be a misfiring in the brain's neural ion channels.

Think of it: a microbial mat and Isaac Newton, separated by hundreds of millions of years of evolution but sharing the same basic unit of currency of thought. The messaging system pioneered by the microbes some four billion years ago is still inside us. It's inscribed in the book of life, written throughout our genes. Your heart beats, and your brain thinks, because those ancient microbes got together and became something much more complex and impossible to foresee. No one looking at a microbial mat three billion years ago could have predicted that the one-celled organisms of life on Earth would evolve into you. That's what happens when living things and environments interact over the course of eons, making it possible for smaller entities to unite and evolve. When the resulting entities become more than the sum of their parts, the phenomenon is sometimes called emergence.

The sea jelly, more commonly known as a jellyfish, is a good example. It doesn't have a brain, or any eyes, or a heart. It's kind of like the stromatolite—a community of much smaller cyanobacteria that have bonded for life. But it's way fancier than a colony of microbes, and with a lot more personality—and 5,600 neurons.

Jellyfish, such as this mauve stinger (Pelagia noctiluca) from Malta, have no brains but rather a diffuse network of nerves throughout their bodies.

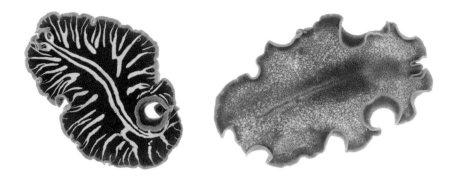

But what's a neuron without a synapse—that junction where bits of information flow between neurons and emerge into heightened states of awareness? Synapses represented a giant evolutionary leap, and some sea jellies have them. Their individual parts can function independently. They can be cut in half and regenerate into two complete sea jellies. I mean, what life-form can do that?

Well, actually I happen to know one that can. You can cut off its head, no problem, it'll just grow another. In fact, you cannot kill it with a knife. It's a creature that looks like a shred of a ruffle from a gaudy dress, but what a story it has to tell.

Long, long ago—some 600 million years ago—life first evolved something new to planet Earth, a command center that could perceive and react to its environment: a brain. We think it first happened inside an ancient flatworm, the first animal hunter. A brain was just what a hunter would need to seek out and plan a strategy for attack. Aiding the process was the emergence of two eyes with overlapping fields of view. This binocular vision allowed this ancient creature to perceive the dimension of depth more sharply and see objects with greater clarity, all the better to triangulate on prey.

The flatworm brain had a pair of dense nerve clusters called ganglia. Cords extended from them, carrying instructions and sensations to the rest of its body via some 8,000 neurons. Not many compared with the life-forms that would come later, but a momentous beginning.

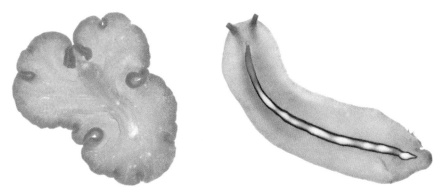

More than 20,000 species of flatworm have been identified, many of them marine invertebrates with brilliant colors, like these. The distant ancestors of these planaria had the first brains.

Flatworms have something called auricles on the sides of their heads where their ears should be, but they're actually noses. We may not look much alike, but we have a lot in common. We share the same chemicals that control our nervous systems, called neurotransmitters. We get addicted to the same drugs. Flatworms can learn. They process information about their environment and act accordingly. We think they were nature's first animals to have a front, a back, and a head—a blueprint that remains state of the art, 600 million years later. And they were true pioneers in the deepest sense of that word. Unlike any life-form before them, they developed the habit of venturing into unknown territory in search of what they craved.

Despite the similarities, there's a big difference between a flatworm brain and ours. How did we get from there to here? We don't yet know. That's mainly because brains tend to be squishy. They don't leave distinct imprints in the fossil record. But the brain itself preserves its evolutionary past.

As we first observed in the original *Cosmos* television series, New York City offers an apt metaphor for the brain, growing from a settlement to a world capital through a series of unplanned developments. As the various systems of roads, water, energy distribution, and communications grew and changed, the city had to remain operational at all times, just as the brain must have throughout its evolution. Neither the brain nor the city can be shut down for repairs and enhancements. The older limbic system must continue working perfectly while the much more recent cerebral cortex evolves.

If all the contents of your brain were transcribed into written language—and I don't just mean knowledge, I mean your ability to breathe, and smell the flowers and remember how they smell, and all the things that the brain accomplishes gracefully behind the scenes, everything your brain knows how to do, and knows anything about—it would amount to more books than are contained in the largest libraries on Earth. The equivalent of more than four billion books are inside your head. As we wrote in the first *Cosmos,* "The brain is a very big place in a very small space."

Those books are written in the neurons pioneered by the undersea microbial mats. They are tiny electrochemical switching elements, typically a few hundredths of a millimeter across. Each of us has something like a hundred billion neurons, comparable to the number of stars in the Milky Way galaxy. The neurons, and their parts—axons, dendrites, synapses, and the cell bodies themselves—make up a network in the brain. Many neurons have thousands of connections with their neighbors. Dendrites, those pathways sent out by neurons to connect with other neurons, extend these nerve cells to synapses until they create a full-blown network of consciousness.

The neurochemistry of the brain is astonishingly busy. Its circuitry is that of a machine more wonderful than any devised by humans. Your brain functions are due to those hundred trillion neural connections that make you, you. Your deepest feelings of love and awe—those moments when we glimpse the grandeur of nature, and all the elegant architecture of consciousness—are made possible by those connections. This is the essence of emergence: tiny units of matter operating collectively to become something much more than themselves, to enable the cosmos to know itself.

But there's a vision of emergence that takes it even higher.

CAN WE KNOW THE UNIVERSE? All those galaxies, solar systems, numberless worlds, moons, comets, beings, and their dreams—everything that ever was, is, or will be? Carl Sagan mused in *Broca's Brain* that he was not sure we could even know a grain of salt. "Consider one microgram of table salt, a speck just barely large enough for someone with keen eyesight to make out without a microscope. In that grain of salt there are about 10 to the 16th sodium and chlorine atoms. This is a one followed by 16 zeros, 10 million billion atoms.

"If we wish to know the grain of salt, we must know at least the three-dimensional positions of each of these atoms." Carl goes on to observe how lucky we are to have a body of knowledge that has mapped the crystal lattice structure and position of every single atom in a grain of salt. This reduces the number of bits needed to know the grain of salt to only 10. If the cosmos is governed by laws, including and similar to the ones we've begun to understand, then the cosmos will be knowable, even if artificial intelligence was needed to augment our own. Carl calculated that there's something like a hundred trillion—that is, a hundred thousand billion—connections in your cerebral cortex. That's a hundred times as many connections inside you as all the galaxies in the visible universe.

We are just at the beginning of a great journey of exploration. Just as biologists succeeded in mapping the human genome, neuroscientists are attempting to map something far more complex and unique to each and every one of us. It's called our connectome—the singular wiring diagram of all our memories, thoughts, fears, and dreams. Once we understand its intricacies, how might we treat each other? Could we heal the brain of its countless torments, and free all the Giovannis of the world? Could we send one of our connectomes on a future interstellar probe, or ever hope to receive one from the being of another world?

Would that be the ultimate realization of emergence—a cosmos interconnected by a connectome of thoughts and dreams?

DR. GONZALEZ FINDS ME in the waiting room after Sam's operation. As he crosses the room I can't tell anything from his expression. He sits down and smiles modestly, telling me the procedure has been a success. It will take time for Sam to recover, but he will remain Sam without any loss of his considerable knowledge and abilities. In the coming weeks when his brain cools down, they will do a much less dangerous follow-up procedure to ensure his safety. All my life I have been writing love letters to science and today Dr. Gonzalez has justified my love.

Can we know a grain of salt? This polarized light micrograph only begins to reveal the crystalline complexity of the salt we shake out every day.

CHAPTER SIX

THE MAN OF A TRILLION WORLDS

April 24, 1956
Dear Dr. Kuiper,
After carefully considering your generous offer
concerning summer research at McDonald—
and after it was pointed out that Europe
will always be as far away from this country
as it is now, which is not the case for Mars—
I accept with delight.
—LETTER FROM 21-YEAR-OLD CARL SAGAN

A scientist who transcended disciplinary boundaries
... and who helped carry us to the Moon and the planets.
—CARL SAGAN'S OBITUARY FOR HAROLD UREY,
ICARUS, SEPTEMBER 17, 1981

The Hubble Ultra Deep Field combined 800 exposures to present a vision of 10,000 galaxies. The farther away the galaxy, the longer ago its image represents. The smallest red galaxies are the most distant, representing the universe at 800 million years old, or mid-January on the Cosmic Calendar.

Once there was a boy who had a special power. He could see farther than anyone else when he gazed at the skies. He saw stars too distant and too faint for others to find without a telescope. When most people looked up at the Pleiades they saw the seven sparkling sapphires and perhaps two or three of the dimmer stars. For our ancestors, the Pleiades had served as the qualifying exam for hunters and scouts. If you could see 12 stars, the job was yours. But this boy could see 14. Gerard Peter Kuiper could see stars that were four times dimmer than those visible to the average human eye.

This was in the Netherlands more than a hundred years ago. Back then, the son of a poor tailor could not hope to become an astronomer. But the boy would not be stopped. In that time, astronomers thought that the cosmos consisted of only a handful of planets—those of our own solar system. Maybe one or two other stars also had planets, they allowed, but our solar system was thought to be one in a trillion. Astronomers saw the great multitude of other stars as barren points of light that had never given birth to any worlds. Even if we weren't the center of the universe, we on Earth could still feel special. Our sun, the scientists believed, was that rarest of stars blessed by worlds and moons.

A Perseid meteor streaks across the sky, seeming to graze the asterism known as the Pleiades, above Yosemite's El Capitan and Half Dome.

Kuiper had a scientist's soul, that yearning to know how the stars and planets had come to be. As a teenager, the young stargazer became fascinated by the ideas of a man who had lived almost three centuries before him: the 17th-century philosopher René Descartes. Descartes described his theory of the origin of the solar system, a vision of colorful, swirling pinwheel clouds with the sun at their center. Featureless planets formed out of the spinning clouds. But Descartes lived in one of those times and places where the penalty for advancing an idea that conflicted with the state's religious view could mean imprisonment, torture, death. He kept his vision to himself, and it was only published 20 years after he was safely dead. Descartes's rudimentary conception predated Isaac Newton's understanding of gravity and its role in the formation of the solar system. But it was more than enough to excite the mind of a future scientist.

Kuiper showed such promise that his father and grandfather pooled their meager resources to buy him a simple telescope. He aced the tests a poor tailor's son was not supposed to pass, and made his way to the University of Leiden in 1924, where a kind of mini–golden age in astronomy was taking place: Willem de Sitter, who collaborated with Einstein on cosmology; Bart Bok, who taught us so much about the evolution and shape of our home galaxy; Jan Oort, who found our sun's place in the galaxy and predicted the existence of the vast cloud of cometary nuclei surrounding our solar system that bears his name; and Ejnar Hertzsprung, who developed the classification system for the stars—these were just some of the distinguished faculty and students there.

Leiden was a special place for astronomers at that moment. It may have been the intense ambient light in this densely populated small country and frequently overcast skies that channeled the Dutch away from optical observations and into radio astronomy, which earthly clouds could not obstruct. Radio telescopes harvest the radio emissions from astronomical objects rather than their visible light. Radio astronomy would extend our vision of the

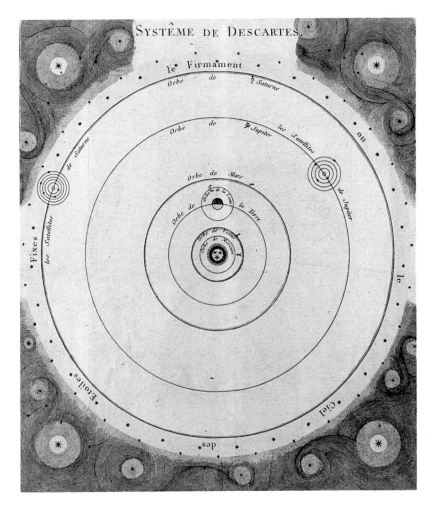

Descartes's 17th-century solar system represented planets orbiting the sun and stars being formed in vortices beyond.

cosmos beyond the narrow band of electromagnetic radiation that our eyes have evolved to see.

Kuiper had rough edges. He was argumentative, and easily drawn into conflict with his colleagues. And he could be careless about properly acknowledging the work of others. His personality quirks would have made life and work in the small pond of Leiden difficult. Kuiper was probably relieved when he was offered an

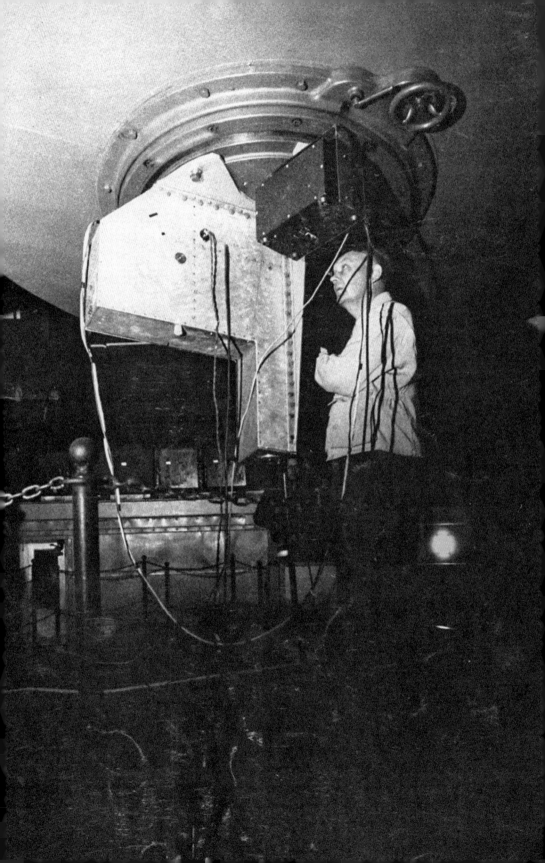

appointment at McDonald Observatory in a corner of West Texas. The prospect of directing a remote observatory, far away from the capitals of scientific culture, must have appealed to him. And besides, you could see the stars better there than just about anywhere else. No cities or towns for miles and miles, just wild darkness.

At the turn of the 20th century, astronomers had discovered that half the visible stars were really gravitational pairs. Most binary stars are like twins, forming from the same womb of gas and dust. Others come of age separately and become gravitationally involved with each other later in their development. And the other half remain single throughout their lives. Kuiper chose to concentrate on the binary stars. He wondered if they could shed light on the way that the planets of our solar system formed, and came to be gravitationally bound to our sun.

AS WITH EVERY DISCOVERY in the history of science, Kuiper was carrying on the search begun by someone else in another time and place. In this case, it was the work of a scientist of great promise who was only permitted the briefest glimpse of the stars.

In 1784, a handsome 20-year-old named John Goodricke visited his friend Edward Pigott's observatory in York, England. Goodricke couldn't hear; a childhood illness left him completely deaf. But like Kuiper, he could see things others missed. The telescope Goodricke used was little more than a wooden tube and a mirror, but what it revealed amazed him: There was something funny about a star called Beta Lyrae.

Goodricke sketched his observations in a log. He continued to observe and sketch Beta Lyrae and its neighboring stars over a

Gerard Peter Kuiper uses an infrared spectrometer at McDonald Observatory to analyze Mars's atmosphere, 1956.

period of weeks. It's clear from his drawings that he was observing Beta Lyrae as it waxed and waned in brightness. This was the second time he'd seen a star behave so strangely, and no other astronomer had ever reported such a thing. The star changed regularly in brightness over a very brief period of time—in only days. It was a subtle effect, but his continuing observations proved that it was real. To Goodricke's surprise, he found that he could predict its variations with great accuracy. The repeating pattern of the numbers on the log was recognizable at a glance.

Goodricke wondered what could cause such a change in a star's brightness, but none of the explanations that came to mind satisfied the evidence before him. And then he thought of a staggering possibility: Suppose there was something orbiting Beta Lyrae that eclipsed the star on a regular basis. But what could it be? Goodricke wrote in his log the following words: *"A world perhaps . . . ?"*

When his discoveries came to the attention of the prestigious British Royal Society in 1786, Goodricke was immediately made a member. Word of this honor never reached him. Only days later, he was dead of pneumonia. He was only 21.

One hundred fifty years later, Gerard Kuiper looked at Beta Lyrae, the same star that had baffled Goodricke, but now with a much bigger telescope. And Kuiper was armed with an awesome power that didn't exist in Goodricke's time: spectroscopy.

Spectroscopy is a way to dissect the light of any single star to find its particular atomic and molecular composition. Kuiper looked at the spectrum produced by the light of Beta Lyrae, which was already known to have a companion star. He saw that, as with all stars, there was plenty of hydrogen and helium. But there was also iron, sodium, silicon, and oxygen.

So far, no surprises there. Now here comes the twist. The dark lines of the spectrum shifted ever so subtly back and forth, as one might expect if a hidden body was gravitationally tugging on the star. But he also observed a set of bright spectral lines that did not move. Something else must be happening. In trying to understand

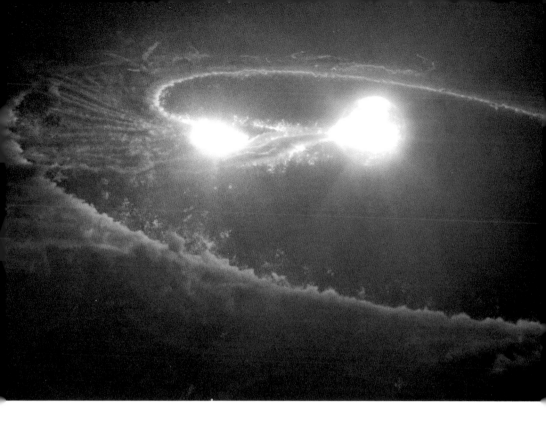

An artist's depiction of Beta Lyrae, a contact binary. This intimate stellar relationship is bound by gravity and connected by an eight-million-mile-long bridge of fire.

what he had seen that night, Kuiper discovered and named the most intimate stellar relationship in the cosmos: a contact binary star system.

Two stars, one large, one small, are connected by a bridge of fire made of starstuff, streaming off the smaller star. That exchange of matter explained the bright lines. The stars are physically locked in everlasting oneness, bound together by gravity, and an incandescent bridge *eight million miles long*. The smaller, blue-white star is six times bigger than our sun. The other orange star is 15 times greater still. Their roiling surfaces pulse with furious intensity. Massive sunspots appear and vanish. Fiery prominences flare and arc into dizzying heights. They are not round like other stars because they're so close to one another. Tidal forces of gravity pull them together, and stretch the two stars into flaming teardrops.

The Beta Lyrae system is about a thousand light-years from Earth. The largest telescopes of the mid-20th century were just not powerful enough to resolve them as individual stars. We needed the new power of spectroscopy to disentangle them.

Kuiper imagined how the formation of the contact binary star system could have happened. He envisioned Beta Lyrae's large and small stars spinning backward in time to the period of their formation from a vast, multicolored cloud of gas and dust. He deduced that they were formed when that cloud became so dense that gravitational whirlpools formed. In thinking about these contact binaries, Kuiper couldn't help but wonder if any of these stellar courtships ever failed to catch fire.

Kuiper asked himself: Was our world, our sun, our moon, and all the planets of our solar system *nothing more than a failed binary star system?* Was the gas giant planet Jupiter, the firstborn world of our sun, more massive than all the other worlds in the solar system, really a *failed* star? And if that's how our solar system came to be, had the same thing happened around other stars throughout the cosmos?

In 1949, Kuiper astonished the world by declaring that our solar system was not so special after all—that half of all the stars had their own family of planets.

A world perhaps?

How about trillions of possible worlds?

But science wasn't ready for that universe. It wasn't even ready to take its first baby step off the planet. Why not?

Science was carved up into little kingdoms—the various scientific disciplines—and scientists of one discipline didn't collaborate with anyone from another. This had to change in order for us to venture beyond Earth. It all came to a head in a feud between Kuiper and another great scientist. Like the two stars of a contact binary system, they could not disengage. But despite their loathing for each other, they co-parented a new kind of science.

A time exposure photograph of the Geminid meteor shower, which the Earth passes through every December

SOMETIMES THE COSMOS just barges right in, and breaks down your door. Like those nights when you thrill to countless streaks of golden light raining down upon Earth. What is going on there?! Our planet is passing through the epic remnants of a comet. A debris field millions of miles long. That's why it looks like it's raining stars. But they're not stars at all, just bits of rock and ice burning up in Earth's atmosphere. It's called a meteor shower, and they happen on the same dates every year. Why? Because it takes a year for Earth to orbit the sun, and return to that same place where the comet streaked by so long ago. That's what a year is.

A bit of an iron meteorite that crashed and formed a crater some 50,000 years ago in today's Texas. Its crystalline pattern shows it was part of a minor planet formed between Mars and Jupiter about 4.5 billion years ago—mid-April on the Cosmic Calendar.

Fragments of comets and asteroids fall to Earth all the time. They come from other worlds, leftovers from the creation of our solar system. But how to understand them? In Gerard Kuiper's time, during the middle of the 20th century, it depended on what kind of scientist you were.

The geologists would bring their hammers, smash it, and look at its dust under a microscope to study its crystalline structure. It was their way of finding out which missing piece in the puzzle of Earth the meteorite could provide.

The chemists were searching for the same answers, but they would drop it in hydrochloric acid to see if it could be transformed from one compound into another. They would torture the meteorite to see if it would give up its secrets about nature on the molecular level.

The physicists would want to see it at its most naked, stripped down to its mass, its density, its hardness, its resistance to heat.

The biologists wouldn't even stop to pick it up. Back then, they would've walked right by it, because they didn't think there was any chance that a meteorite from space had anything to do with them. In their view, life could only be from one place—Earth.

But the craziest thing of all is that back then, the astronomers would have walked right by it, too. Their sights were focused on the distance. And you can't really blame them. What was happening in astronomy back then? Big ideas about events and objects far beyond our solar system. Einstein's theory of relativity, with its vision of riding a light beam across the cosmos, and Edwin Hubble's discovery that distant galaxies were flying away from one another as the universe expanded—that's what raised goose bumps in those days, not looking at a rock lying in your own backyard. Studying the planets, moons, comets, and meteors of our own tiny solar system seemed like Little League.

That was, until Kuiper dared to venture into territories off-limits to astronomy. Night after night, he would stay up, a virtuoso playing the 45-ton, 82-inch telescope like a violin, searching the solar system for clues to its origin. This was a mystery that he recognized was insoluble without the cooperative enterprise of all the scientific disciplines.

But the scientists didn't know they needed one another.

The geologists and the astronomers didn't speak a common language, and there was no university department on Earth where a chemist and a biologist could cross-pollinate their knowledge and ideas. So here, in the middle of nowhere, in a corner of West Texas, Kuiper conducted his one-man exploration of the solar system.

He looked at Titan, one of Saturn's moons, and discovered that it had an atmosphere. It was thick with methane. A point of light in the sky had suddenly become a possible world. Kuiper used the spectroscope to probe the acrid clouds in the upper atmosphere of Jupiter, to see what they were made of, to discover their chemical and atomic structures. And when he looked at the red planet Mars, he found carbon dioxide in its atmosphere. And he wondered: Am I looking at my own planet's future, or its past?

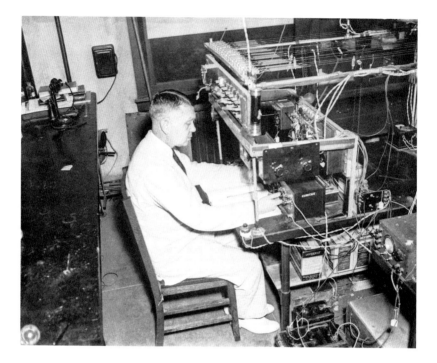

Harold C. Urey, who won the Nobel Prize for discovering deuterium and played a leading role in the exploitation of the atom and the exploration of the solar system

But to some people, Kuiper was doing nothing more than trespassing, butting into chemical matters where an astronomer had no business. One of those people was Harold Clayton Urey.

Urey was a chemist. Like Gerard Kuiper, he'd had to fight his way into science. Born in a small town in Indiana in 1893, Urey's family was poor, like Kuiper's. It only got worse when Urey was six. His father died. College was out of the question, so he took a job teaching grammar school in a mining camp in Montana. His brilliance seemed out of place there. The parents of one of his students urged him to find a way to get to college. He was already in his mid-20s, but it was not too late. Urey took that advice all the way to a Nobel Prize, awarded to him in 1934 for his discovery of deuterium.

By 1949, Urey was riding high, a distinguished professor at the University of Chicago, then and now one of the world's great capitals of science. But something soured inside him when press accounts of Kuiper's pronouncements began to reach him. First, a pang at a fellow scientist's heightened celebrity. Well, that was normal. But the part about the origin of the planets . . . He was horrified that an astronomer was making pronouncements about the chemical nature of the solar system. That was his turf.

Scientists are human. Primates, actually. They carry the same evolutionary baggage as the rest of us. Kuiper and Urey were two alpha males who chose scientific argument as their weapon of combat. And the two men held a single hostage, a promising young student with an all-consuming desire to know the universe.

IN 1910, AT THE AGE OF FIVE, Carl Sagan's father, Sam, embarked on an epic voyage with his 15-year-old half brother, George. The two boys left Kaminetz-Podolsk, a small town in Ukraine, and made their way to Ellis Island. Despite the loss of Sam's mother in child-hood and a hardscrabble youth, he somehow managed to retain a sunny sweetness throughout his life. That openheartedness com-bined with his quicksilver wit was a winning combination. He put himself through two years at Columbia University with his earnings from shooting pool. He hoped to become a pharmacist, but there was just no money to continue his education. So he went to work for George's New York Girl Coat Company as a cutter.

He fell in love with another motherless child, Rachel Molly Gruber. She was born in New York City, but her father exiled her to Austria to live with her grandparents when her mother died in childbirth. She was only two. This, and other catastrophes, shat-tered her trust and channeled her brilliance into emotionally defensive strategies. Her wounds made her fierce and hard to reach. She was one of the many thwarted women of her time who would've made her mark if given a world where females were held in higher

Chicago News - Nov 3, 1944
NEW NAZI WEAP
V-2, New rocket with Ne
3000 m.p.h. terrorizes Br... 1953

San Francisco
XS-1 BREAKS SONIC B
White Plains, N.M. 1948 (AP)
The Army's XS-1 rocket t
passed the speed of sound. It b

see space flight, said Mr
Glenn L. M... today. Mr
...art... believes this since he

Wilkes-Barre Sun - Sep
O.S.R.D. DEVELOPS ATO
DRIVE FOR AVIATION
NEW DISCOVERY HE

Chronicle, 1953
ATOM DRIVEN SHIP
SPEED OF 5 MILES A S
INS the amazing

Denver Star - Apr 17, 1955
SOVIET AND AMERICAN
GOVERNMENTS AGREE
ON MUTUAL COOPERATION
IN PREPARATION
FIRST MOON
SHIP

Newark - 195
ANTI-
METEORITE
SPACE-ARMOR

PHILADELPHIA RECORD Jan 4, 1955
SPACESHIP REACHES
MOON!!!

(UP) It was proven to
U.S and U.S.S.R. get t

SHINGTON TRIBUNE
1959 EXTRA
ENON - 1959 - EXTR
ON MOON - TWO
SIANS - TWO AMERICA

N ORLEANS PO
MARS REAC
1960 - The red pla

NORTH AMERI
Division 74, Level
Newsletter for A...
JUPITER AND S
TURN ARE NE

1961 - CLEVELAN
LIFE FOUN
ON VENUS
- Prehistoric-like
reptiles are kno

NEWSLETTER for 7/4/65
ERICA, Division 23, Level N
PLUTO AND PROSP
HAVE BEEN EXPLOR
WHAT NEXT?

evel D' Newsletter for 11/9/67 - N
EPSILON ALTAIR VII SEEN FIT
FOR HUMAN HABITATION!!
IP) A new organization, Interste
Spacelines plans to explore and colo
new planets on other stars. An expe

RICA, Division 1, Level A-
Newsletter for 4/29/68-
"LITTLE STAR, how I
wonder what you are." so
Have you ever said
this rhyme? If you have and are inter
ested in joining the crew of a spaceship
like M-1, contact the ISS office
nearest you Young men and couples
from 22 to 32 years in top physical

esteem. Sam's love was even more powerful than all the traumas she'd sustained. They made a great life together and had two children, first Carl and then, six years later, a daughter, Cari.

It was in their modest apartment in Bensonhurst, a working-class neighborhood of Brooklyn in the mid-1940s, that Carl lay on the living room rug, tracing and freestyling a recruiting poster for an interstellar space fleet.

Once there was a boy who had a special power. He could see further than other people: into the future. His drawing featured the mastheads of famous newspapers of the time, and their fanciful headlines, stretching into distant decades, proclaiming the swift and ambitious exploration of the galaxy. In an era when life here was in the last seconds of its four-billion-year captivity on Earth, he dreamed of going to the planets, and even to the stars.

And so on that afternoon, the boy's drawing made a startling announcement: "A NEW ORGANIZATION, INTERSTELLAR SPACE LINES, PLANS TO EXPLORE AND COLONIZE NEW PLANETS ON OTHER STARS."

His dream was rooted in the terrible but distant reality that had dominated his childhood, the Second World War that had recently ended. He correctly deduced that the Nazi's weaponized rockets of the Blitzkrieg contained the potential for more benign applications in space exploration.

Chicago News, November 3, 1944: "NEW NAZI WEAPON. V-2, NEW ROCKET WITH SPEED OF 3,600 M.P.H. TERRORIZES BRITAIN," he wrote.

But then he bolted seven years into the future to imagine the scientific and technological might of the victors joining forces to explore the cosmos. *Denver Star:* April 13, 1955: "SOVIET AND AMERICAN GOVERNMENTS AGREE ON MUTUAL COOPERATION IN PREPARATION FOR FIRST MOON SHIP." And from the

"The Evolution of Interstellar Flight" as envisioned by a kid in Brooklyn in the mid-1940s: Carl Sagan's prophetic dream of the future exploration of the galaxy

moon, that first stepping-stone to the stars, he imagined the course of human progress through the galaxy. *New Orleans Post,* 1960: "MARS REACHED!" "Level D Newsletter," November 9, 1967: "EPSI-LON ALTAIR 8 SEEN FIT FOR HUMAN HABITATION!"

But the dream didn't end when it was time to clear away his little project so the family could have dinner. Carl didn't want to just go in his imagination, he wanted to *really go;* he wanted to know what those worlds were really like. And he knew that the only way to do that was to become a scientist.

Carl would later come under the wings of the two warring giants, Kuiper and Urey. As much as they hated each other, he loved them both. Together, the three of them would tear down the walls between the sciences. And Carl would do everything he could to tear down the tallest wall, the one between science and the rest of us.

THE SAGAN FAMILY'S FORTUNES improved when Carl was a teenager, and the family now lived in a small house in the suburbs. When Carl was still a student at Rahway High School in New Jersey, he wrote a paper about his speculations on the origin of life. He wanted an expert critical opinion of his essay, but he'd never met a scientist and didn't know who to ask. So Rachel sent his paper to the closest thing to a scientist they knew, the son of a friend, Seymour Abrahamson, who was a grad student in biology at Indiana University.

Abrahamson was so impressed, he showed Carl's paper to a distinguished professor on the faculty, H. J. Muller, who had won the Nobel Prize for his discovery that radiation causes mutations in genes. (Muller had been one of Nikolay Vavilov's closest friends and colleagues. He, too, spoke out against Lysenkoism in the most repressive days of the Stalin era. He pleaded with Vavilov to leave the Soviet Union with him and barely escaped with his own life.) To Carl's astonishment, Muller liked his ideas and invited him to Indiana to discuss them. This led to Carl's very first scientific appointment, a summer job in Muller's lab.

Carl told me how many embarrassing, rookie mistakes he made that summer. But Muller's encouragement was unflagging. He urged Carl to pursue his passion to know how life got started here and whether it had happened elsewhere. He helped Carl get his first two scientific papers published. And when Carl was admitted to the University of Chicago, Muller sent word to Harold Urey that a budding scientist of great promise was coming his way. Would he please take this fledgling under his wing?

But Urey's idea of mentorship was different from Muller's. Where Muller was gentle and reassuring, Urey was gruff and quick to anger. By the early 1950s, when Carl arrived at Urey's lab, the chemist was now doing the thing that he had resented Kuiper for— trespassing on the turf of another scientific discipline. This time it was biology. Urey and his team wanted to know how life could have originated from lifeless matter. Working with another student of his, Stanley Miller, Urey designed an experiment to simulate the chemical conditions of the atmosphere on the early Earth. They wanted to see whether those basic chemicals could have led to amino acids, the building blocks of life. Could lightning have provided the spark that awakened matter into life?

"And if it could happen here on Earth, where else could it have happened?" Carl wondered. When he wrote a paper speculating on that possibility, Urey responded harshly. He scolded his apprentice for venturing beyond his expertise. But still, Carl revered Urey because he knew that this toughness would make him a better scientist.

When Carl completed his master's work in 1956, he decided to remain at the University of Chicago for his doctorates in physics and astronomy. The Doctoral Astronomy Program was based at Yerkes Observatory in Williams Bay, Wisconsin, then under the directorship of Urey's nemesis, Gerard Kuiper. That summer of 1956, Kuiper invited the 21-year-old to join him at McDonald Observatory for a couple of months of looking at Mars. At that time, Kuiper was the only planetary astronomer on the planet.

Mars was in a favorable opposition to Earth—the two worlds would be the closest they'd been in 30 years. Kuiper and Sagan took turns looking through the telescope eyepiece, invariably shaking their heads in disappointment. The weather didn't cooperate—not in Texas, but on Mars. A global, windblown dust storm there prevented Kuiper and Sagan from seeing anything new. So instead, they spent those summer nights talking of many things. The older man taught the young scientist the most efficient ways to test his bold new ideas and how best to make a "back of the envelope" calculation, methods Carl would use daily for the rest of his life. They fantasized about what those possible worlds, circling other stars, might be like. These two fearless scientific imaginations ventured throughout the galaxy all that summer. The gates to the wonderworld were swinging open for Carl.

To conjure up the cosmos of that summer is to know how far we've come since. Pretend that we live in a time before any spacecraft or human had ever left Earth. No one had ever even seen our own little world from space. And then, in one instant, on a single day in the following year, everything changed. On October 4, 1957, a Vostok rocket was launched from Baikonur Cosmodrome in the U.S.S.R. into space, releasing its payload before falling back to Earth. The launch package opened and sent forth a gleaming futurist orb trailing streamlined silver antennas. Sputnik 1, a simple radio transmitter, circled Earth every 96 minutes. People all over the world came outside at night, climbing to their rooftops to look for a tiny man-made moon that declared nothing could stop us from achieving our most daring dreams. Think of it: Something we made was a new light in the night sky, something like a star.

It scared the hell out of the United States. The Cold War was a contest between dueling ideologies about property and free-

The space age begins: On October 4, 1957, the Soviet Union launches Sputnik 1, the first man-made satellite.

dom. When the Russians succeeded by getting into space first, it seemed to reflect badly on the Western worldview. And if they could send Sputnik into orbit, above American heads, they could easily send other more dangerous things. America, long protected by two oceans and weak friendly neighbors to the north and south, was vulnerable to attack for the first time. It could no longer defend the skies overhead. Suddenly, there was a new orbital route for spying and sending nuclear weapons. Nowhere on Earth could be safeguarded against espionage or attack. The United States needed a space program of its own. The National Aeronautics and Space Administration was founded less than a year after Sputnik, in 1958.

And there was another by-product of Sputnik. Science was at last ready to see Earth as Kuiper had been seeing it for years: as a planet. That may seem obvious to us now, but in a time of fanatical, fight-to-the-death nationalism, it was an intellectual and spiritual thunderbolt.

A human footprint on an alien world

MEANWHILE, KUIPER'S FEUD WITH UREY still raged, even as each took leadership roles in the fledgling space program. Carl continued ferrying between their warring labs. The enmity between the two men was emotionally so corrosive that he said at the time he felt like the child of divorced parents. And he, their sole graduate student in common, was the only bridge left between them.

Urey fought hard for NASA to go to the moon. Among his reasons was a desire to know, at last, how the solar system formed. Kuiper predicted what it would be like when we got there—it would feel like walking on crunchy snow. Neil Armstrong later said that he felt Kuiper's crunchy snow beneath his boots when he first stepped on the moon.

Thanks to Urey and Kuiper, Carl was part of this great adventure. The first of the triumphant headlines of his childhood drawing—Spaceship Reaches Moon—was beginning to come true and he was part of that event. He briefed the Apollo astronauts before they left for the moon, and he was there when scientists first met to evaluate the information gained from the dawn of space exploration.

For the first time ever, the biologists, the geologists, the astronomers, the physicists, the chemists—they were all talking to one another. Well, actually, mostly shouting.

The young Carl Sagan stood up at one of their first joint scientific meetings and famously said, "Hey, guys, we're the first generation of scientists to receive these riches. We're all in this together." He set a tone for planetary science in its formative period that still holds today. He edited the first modern interdisciplinary journal for researchers studying the worlds of the cosmos—*Icarus*—which still thrives. He was one of a handful of scientists who made the search for possible worlds, for extraterrestrial life and intelligence, respectable scientific pursuits. He conducted a lifelong campaign to bring their revelations to all of us.

Gerard Kuiper and Harold Urey never lived to see the discovery of the first exoplanet, first observed in 1995. Carl died the following year, long before NASA's Kepler mission and other observatories confirmed the existence of thousands of worlds circling other suns. Thanks to those three scientists, and many others, we now know that it takes just a few million years for a star to evolve, and planets and moons to coalesce out of a cloud of gas and dust—in other words, to form a solar system.

It's a long period of gestation, but far from rare. In the Milky Way, it's a roughly monthly occurrence. In the visible universe of perhaps a trillion galaxies, containing as many as a hundred million trillion stars, every second may bring the birth of a thousand new solar systems.

Snap your fingers. That's a *thousand new solar systems* right there. Snap. *A thousand new solar systems* . . . Snap. *A thousand new solar systems* . . .

Snap. *A thousand new solar systems* . . .

Snap. Snap. Snap.

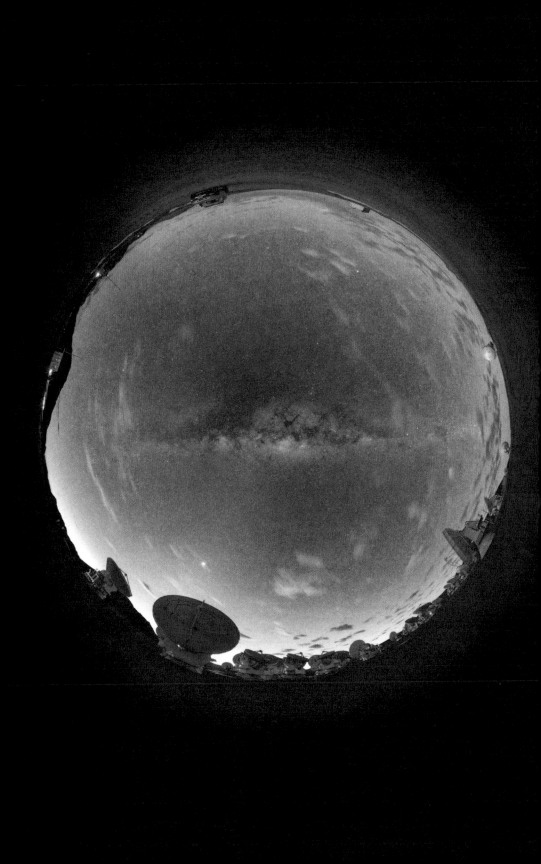

CHAPTER SEVEN

THE SEARCH FOR INTELLIGENT LIFE ON EARTH

*It is hardly an exaggeration to say that the tip of the radicle
[the root] thus endowed [with sensitivity], and having the power
of directing the movements of the adjoining parts, acts like the brain
of one of the lower animals; the brain being seated within the
anterior end of the body, receiving impressions from the
sense-organs, and directing the several movements.*
—CHARLES AND FRANCIS DARWIN,
THE POWER OF MOVEMENT IN PLANTS

*And you? Remember how the crickets came
Out of their mother grass, like little kin,
In the pale nights, when your first imagery
Found inklings of your bond to all that dust.*
—WALLACE STEVENS,
"LE MONOCLE DE MON ONCLE"

A 360° fisheye-lens view of the Milky Way over Chile's Atacama Large Millimeter Array
(ALMA) radio telescopes

W e search the heavens for signs of intelligent life. But what would we do if we found it? Are we ready for first contact? Would we be smart enough to even know if someone was sending us a message?

We've only been able to detect radio signals for a little over a hundred years. Extraterrestrial civilizations could have been bombarding Earth with radio signals for millions or billions of years before then, and nobody here would have had any inkling that it had ever happened. Maybe the day after you read this, someone will come up with a new way of listening to the cosmos, another physical medium of communication, one we haven't been smart enough to discover yet.

And what if, to aliens, we seem just like ants? We all know how we treat ants. What if the extraterrestrials are smarter than we are? What if they have technology, weapons, microbes, and viruses that render us helpless? The history of first contact among terrestrial civilizations—the humans of east and west, north and south—has been stained by genocide. In all of the cosmos, is there such a thing as a first contact story between cultures of disparate levels of technological development with a happy ending?

I know of one first contact story, but it's too soon to know how it will turn out.

The Five-Hundred-Meter Aperture Spherical Radio Telescope, or FAST, in southwestern China, the world's largest telescope

In Dawodang, Guizhou Province, in southwestern China, there's a wonder of the world. The Five-Hundred-Meter Aperture Spherical Radio Telescope (FAST), the largest telescope of any kind on Earth, sits in a lush green valley surrounded by thick trees densely packed together like broccoli florets on mountains shaped like peaked loaves of bread. It received its first light, the official beginning of a telescope's life, in September 2016.

FAST is able to see objects that are three times dimmer than the next largest telescope, also a radio telescope, the Arecibo Observatory, completed in 1963 in Puerto Rico. And it can do something else that the Arecibo telescope cannot. It can change shape. Its vast dish consists of aluminum panels that move at a computer's command to shift focus to a different part of the sky.

FAST's mission is to solve unanswered questions about the origin of the universe, and its early history. It will search for pulsars, those rapidly rotating neutron stars, and use the frequencies of their rotation to search for signs of gravitational waves, ripples in the fabric of spacetime.

And FAST will also search for signs of alien civilizations, but only those very far from Earth.

THERE'S ANOTHER FORM OF INTELLIGENCE, one that's much closer. We didn't even know it existed until recently. Complex beyond our wildest imagining, it was built by a community whose population is inconceivably vast. Here rays of light filter down through the canopy of birch, maple, tung, fir, pine, oak, and poplar, and the rich carpet of moss and twigs crunches beneath our footsteps. Our distant ancestors, tiny shrewlike animals, came of age in places not too different from this one. Forests. Maybe they knew what we've only recently discovered. The secret life of this place is filled with drama, abuzz with conversation. Much of it is

The World Wide Web beneath our feet: the mycelium, a grand collaboration of the kingdoms of life

spoken in an electrochemical language, and it takes place on a scale too small, and in motion too slow, for creatures like us to even notice.

There's something even more amazing going on right beneath our feet. It's an ancient, subterranean World Wide Web, a vast neural network binding the forest together, making it an intercommunicating, and interacting, dynamic organism, one with agency, and the power to influence events above ground. This glowing matrix of intricate filaments, radiating outward in all directions, stupefying in its complexity, is called the mycelium.

It's a hidden communication and transport grid, the creation of an ancient collaboration between fungi, plants, bacteria, and animals. Ninety percent of all the plants and trees on Earth are involved in the mutually beneficial relationship made possible by the mycelium. They exchange nourishment, messages, and empathy with one another, across species, and even across the kingdoms of life.

Mushrooms are the reproductive organs, the fruiting bodies of the mycelium. To see a mushroom growing wild in the forest is to know that the great natural internet is online beneath your feet. Some mushrooms spread trillions of spores on the breeze, each spore a paratrooper carrying life's message. A single spore will arc across the forest to land in a clump of velvety moss. Another spore will land nearby. The two spores will send out branchlike hypha until they merge into the white, cottony filaments of the mycelium. This is mushroom sex. After a while, in the search for moisture, this new segment of the mycelium will return down to the underworld, and link up to the greater network.

The secret worlds of trees have been long hidden from us. For them, the mycelium is their lifeline to one another. It makes the forest a community. The extent of the tree's root structure below ground is even larger than the tree itself. The tips of the tree's roots interdigitate tenderly with the flossy connectome of the mycelium. The roots plug in to it to parent, to nurture each other, and even to devise a stay of execution, a reprieve from the ax. When a tree is cut down in the forest, other trees reach out to the victim with their root tips, and send life-saving sustenance—water, sugar, and other nutrients, via the mycelium. This continuous IV drip from neighboring trees can keep the stump alive for decades, and even centuries.

And they don't only do it for their own kind. They sustain the trees of other species. Why? What's in it for them? The tree stump rarely grows back into a healthy tree that will give off new seeds to spread its DNA. Can it be affection? Fellowship? Is it because their lives depend on the health of the whole forest, and even on beings

Cloud forest near the summit of Manuoha, in Te Urewera, New Zealand. Now that we have begun to perceive the lively conversation of the forest, do the trees and plants look different to you?

very different from themselves? Is it possible that the trees can act on longer terms than we can?

We know that trees have excellent parenting skills. The parent will send nourishment from its root system. A pine tree will lavish constant attention on its offspring, even though it is hardly young by our standards, some 80 years old. But trees don't live at the speed of humans.

The young have a tendency to want to grow up quickly. They don't grasp that if they do, there will be too much air in the cells of their trunks. Later, when the stormy winds and predators come, they'll be weak and vulnerable. The mother pine shades the younger

In places like Tanzania's Tarangire National Park, acacia trees defend themselves against the giraffes that find their leaves delicious by spoiling the flavor and warning other nearby acacias to do the same.

tree with its branches so that it cannot binge on sunlight, and grow up too fast for its own good.

How many forests have I been in without any awareness of what was really happening all around me? Who are we to search for alien intelligence when we can't even recognize, or respect, the consciousness all around us, and even beneath our feet?

It wasn't until the latter part of the 20th century that scientists first became aware of how an acacia tree in South Africa defends itself against a predator, and sounds the alarm to other members of its community. A group of giraffes amble by and begin to nibble on its uppermost leaves. At the first twinge of a nibble, the tree releases toxic chemicals that the giraffes find unpalatable. But that's not all the acacia tree does. It sends out a chemical scream, a cry composed of ethylene to its fellow acacias: "911! Trouble coming!" From the suddenly unpleasant taste of the leaves, the giraffes know that the acacia is aware of their presence, and actively alerting the other trees to the danger.

The giraffes move briskly away from the stand of acacias, bypassing other nearby acacias, to feed on trees much farther away. It's not enough for a giraffe to move on to the next tree because it, too, now knows to produce the poisons that can ruin a giraffe's meal. The giraffes have to travel some distance to find acacia trees that have yet to hear the call to arms: "Hungry giraffes are coming!"

A mighty oak with many thousands of leaves can sense a small caterpillar traversing one of them. An electrochemical signal is sent through the tree, just as it would go through our own nervous system, but not nearly so fast since the trees live on a much slower time scale. The speed of "ouch" for a tree is only an inch every three minutes, so it will take at least an hour for the tree to react by generating the chemical that will chase this pest away.

When a predator strikes, the first thing some trees do is to take a saliva sample in order to sequence the DNA of the invading species. It then tailors its chemical response to the special vulnerability of its enemy. In certain cases, it releases the precise pheromone that will attract its enemy's enemy to do the tree's fighting for it. Is it fair to say that the trees have a deep knowledge of chemistry, entomology, and other earth sciences? How exactly is their knowing different from ours?

Are trees conscious? Are they intelligent? Or is it nothing more than the interaction of all those life-forms being tested by the environment over the eons, and evolving behaviors through evolution by natural selection? Are these remarkable capabilities of the trees just another by-product of DNA striving to perpetuate itself? Is it any different when we do these things?

THROUGHOUT NATURE, we find these electrochemical conversations between the life-forms of different species and kingdoms. But what of a conversation between two different worlds? What could we possibly have in common with beings that came of age on a different world, with a completely different evolutionary history?

The natural laws of the cosmos that scientists hunt for are so powerful because they cannot be repealed, or broken. They are true, no matter what we want to believe. Laws that apply not just locally but throughout the universe and across all of time. What might we share with the intelligent civilization of another world? Science and mathematics. The symbolic languages of the scientist, the mathematician, and the engineer avoid those things that are lost in translation from one culture to another. Symbolic languages, including those used in programming, have a much higher degree of precision than words do. They are not as open to misinterpretation.

I know of only one nonhuman symbolic language, and only one instance when we humans made contact with the life-form that uses it. Their knowledge of astronomy and mathematics would put most of us to shame. Their commitment to resolving their differences democratically, and reaching the broadest consensus through debate, is unequaled by any human society. They are explorers who use their symbolic language to tell each other about the things they have discovered on their travels. Tens of millions of years ago, they had been carnivores, but they gave that up to become vegans. It transformed this world, and resulted in surpassing beauty wherever they wandered.

There's no predictive theory of evolution. Not yet, anyway. If you'd looked at our ancestors of 480 million years ago, there would be no hint of family resemblance. And so it is with the heroes of this first contact story. The Cosmic Calendar is a useful yardstick for how large a portion of cosmic evolution nearly half a billion years is.

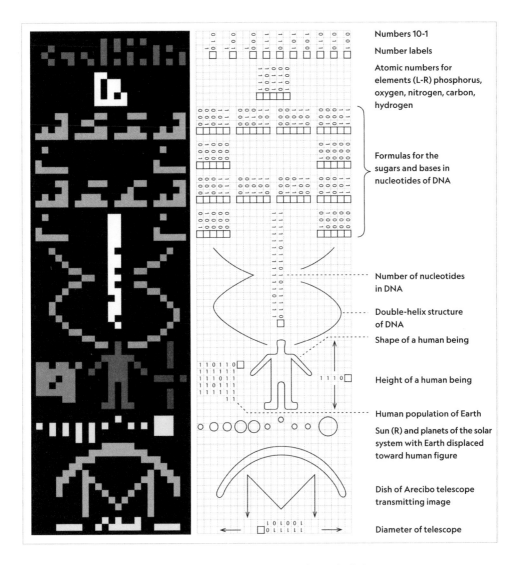

A message to another star system written in symbolic language:
Frank Drake's Arecibo message of 1974

Imagine it is the morning of December 20 in the cosmic year. Small waves from the Panthalassic Ocean, a sea that covered Earth's entire Northern Hemisphere in a period named the Ordovician, lap at our feet. The Northern Hemisphere is still completely covered with water. Gondwana, the mostly flat supercontinent, sprawls across the Southern Hemisphere up to the Equator, broken here and there by small interior bodies of water.

This was the time when life began another binge of diversification, to bust out into astonishing new forms, to experiment with eyestalks, antennae, armor plating, pincers, blades, and all kinds of crazy anatomical features—the vocabulary that life still uses today. It's remembered as the Great Ordovician Biodiversification Event. It came 40 million years after the Cambrian explosion, life's first big leap into diversification.

The simple organisms that made up the sturdy trunk of the tree of life began to mutate and adapt to their different environments. The trunk grew new shoots and twigs, as life spread out. In the ocean alone, new kinds of life tripled. This was the dawn of the arthropods, the invertebrates who wear their skeletons on the outside, instead of on the inside, as we would one day do hundreds of millions of years later. The arthropods of the Ordovician pioneered the most successful body plan ever evolved by life. Even today, more than 80 percent of all living animals are arthropods.

In the Ordovician period, miniature moss forests covered a landscape dotted by streams and lakes, which themselves were lined with plants that were more marine than terrestrial. On the coastline of the shallow sea, tiny crustaceans that looked like ghostly millipedes emerged tentatively from the water and made a home in the new world of the land.

Insects evolved from these crustaceans (a thought I do my best to hold at bay whenever I'm dining in a seafood restaurant). Eighty million years passed and it was now the morning of December 22 on the Cosmic Calendar. Giant mushrooms, some 24 feet high and three feet around, dominated the landscape. They dwarfed the tallest trees, which were then only a couple of feet high. (Mushrooms that gigantic make you wonder just how big the underground network that supported them must have been.)

As we move over to December 29, the trippy, giant mushrooms give way to increasingly taller trees. A new sound debuts on the planet: the rush of the breeze through the branches and leaves.

This was the time on Earth when life learned how to fly. The air was a wide-open, untenanted ecological niche for life. The insects would have it all to themselves for another *90 million years*. No flying reptiles, no birds, no bats to gobble them up . . . just other bugs. Powered flight was a huge evolutionary leap for insects, allowing them to spread all over the planet. The insects put human pretensions to shame. Their tenure on Earth is hundreds of times greater than ours. They look much the same to us today as they did to the dinosaurs in the late Cretaceous. These are masters of time, traveling across a hundred million years, and none the worse for wear.

Even back then, you didn't want to mess with a wasp. Think of it, by a hundred million years ago, they'd already been around for *150 million years*. They were voracious hunters even back then, on the prowl for a hapless fly to take back to the nest, dinner for their youngsters, the larvae.

The wasps did their thing for 150 million years. Back then, there was no such thing as an animal partner to aid the plants in their fertilization, to efficiently transport their seed to the reproductive organs of distant plants—in other words, to play cupid for them. But then something happened on an almost microscopic scale that would paint Earth in a whole new spectrum of colors. Maybe a wasp attacked a spider clambering across the drab female sexual organ of a plant and it inadvertently became peppered with the plant's pollen. Tiny particles of brown dust adhered to the wasp's legs.

The drama unfolding here was not the struggle between the spider and the wasp: It was those tiny particles sticking to the wasp's legs. Nothing much to look at, just a few grains, but this magic dust—pollen—contained the power to transform the world, and to make possible some of the most beautiful sights ever seen on this planet. Even today, more than a hundred million years later, this is still true.

Found in northeastern Brazil, this fossilized wasp coexisted with dinosaurs in the late Cretaceous, about 90 million years ago. Its form was so brilliantly adapted to the environment, we can barely distinguish it from contemporary wasps.

Consider a single mote of pollen dust. It's astonishingly intricate, Escher-like in its mesmerizing geometry. You have to be able to see nature on the nanoscale to discern the bold geometry, and unceasing variation, of the seed that issues from the male plant's genitalia. Each grain of pollen sculpted differently by evolution represents a novel strategy for survival, sharpened over vast expanses of time. Some looking like land mines, some covered with daggerlike projections, but all strikingly different. Pollen is tough. It has to be. It's often spiky, always enclosed by two thick fortress walls. It's so well built that you can fire it from a gun, and it will emerge unscathed with its identity and capacity to propagate its own kind, fully intact.

Imagine a single grain of pollen as a single dot carried inadvertently on the tip of a filament attached to the body of a wasp resting for a moment on a plant. The wasp takes off from the plant, and circles indecisively before plotting its course. Our wasp approaches the female sexual organ of a Cretaceous plant and lands on its brownish green, flower-shaped structure. As the wasp takes off again, the tiny pollen grain bobs on the filament before being launched into the air like a daring trapeze artist. A moment of suspense as the pollen grain arcs through the air. Will its trajectory take it to that one tiny place where new life can begin? The male pollen grain sails like a three-pointer at the buzzer, right through the narrow opening of the stigma, the germination platform for a female plant. Or, maybe that very first time, it was some crazy accident—a grain of pollen hitchhiking to the next plant on the back of a clueless beetle.

All this happened during the Cretaceous period, some 65 million years ago. But now imagine you have hundreds of thousands of years, millions of years, tens of millions of years, for this collaboration between insect and plant to emerge from a series of hits or misses, into a formal partnership. Whole new species of insects evolved. They brought this compact between the animal and plant kingdoms to new heights.

Now, another wasp flies home to the nest. It carries a fly slumped in the clutches of its mandible, food for its larval offspring. But its body carries some pollen, too, that rubbed off on it as it brushed past a flower. As the wasp lingered at the nest, a few pollen grains fell off her and the larvae eagerly devour the protein-rich pollen as well. Over the eons, a new kind of life-form evolved, one that stopped bringing meat home for dinner. This new creature brought the magic dust that the flowers made: bees.

Bees had no appetite for the mangled parts of dead insects. They went on the all-pollen diet, and it was no fad. The bees became fully committed pollinators. The plants rewarded them handsomely by evolving ever more alluring female sexual organs, in outrageous colors and seductive forms. They concocted delicious secretions, sweet nectars, that would keep the bees coming back for more, again and again. The age of the flowers had begun.

FOR US HUMANS, bees have been symbols of mindless industry. We tend to think of them as being nothing more than biological robots, doomed to live out their lives in lockstep, shackled to the rigid class roles assigned to them by nature. But this conception of bee existence owes more to our self-centered view of nature than anything else.

Here is our first contact story. It began in a postcard landscape, a lake surrounded by lush green mountains and trees, called Brunnwinkl in rural Austria, in the early 1900s.

From the time Karl von Frisch was a child, he longed to understand what the other animals knew, how they perceived the world. He wanted to know if tiny fish saw color, or had a sense of smell. He invented experiments to explore animal experience, and he filmed them. He was the first to use the new medium of motion pictures to create popular science communication.

For thousands of years, humans have noted the spasmodic, darting maneuvers of the bees. But no one had ever looked at them with the kind of respect that assumed there was a reason for their dancing. Before Frisch, no one ever thought to ask questions such as why they moved this way and that way in a succession of elaborate figure eights.

Beginning in the 1920s, Frisch studied every tiny bee gesture, and became fascinated by a mystery he couldn't explain. He would set out a dish of sugar water for a bee from his experimental hive and dab a bit of paint on the bee's back when it lighted there. The marked bee would feast upon the sugar water before flying back home, where she (all bees except drones are female) would pause outside the entrance to the hive, and perform a dance in the sunlight.

The marked bee would later return to dine on the delicious sugar water. Frisch noted that in just a few hours, a multitude of other bees would join her there. They were always her fellow hive mates. But here was the really amazing thing: Frisch knew that the other bees had not followed the marked bee to the feeding place. How? Because he had the hive closely watched at all times. He had

Karl von Frisch, cryptologist of the symbolic language of bees

been careful to use sugar water, and not honey, so that the bees' sense of smell could not guide them to the reward. He continued to move the dish of sugar water farther away, until it was several kilometers from the hive. Still, the hive mates would find their way to it. So, how did the painted bee reveal the exact location of the sugar water with such precision that her hive mates could unerringly find their way there?

Frisch studied the painted bee at the entrance to her hive, dancing in the sunlight, making her seemingly nonsensical turns left and right. As Frisch stared at the bee, he decided to sketch the seemingly erratic pattern of the bee's dancing in his notebook with the sun's position carefully noted.

He tracked the bee's dance moves, down to every turn, left and right, until there was no doubt about it. There was a secret message in her choreography. The bees were speaking a *dance language* with their movements, what Frisch called in German, *tanzsprache*. And it could be expressed as a mathematical equation. Frisch discovered that one second of waggle equaled one kilometer of distance or $1s\,w = 1\,km$. When combined with the location of our star and the direction of the waggle turns, it's a surefire coded message for the location of a single tree in a forest filled with them. If that equation ever came across the monitors at FAST from some other part of the galaxy, it would ring all the bells for a message from an alien intelligence.

What had seemed to countless generations of observers to be nothing more than the meaningless, spasmodic motions of a dumb animal was actually a complex message—an equation informed by mathematics, astronomy, and an acute ability to measure tiny increments of time, all synthesized to convey the location of the riches she hoped to share with her sisters. The dancer used the angle of our star, the sun, to indicate the general direction of the food's location. Frisch noted that when a bee danced straight upward, she meant "fly toward the sun." And when she moved downward, she meant "fly away from it."

Her swivels left and right conveyed the food's exact coordinates in space, sometimes kilometers away. The duration of her dance—down to a fraction of a second—indicated the length of time it would take her fellow bees to get there. She even factored in wind speed to more finely calibrate the message she danced. And this was true at any time of the year, and from hive to hive, from continent to continent. All social bees know how to calculate and communicate the navigational equations for travels in space and time. In different regions of the world, they may dance different dialects, but translation seems to come easily.

Why do I call this a first contact story? Two species as different as any you can imagine—humans and bees—evolved on evolutionary pathways that diverged several hundred million years ago. And yet, these two species—and as far as we know, only they and we on this planet—managed to create a symbolic language written in mathematics and informed by knowledge of physical laws—science. This is the only kind of language that, scientists speculate, we are likely to share with an extraterrestrial civilization.

We lived side-by-side with the bees for eons, never dreaming of the complexity of their communications. What we've learned about bee society in the decades since Frisch puts some of our loftiest human aspirations to shame, and changes our idea of intelligent life on Earth.

AS I WRITE THIS, the world's democracies seem more fragile than ever. But there are places on Earth where that's not true. Where every individual has a voice. Where corruption is unknown. Where the community acts when it has arrived at consensus through debate. Wherever the bees gather is one of those places.

Contrary to popular belief the hive is no monarchy. The queen is no absolute ruler controlling the other bees. The queen's role is almost entirely reproductive. Any female bee can ascend to the throne given the right food and the space to grow.

When the weather warms, and the trees bloom, she passes her scepter to a new generation of queens. That's the time in the life of a hive—in late spring or early summer—when about half the hive's bees, around 10,000 of them, grow restless. They decide it's time to leave the mother hive, to found a new colony, they know not where. Once they depart, there's no turning back.

It takes courage to leave home with no way back, to risk everything, and choose the unknown. The momentous decision to swarm sets all kinds of activities in motion. Virgin queens begin growing in their special nursery cups. The reigning queen is

surrounded by workers, who keep prodding her constantly. The pushing and shoving is not meant to be hostile. The workers are putting the queen on a rigorous exercise program so that she can lose weight, and get back into flying shape. When everyone's ready, it's time for the first leg of their odyssey. It's time to swarm.

Suddenly, a single black cloud—a massive exodus of thousands of bees—emerges from the hive. With a new queen now installed on her throne in the original hive, the old Queen Mother has pride of place at the very center of the adventurers. They regroup as a dense, teardrop-shaped swarm, vibrant with the activities of the milling bees, hanging heavy from a nearby tree branch, a single organism composed of a multitude of individuals.

Hundreds of their most senior members—scouts—are dispatched in different directions on missions of reconnaissance over a three-mile radius. The scouts reconnoiter the local trees for the best possible new home. And they're extremely picky. Not just any place will do. The front door, a hollow in a tree, must be too high for bears and other marauders to easily reach in and plunder their precious honey. And the features of the interior are just as important. The bee scouts painstakingly measure the hollow, crawling along its walls, flying back and forth between the inner bark of the tree. Total square footage is of critical concern. Bees don't hibernate. They'll have to heat the place for the long winter, and be sure to produce enough food—honey—to see them through. Each scout must measure the exact dimensions—height, width, and depth. If it's even slightly too small, or too large, the entire swarm will be wiped out before the next spring. Once all the measurements have been taken, the scouts return to the swarm to report their findings.

When all the scouts return, the bees are ready to hold their annual convention. Each scout finds a place to stand on the swarm. She presents her argument for the best site she has discovered. This

---

A political convention of the hive: The scouts of the swarm report their findings regarding potential locations for their next outpost. A great debate ensues.

house-hunting discourse is conducted in their scientific and mathematical symbolic language. Hundreds of scouts now use the waggle dance to advertise the home that they've found.

At first, each one attracts an audience. Opinions vary widely, as each advocate draws her share of followers. At our political conventions, people routinely lie. They press our buttons—demonizing, scapegoating, appealing to our fears, exploiting our weaknesses. But the bees can't risk that. In both cases, ours and theirs, the future depends on seeing reality clearly. But for some reason, we are easily manipulated and deceived. The bees somehow know that they have to stick to the facts. They have to be accurate. They can't oversell. They act as if they understand that it matters what's true. That nature won't be fooled.

Certain scouts attract larger numbers of followers, while other scouts are left to dance for no one, until they, too, cave, and join the supporters of another scout. The scouts who have found the optimum sites for the swarm's new home are the most passionate waggle dancers. Close scientific observation over many decades affirms this fact: Each bee has a platonic ideal of home in mind. Just as with our party primaries, some waggle dancers drop by the wayside as the process unfolds until only a few contenders are still standing.

The members of the swarm don't take the testimony of the most popular dancers on faith. Many of them go to see for themselves. *Skepticism is a survival mechanism.* The fact-checkers fly off to the site to make independent evaluations. Just think for a minute how articulate the waggle dance messaging has to be. It's the coordinates for one particular tree in a whole forest of them. The scouts make a beeline for it every time. If the hollow turns out to be as good as advertised, they will return to the swarm, where they, too, will dance its praises.

As more scouts come in for landings, returning from their verification missions, they waggle dance in unison with the original dancer. The last few holdouts of the rival dancers begin to drift toward the majority. Without deceit, or violence, or back-hive deals, the scouts are the first to arrive at consensus. But the larger population remains to be persuaded. Once they align behind one dance, once they've achieved virtual unanimity on the best new place to call home, the great migration can begin.

Now, the mood of the swarm changes into one of frenzied activity, and the sound of buzzing grows ever louder. It all starts with a roar. The buzzing bees rev their engines before takeoff to achieve an optimal flight temperature of 95 degrees Fahrenheit. Now, the scout bees take the temperatures of the others to make sure they're flight ready, too. Within 60 seconds of the first takeoff, 10,000 bees depart in formation for their new home, with their queen at the heart of their school bus–size formation. If she drops short of their goal, the swarm cannot continue and all is lost. With the sun as their compass, the airborne colony is wholly dependent on their queen and her leadership.

Once they arrive at their destination, the entire swarm disappears inside the hollow of the tree, and the buzzing air grows strangely still. The swarm is a kind of mind, a collective consciousness to which each individual bee makes a contribution.

Now that the move is complete, it's time to unpack, decorate the nursery, stock the pantry in honeycombs that are flawless geometry lessons, and make the place their own . . . until the weather warms, and the trees bloom again. And so it has been for tens of millions of years.

This intimate knowledge of the lives of the bees is the legacy of Karl von Frisch, who was the first to decrypt their symbolic language—to make contact with a completely different kind of mind.

IN THE DECADES SINCE, other scientists have continued Frisch's quest by studying bee brains. We now know that bees sleep, and some scientists suspect that they dream. We are building a bridge over the

chasm that has separated species for half a billion of years. And yet, after all that time, there are places where our species and theirs converged—agriculture, architecture, language, and politics. We have lived with bees for eons, but we never looked at them beyond what they could do for us. The honey they could provide, and the crops they could pollinate. Our human-centrism blinded us to their complex culture. What knocked us out of our trance so that we could finally recognize another intelligence that had always been there?

I think it was one man who did more than any other to open the way. For me, he was the greatest spiritual teacher of the last millennium. It was he who figured out how the Palace of Life could evolve from a modest one-room structure to an edifice of soaring towers, reaching to the stars. And it was he who first glimpsed the secret lives of our fellow Earthlings.

Somewhere, there's a place called the Halls of Extinction, a shrine to all the broken branches on the tree of life. But that tree still lives—even as scientists continue to revise their view of its structure. It has seen four billion springtimes since it first took root. Its flowers burst forth with unforeseeable possibilities. A tiny, one-celled organism evolves into you and everything else that is Earth life. There's just no way of predicting—for now, anyway—where life can lead. No way of foretelling the forms and capabilities that can issue from simpler organisms over vast expanses of time. Life itself can be seen as an emergent property of chemistry, science as an emergent property of life—a way that life has found to begin to know itself.

It didn't go in that direction on purpose. Evolution is not purposeful. Life staggers and lurches across the eons, randomly

Charles Darwin traveled around the planet to study its life. Upon his return to England, he published a massive illustrated record of the zoology he observed, including these images from the 1839 and 1841 editions: **LEFT TO RIGHT**, Darwin's fox, Darwin's leaf-eared mouse, Pampas cat, and Andean goose.

checking every door to find the one that opens to the future—rushing through it to keep sending its message further on in time.

Nobody knew this palace existed. It was hidden by the mists of time, and enshrouded in myth. But one man parted that curtain. He studied as many kinds of life as he could. He sailed to a group of islands on the far side of the planet in search of exotic species. He studied the bees, the flowers, the finches, mollusks, and earthworms—for 30 years. A radical pattern emerged, one that would shake our world.

Darwin's work revealed that humans are not the kings of life, created separately, and charged with its management—but instead the upstart offspring of its stately, ancient family. Darwin waited to tell the world what he had discovered until he could demonstrate its truth beyond a shadow of a doubt. But then he made another great leap: Darwin was also one of the first to recognize that if all life is related, there are certain philosophical implications. If we were not created separately from the other animals, must we not share more of who we are with them? Our awareness . . . our relationships with others . . . even our feelings?

Instead of a single island of human perception in the universe, Darwin realized that we are surrounded by other ways of being alive and conscious. For Darwin, science was a pathway to a deeper level of empathy and humility. When word reached him that a local

One of science's proudest achievements: We have traced our lineage all the way back to what we think is the earliest ancestor we share with other animals. Shown here in an artist's conception, *Saccorhytus coronarius,* recently discovered as a microfossil in China, was only a millimeter wide when it lived 540 million years ago.

farmer was mistreating his sheep, Darwin dropped his research to make a citizen's arrest of the man. He exposed the horrendous suffering of wild animals caught in the jaws of steel traps, and those experimented on surgically without benefit of anesthesia. Throughout his entire life, he was haunted by an image of the helpless dog that licked his tormentor's hand while being dissected by a scientist. And this compassion extended even to our own species. He recognized the blindness of his 19th-century contemporaries. In his autobiography, he recounted the story of an African woman who jumped off a cliff to her certain death rather than submit to being enslaved in Brazil. Darwin observed that if she had been a Roman matron from classical antiquity, she would be viewed very differently. We would be naming our daughters after her.

It was he who began the scientific study of the hidden world beneath the forest floor. He realized that the tips of tree roots acted like brains, sensing and directing the trees' actions, however slowly. He read the facial expressions of the other animals, seeking to find out if they experienced pleasure, pain, and fear the way we do. Darwin was a supplicant to nature whose knowledge of science informed and drove his compassion to new heights.

I think of Darwin as I stare at a picture of *Saccorhytus coronarius*. When it lived, 540 million years ago, it was microscopic. But for us now, it looms large because this creature is the earliest common ancestor we share with other animals that we have yet found.

If we could only take that connection to heart. If some day we could synthesize all our knowledge of life and use it to build an Arch of Experience, a place for us to stand beneath so that we could really feel what it's like to be the other. What if we could know the joy of a giant condor riding the thermals high above the Andes mountain range, or the anguish of a humpback whale singing to its lover across the vast Pacific, or the fear in the heart of our most hated enemy? How would that change this world?

All of them, and each of us, made from the same toolbox . . . with the same genetic material . . . but on different evolutionary voyages.

Are there other possible worlds in the cosmos where life's pathways converge and intersect? I am thinking about the tardigrades, those microscopic creatures that rise from the dead to thrive on Earth in those hellish places where no one else can live. They have survived all five mass extinctions, and they can even live in the vacuum of space without protection. These creatures, too small to see with the naked eye, have been filmed at the Senckenberg Research Institute and Natural History Museum in Germany, spending an hour appearing to pleasure each other. See for yourself. It's hard not to think that what is happening between them is affection, tenderness.

If bees dream, and tardigrades snuggle, are there countless roads in the universe that life can take to wonder and to love?

If only we could stand beneath the Arch of Experience, or build one inside ourselves.

CHAPTER EIGHT

THE SACRIFICE OF CASSINI

*In the seventeenth century there was still some hope that,
even if the Earth was not the center of the Universe,
it might be the only "world." But Galileo's telescope revealed that
"the Moon certainly does not possess a smooth and polished surface"
and that other worlds might look "just like the face of Earth itself."
The Moon and the planets showed unmistakably that they had as
much claim to being worlds as the Earth does—with mountains,
craters, atmospheres, polar ice caps, and, in the case of Saturn,
a dazzling, unheard-of set of circumferential rings.*

*Voyager 2 took advantage of a rare lining-up of the planets:
A close flyby of Jupiter accelerated it on to Saturn, Saturn to
Uranus, Uranus to Neptune, and Neptune to the stars. But you can't
do this anytime you like: The previous opportunity for such a game
of celestial billiards presented itself during the presidency
of Thomas Jefferson. We were then only at the horseback,
canoe and sailing ship stage of exploration. (Steamboats were
the transforming new technology just around the corner.)*
—CARL SAGAN, *PALE BLUE DOT*

Enceladus setting behind Saturn, one of the final images sent from NASA's Cassini
spacecraft before its final dive into the planet's atmosphere

NASA

Jet Propulsion Laboratory
California Institute of Technology

There's a room in Pasadena, California, where women and men sit at consoles ordering robots around on other worlds and communicating with the ships that sail the bottomless sea of interstellar space. The Deep Space Network at the Jet Propulsion Laboratory is chilled and lit like a movie set, and dimmed to an arresting darkness that makes the self-illuminated frosted glass titles at each station gleam like ice sculptures. Unlike the NASA of old, this place embraces its mystique—maybe a little too much. A console title reads "Voyager Ace," designating the person who communicates with the spacecraft as if they were a fighter pilot. Wide tilted flat screens line the upper front wall of the room. They tell us which global tracking station is currently communicating with which particular craft out by which distant world. The way the air temperature is maintained at a morgue-like chill makes you feel you must be underground at some secret government installation. It contributes to the heroic atmosphere of a species doing big things. But it's the constantly changing odometers of the Pioneers and Voyagers, logging their mileage in light-hours after more than 40 years, that make the most profound statement of human ambition.

Some of the original team leaders of NASA's Cassini mission, **LEFT TO RIGHT:** Torrence Johnson, Jonathan Lunine, Jeff Cuzzi, Carolyn Porco, and Darrell Strobel gather in the VIP viewing area overlooking the Space Flight Operations Facility of JPL's Deep Space Network in September 2017. They had conceived and executed its ambitious odyssey and now they were there to say goodbye.

On the evening of September 15, 2017, eight scientists stood in the gallery overlooking the Deep Space Network. Each one of them was coping with the imminent, violent, irrevocable end of a relationship that had lasted throughout their professional careers. Did it make it worse that they themselves had ordered their longtime avatar, NASA's Cassini spacecraft, to commit robotic suicide on a distant world?

They'd all been so young when the mission was first conceived. Back in the early 1980s, as team leaders of the mission, they'd stood at the lectern and looked into the camera to outline their specific goals for an ambitious robotic journey to Jupiter and Saturn. Now, decades later, they peered into the glass that enclosed the distinguished visitor's gallery. Perhaps, they were startled by their reflections and marveled at what time does to us. Maybe they looked past the glass to the "Cassini Ace," seated below, the designated executioner, whose fatal command would be tapped out on a keyboard as ordinary as the one that an airline representative uses when you check in.

GRAVITY HAS A BIG BAG OF TRICKS. Some of the loveliest are the rings around worlds. Half the planets in our own solar system are ringed. But of the thousands of extrasolar worlds we've discovered since 1995, we weren't able to discern a single ringed planet until we found J1407b in 2012. And, wow, is it a doozy.

Imagine a world *20 times as large as Jupiter,* with a ring system that would more than fill half the 93 million miles between Earth and the sun. That's what awaits us 420 light-years from Earth, in orbit around an infant yellow dwarf star, a ring system so extensive it makes its gigantic planet look tiny. Why haven't we found more ringed planets in our galaxy? Is it that rings are so unusual, or are the methods we use to find exoplanets not very good at seeing the ring systems that may surround them?

Artist's conception of the exoplanet J1407b, a world at least 20 times the size of Jupiter, made to appear small by a ring system that extends for 40 million miles in all directions

One method of searching is to look at a star with a spectroscope, which produces a picture of the signals hidden in the starlight. Looking at J1407, we see thin, dark vertical lines running across the spectrum are shifting back and forth by a small amount. That's the gravity of the exoplanet tugging on its star.

And then there's the transit method, a kind of interstellar electrocardiogram, or EKG. A graphic exhibits a series of blips against the blackness of the graph, and the yellow dwarf star at the same time. As the planet transits across the disk of the star, the light blips stop because the planet's rings are blocking out its star's light.

A light curve is a measure of the variations of brightness from a distant object. The most interesting part in the one from J1407 is the darkness. It tells us that something mysterious is passing

between us and the star . . . something very large. J1407b's ring system is so vast that it eclipsed its star for days. These rings extend across an astonishing 112 million miles. But as enormous as they are, they're shockingly thin. If the ring system of J1407b were the size of a dinner plate, it would have to be a hundred times thinner—as thin as a human hair. This surprising contrast between the immense territory of a ring system, and its thinness, is just as striking in our own solar system. The outermost ring of Neptune is so dainty that it was first thought to be the fragments of a ring. Not a ring, but a collection of arcs. That was, until NASA's Voyager 2 spacecraft revealed that the so-called arcs were clumps, the thicker parts of a fainter, complete ring.

Uranus also has rings. Why is it that the weirdest planet in the solar system has attracted the least attention? Voyager 2 is the only spacecraft that has ever been sent on a reconnaissance mission to Uranus, one of the two ice giant planets that circle the sun. Uranus looks like it's on its side, skating around the sun on the blade of its rings. Amid its 13 faint rings are 27 small orbiting moons. During Uranus's 20-year-long summers, the sun never sets. The winters are equally as long—20 years of unbroken night. Unlike its fellow gas planets, Uranus is cold-hearted. It doesn't generate any internal heat.

Uranus is one crazy world. The outer edge of Uranus's atmosphere is hot—hotter than 500 degrees above zero. If we could dive into them we would find that the clouds become thicker, more blue, colder. Uranus also has the coldest clouds in the solar system—nearly 400 degrees *below* zero. Scientists speculate that its vast, interior ocean might be made of ammonia, water, or liquid diamonds. It may rain diamonds on this world.

Uranus revolves around the sun at a roughly 90-degree angle to the plane of the orbits of the rest of the other planets. What could have happened to Uranus that it got knocked sideways? Our best

Uranus, our sideways planet, with its skimpy rings and six of its 27 known moons, as captured in an infrared image from the Hubble Space Telescope

guess is that it went something like this: Uranus must have sustained a wicked one-two punch by two separate massive objects that collided with it. Before it could stabilize after the first one, it must have been hit by the second, and it's been rolling around on its "side" ever since.

Jupiter's system of four main rings is completely different from those of the other worlds we've just looked at. The rings are mostly red except for the innermost ring, which is bright blue, and much thicker than any of the other rings in our solar system. The outer rings are gossamer in their faintness. The rings of Jupiter are so flimsy that no ground-based telescope had ever seen them. They were discovered when Voyager 1 came flying by.

SATURN IS GRACED BY the loveliest, largest, and brightest ring system of any in our solar system. It's the most distant planet that can be clearly seen with the naked eye, and it made quite an impression on our ancestors. What those points of light meant to them—going all the way back to the Babylonians, and beyond—is part of a great and terrible human tradition. We use our imagination to project meaning, portent, and our fears onto those things that we are helpless to understand. Still, over the eons, we find our way, and now, a few thousand years later, the Deep Space Network room at NASA's Jet Propulsion Laboratory (JPL) is filled with humans riveted by the same planet.

The pathway from our earthbound helplessness during the period of ancient astronomy to our presence in Saturn's skies was long stretches of uneventfulness culminating with a short burst of feverish activity. Nothing much happened until 1609, when Galileo looked through his first telescope and found the cosmos. The following year he turned his new telescope on Saturn and asked himself: What is that shimmering, unsteady thing I'm looking at?

He was the first human ever to see Saturn as more than just a point of light.

Galileo guessed wrong at what he thought he saw, believing that Saturn sported two symmetrical moons on either side of it. Later, in 1612, when he looked at Saturn again, the "moons" were gone. This was because both worlds, Earth and Saturn, are in motion, and the two worlds had changed in position to each other. Unbeknownst to Galileo, he was now looking at Saturn's rings edge-on. They were too thin for Galileo's primitive telescope to see. The Saturn ring system is 175,000 miles across but on average only a few hundred feet thick. Two years after that, he took a third look. In 1614, the planet appeared to have two handle-like appendages. Now, Galileo thought that the planet had . . . arms.

Another 40 years passed before the Dutch astronomer Christiaan Huygens looked at Saturn with his own greatly improved telescope. Huygens's 1655 view of Saturn was still fuzzy, but it clearly revealed a world with a ring system. He was the first to know that worlds could be circled by rings, and Saturn was one of them. He also discovered Saturn's largest moon, which would come to be known as Titan 200 years later. When it finally came time for us to visit that world, the European Space Agency's spacecraft bore Huygens's name.

In science, there are the Galileos, the Newtons, the Darwins, the Einsteins—although precious few of them. And then there's another kind of great scientist. Not the kind that paints a whole new picture, but, like Christiaan Huygens, someone who has much to contribute, filling in more than a blank or two on the vast canvas of nature. Such a scientist was Giovanni Domenico Cassini. He was born early in the 17th century in the hill town of Perinaldo, in what is now Italy.

Cassini didn't start out as a scientist. He began his career as a pseudoscientist—an astrologer. Astrology is a collection of ideas based on the notion that worlds have certain human personality traits, and that the influence of these distant worlds, depending on which are rising and falling at the time of your birth, will determine who you are and what your fate will be. It's another form of prejudice: making unfounded assumptions about who a person is based on one aspect of their being—it could be as trivial as the amount of melanin in their skin, the shape of their nose, or where the planets and constellations (also baseless human projections on the cosmos) happened to be on the date of their birth—without bothering to get to know the person. Astronomy and astrology used to be the same thing—until there was a great awakening to our actual circumstances in the cosmos.

In 1543, Nicolaus Copernicus, a Polish cleric, demonstrated that, contrary to popular belief, we were not the center of the solar system. Earth and the other planets traveled around the sun. Demoting Earth from the center of the solar system was a severe blow to human self-esteem, the first in a long series dealt by science. More than a century later, some people still hadn't gotten over it. Giovanni Cassini was one of them. He accepted a terrific job offer—an appointment by Louis XIV, the legendary Sun King of France. Louis believed himself to be an absolute ruler whose dominion was God's will. But he was also the first monarch in Europe to recognize the great power of science and its potential value to national security.

Louis XIV founded the first modern, governmental, scientific research institute: the Académie des Sciences. Upon his arrival at court, Cassini told the absolute ruler that he would not be staying long in Paris—a year or two, at most. But when the king placed his new observatory at Cassini's disposal, Cassini began to lose all interest in returning home to Italy ever again. It's not often in science that a position becomes hereditary, but for the next 125 years, the Paris Observatory would be led by a Cassini. Cassini rewarded his patron with a map of the moon that remained cutting-edge for a century. King Louis financed a research expedition to South America to obtain more accurate observations of longitude—navigational intel of enormous value to the captains of his far-flung fleet, hungry for trade and territory.

The ratios of the distances between the planets, but not the distances themselves, were known in 1672 when Cassini set out to

Giovanni Cassini created this map of the moon, published in 1679.
It was not improved upon for more than a century.

calculate the size of the solar system. King Louis's expeditions had produced more precise measurements of distances between places on Earth. Cassini was able to use his knowledge of exactly how far apart two points were on Earth to perform a geometric calculation that gave him the distance to Mars. If you know the ratios of the distance between the planets, once you know the distance to one, you can calculate the distances between each of them. With this method, Cassini discovered the true scale of the Copernican solar system that he had once rejected. Cassini discovered Jupiter's Great Red Spot independently of Robert Hooke in England, and to this day, they share the credit.

With his increasingly powerful telescopes, he discovered the length of a day on Jupiter and documented its distinctive bands and the spots on the gas giant's surface. Cassini went on to determine the length of a day on Mars. He was off by only three minutes. A Martian day, it turned out, was almost an hour longer than one on Earth.

When he returned to his observations of Jupiter, he came excruciatingly close to making what would have been his most profound discovery. But character is destiny, and Cassini's conservative nature prevented him from following the evidence where it should have led him.

He was stumped by a recurring problem: The eclipses by Jupiter's moons did not begin when they were supposed to—their timing varied from observation to observation. Could it be that it was due to changes in the distance of Earth from Jupiter, as the two worlds followed their independent orbits around the sun? Scientists of the time assumed the speed of light was infinite. But, if that were true, the varying distance between the two planets wouldn't affect the timing of Jupiter's eclipses. *Could the speed of light be finite?* Out of the question. All the experts thought light traveled at infinite speed. They couldn't be wrong. The very idea was just too crazy for Cassini, too revolutionary. He rejected it out of hand. If he had simply trusted the evidence, instead of the prevailing scientific view, he would have given us the yardstick for the cosmos that we still use 350 years later. But Cassini dismissed the idea as being just too wacky.

Several years after this unfortunate assumption, a Danish astronomer, Ole Rømer, became Cassini's assistant at the Paris Observatory. Rømer made his own observations of the eclipses of some of Jupiter's moons and found the same discrepancies in the data that Cassini had dismissed. But Rømer recognized them for what they were: pieces of evidence for the finite speed of light.

There was a time, however, when Cassini exhibited an exemplary faithfulness to the data. He was willing to risk the displeasure of an absolute monarch, King Louis, who had the absolute power to punish or execute anyone. The king asked Cassini to calculate the exact area of his realm. No one had ever attempted to make an accurate map, much less a topographical one that would feature all the mountains and rivers and valleys of France, or any other country, for that matter. Cassini rose to the task, but he discovered results that could not possibly please the king.

Despite this, Cassini appeared at court and told Louis words to this effect: "I have some rather disappointing news for you, Your Royal Highness. We all thought that France was much bigger than our studies revealed. I'm afraid, Your Majesty, your kingdom is much smaller than heretofore thought." The king's face grew serious and the courtiers trembled. But Louis surprised everyone with his good humor when he laughed and chided Cassini for robbing him of more land than all the armies of his enemies combined.

WHY DID A 21ST-CENTURY SPACECRAFT bear the name of Giovanni Cassini? Because he was the first person to know what the rings of Saturn really were. He proposed that they were not solid but instead composed of countless satellites orbiting the planet, and he observed that there was a division between the rings, one that bears his name today.

But how to get there?

The lineage of a spacecraft mission to the outer planets requires the questioning and research of countless minds, some of whom are famous, most of whom are not. But the one person most responsible for the exploration of the solar system is virtually anonymous.

Weighing in at more than 12,000 pounds at launch, the Cassini spacecraft was the size of a bus, the largest spacecraft ever launched by NASA. That figure included 70 pounds of plutonium-238 fuel, enough to last it for more than 20 years. But that was not what powered the spacecraft's odyssey. It rode gravity's rainbow all the way to the outer solar system. The roots of this human achievement stretch further back than we might assume. Some of them were buried deep inside the tomb of lost hope. But somehow, dreams rise. The epic missions of the first golden age of space exploration, and likely the next ones, were made possible by a man whose two names—one real, one fake—are equally forgotten.

Aleksandr Shargei was born in 1897 in Poltava, Ukraine, then a part of the Russian Empire. His mother was a proud trouble-maker, a fearless participant in political demonstrations against the tsars. When Aleksandr was five, she was taken by the tsar's police and imprisoned in a mental hospital. When the authorities dragged his mother away, the little boy was left alone in their shabby cottage. He took refuge in his father's physics and mathe-matics textbooks. By the time Aleksandr was 13, he had lost his father, too. He lived with his grandmother, and despite great hard-ship, he managed to be accepted at a prestigious high school. Upon his graduation, he gained admission to the best engineering insti-tute in the Ukraine. But only two months after he arrived there, in 1914, he was drafted into the tsar's army to fight in the First World War. It was there, at the front in the Caucasus in 1914, amid the ceaseless artillery fire, in a trench filled with sewage, corpses, and rats, that the 17-year-old Shargei looked up at the moon and figured out a way to get there.

Dreams are maps. In the hell of war at the front, Shargei con-ceived a scientific strategy for reaching and exploring the moon—not intended as fiction, but as blueprint. Shargei imagined how a rocket could be launched from Earth into orbit around the moon. Upon arrival, one explorer would remain in the orbiter while it deployed a modular vehicle, a lander carrying two human explor-ers. The orbiter would continue circling the moon, while the explor-ers in the lander touched down on the lunar surface. After their reconnaissance was completed, the lander would lift off from the moon to rendezvous with the orbiter, which would then head home. Sound familiar?

World War I ended, but Shargei's hell continued. Now, Shargei was forced to navigate the treacherous political minefields of revolutionary Russia. He was much better at figuring out how to get to the moon. People such as Shargei, who had joined the counterrevolutionary White Army, were assumed to be "enemies of the people." He went from place to place searching for a day's work, but he would be turned away as soon as he presented his papers. Shargei could find no peace in the Soviet Union, so in 1918, he tried to escape to Poland. By then he was so emaciated and sick, the border guards who apprehended him decided he was close enough to death that they need not speed up the process. The skeletal Shargei was allowed to stagger away.

Somehow, Shargei made his way back to the modest cottage of his childhood in Poltava. There, a neighbor lady with a small daughter is thought to have nursed him back to health. No one knows where he spent the next three years. He simply vanished. When at last he emerged, Aleksandr Shargei was no more. In his desperation to be left alone, he took the name and the papers of a dead man, one without an incriminating counterrevolutionary past. He was now Yuri Kondratyuk, author of a book entitled *The Conquest of Interplanetary Space,* the book he had written years earlier during the First World War. No publisher had been interested, so he had printed it at his own expense. It was Kondratyuk's letter to a future no one else could see. He wrote it for "Whoever Will Read This Paper in Order to Build an Interplanetary Rocket."

To read this book is to feel Kondratyuk's confidence in the future, especially impressive in view of his own miserable circumstances. His voice in the book is an act of scientific faith. With his words, he reaches out to take the hand of a lucky stranger, living in a better time. They are bound together by the fellowship of aspirations that binds the generations to each other—that desire to know the cosmos.

The opening words are a therapeutic appeal to transcend discouragement. "First of all, to the question of the work, let it not frighten you . . . " writes Kondratyuk. "Speaking about the possibility of flight implementation, just only remember that there is nothing improbable on the theoretical side of the flight of a rocket into space."

Kondratyuk backed up these bold assurances with a practical method for getting to the moon. But there was something else in the manuscript of even greater significance. He included the means of getting from world to world and star to star: the gravitational assist. A spacecraft could use the gravity of a planet or moon to get a boost as it swung by them.

Kondratyuk wrote these words 40 years before the idea was first tested by Luna 3 in 1959, the Soviet spacecraft used to photograph the far side of our moon, which we never see because it is tidally locked to face away from Earth. All of NASA's interplanetary craft since Mariner 10, launched in 1973, have used Kondratyuk's gravitational assist. The Voyagers hitched a ride on massive Jupiter's gravity to slingshot out of the solar system into the vast interstellar ocean.

In the late 1920s, Kondratyuk was enlisted by the Soviet Union to design a grain elevator. It was during a time that the U.S.S.R. was going through a metal shortage, so Kondratyuk's challenge was to build the largest grain elevator possible without using more than a single nail. It ended up being so big, they named it the "Mastodon." But upon its completion, he was arrested by the secret police, charged with sabotage for accomplishing this impossible feat. *Who but an enemy of the state would do such a reckless thing as building a colossal grain elevator with only a single nail!* Such was the nightmare logic of Stalin's Soviet Union. It made no difference to Kondratyuk's fate that the grain elevator functioned for another 60 years until it burned down.

Kondratyuk, now in his early 30s, was sentenced to three years in a special labor camp. It was a new kind of prison, called a *sharashka*, strictly for scientists and engineers, where they worked on the nation's most ambitious projects. He was assigned to a wind power project, but in his fantasies he launched spacecraft to the

Yuri Kondratyuk, born Aleksandr Shargei in 1897, envisioned a scientifically sound round-trip lunar mission during World War I that would be successfully executed by NASA's Apollo program 50 years later. He was also the first to conceive of the gravitational assist as a means of deep space travel. He died without knowing how vital his contributions would be to the space age.

planets and moons. He met Sergey Korolyov, who also dreamed of leaving Earth to explore the cosmos. Korolyov would later become the chief engineer of the Soviet rocket program. Korolyov recognized Kondratyuk's brilliance and wanted him in the rocket program he hoped to lead someday, but Kondratyuk was terrified that any change in his status might result in closer scrutiny by the secret police. He dreaded what would happen to him if he was revealed to be Shargei. So he rebuffed Korolyov.

When Germany attacked Russia in the Second World War, Kondratyuk volunteered for armed service at the front, where he led a communications outfit. His precise fate is unknown, but he is believed to have disappeared in the fire and smoke of a ferocious battle on the defensive line of the River Oka on a February night in 1942. Aleksandr Shargei, aka Yuri Kondratyuk, was only 44. That was the end of his story, but not of his dream.

DECADES LATER, IN 1961, a handsome crew cut, Iowa-born engineer named John Cornelius Houbolt was burning the midnight oil at Langley Research Center in Virginia. He was stumped by a seemingly impossible challenge. In the early days of the Apollo program, the scientists and engineers struggled to figure out how a rocket could leave Earth and land directly on the moon. It would take a big powerful rocket to escape Earth's gravity and reach the moon. How would you land such a thing on the lunar surface without crashing it? Being able to guarantee that it could take off again and bring your crew safely home was even more of a long shot. This approach, known as direct ascent, seemed unworkable to John Houbolt and his colleagues.

As one version of the story goes, used coffee cups were everywhere and the wastebasket was overflowing when two European scientists knocked on Houbolt's office door. One of them was carrying a worn, hand-typed manuscript: an English translation of Kondratyuk's 40-year-old book. These two men had kept the spark of Kondratyuk's dream alive.

There are other versions of the story, including NASA's official story in which the space agency doesn't obtain a copy and translate Kondratyuk's work until 1964. I have enormous respect for NASA, but I can't help but wonder about the official version. I was 12 in 1961 and I can recall the fever of the Cold War and the willingness to destroy everything in the service of that competition. Can we really imagine NASA or any other U.S. or Soviet agency crediting a citizen of the other side, even a long dead one, with making possible its greatest triumph?

NASA engineer John Houbolt built on Kondratyuk's ideas and developed a lunar orbit rendezvous plan, on the blackboard, that was essential for travel to the moon.

Whether by design or coincidence, Apollo 11 followed Kondratyuk's plan to what remains the most mythic achievement in human history. And not just the moon landing and the successful return home to Earth. No one disputes that Kondratyuk discovered the gravitational assist. He was the first to dream that we would swing from world to world just as our ancestors had done from tree to tree. So, in some measure, all the discoveries of the space age from 1973 onward belong to him. The Cassini mission was no exception. The spacecraft used gravitational boosts from three worlds to get to Saturn: Venus, Earth, and Jupiter.

BESIDES EARTH, SATURN, the *art deco* planet, is the best loved world in the solar system. It's those majestic rings, visible from Earth with the feeblest amateur telescope, that make the planet synonymous with space travel and the future. Sometimes on a summer night with a full moon, I look up and wonder what it would be like if our planet had rings. What crazy shadows would they cast on the lovers seated on the park benches of this world? Could we make out the individual icy boulders tumbling within them?

Why do some worlds have rings, and others don't? Why none for ours or Mars? We wouldn't recognize Saturn without them. The planet would look naked without its rings, but how did it get them in the first place? This is exactly what the French astronomer Édouard Roche asked himself when he looked at Saturn through his telescope in 1848. Roche speculated that Saturn's rings were the debris of a moon, or moons, that had ventured too close, and were pulled apart by the massive planet. As the orbit of this careless moon began to decay, the moon itself started to elongate and distort, until it became stretched into an arc curving partially around the planet and broke apart completely.

Roche was able to devise an equation that applies to all worlds. It tells you how close an asteroid, comet, or small moon can come to a planet before it's pulled apart by the planet's tidal forces of gravity, and is turned into a ring. That's the Roche limit. But until NASA's Cassini spacecraft executed a series of daredevil maneuvers in the Saturn system, there was a vigorous scientific debate about when the rings formed. Some astronomers suggested they were nearly as old as the planet itself. They conjectured that more than four billion years ago, when the planet coalesced out of the disk of gas and dust that surrounded the newborn sun, a moon, or moons, likely violated Saturn's Roche limit. Other scientists thought the rings to be fairly recent. Perhaps only a hundred million years old or so. And Cassini proved them right.

But what is Earth's own Roche limit? If the moon were ever to come closer than 12,000 miles—which, by the way, it's absolutely

The methane lake-dotted surface of Titan as revealed in a radar image by NASA's Cassini spacecraft, 2006

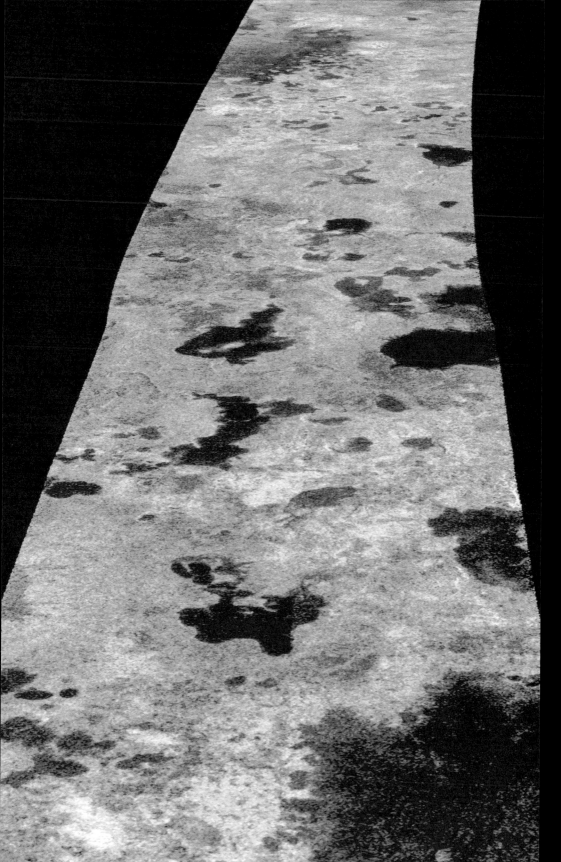

in no danger of doing—it would suffer the penalties of violating the Roche limit. But in that case, the loss of the moon as it is would be the least of our problems. And it's a good thing, too, because I like our moon right where it is. There's only one other moon in the solar system that moves me like ours does. Maybe that's because it's the only one that has a thick atmosphere like Earth's, and the kind of surface features—lakes and mountains, and rain—that remind me of home. All of it was hidden from view by a dense layer of orange smog until the European Space Agency collaborated with NASA to send the Huygens probe along with Cassini.

On the first of July 2004, after an interplanetary voyage of seven years, the Cassini-Huygens spacecraft arrived in the Saturn system. It was the fourth of our ships to venture there, but the first to send a probe to explore the surface of Saturn's moon Titan. Huygens's namesake spacecraft parted from its mother ship and braved the atmosphere of Titan, becoming a flaming shield of fire. Its braking system worked flawlessly, jerking it momentarily before

Cassini flies over the north pole of Saturn. An artist's rendering imagines the scene as the seven-year-long mission nears its end.

the landing chute could be deployed. Now, with its descent slowed, the probe penetrated the thick, obscuring orange clouds, to reveal a stunningly complex surface of mountain chains and methane lakes. As Carl Sagan and others had predicted more than two decades before, there were seas of methane, and ethane, and there was water ice. Here was a moon of far greater complexity and splendor than our own rather dull and lifeless one.

When Cassini first arrived at Saturn's northern hemisphere, it was in the depths of winter. And the sun didn't come out until five years later, when Saturn's northern spring began. The sunlight revealed an astonishing sight: a bright pink and purple churning hexagon. The geometrically regular hexagonal shape of this feature brings to mind the handiwork of intelligence, terraforming, reworking the surface for some unknown purpose. But it's actually the result of the sudden change in wind speeds as vast upwellings of ammonia rise near the poles. It's the mother of all hurricanes, a frenzy of thunder and lightning, containing countless hurricanes within it.

Spring can be a violent, stormy season on Earth, too. But it was during Saturn's seven-year-long summer that Cassini was commanded to self-destruct. From the time of its launch in 1997 and throughout its voyage to Saturn, the spacecraft had utilized the gravity assist, although it was a supply of rocket fuel that made it possible for Cassini's earthbound controllers to steer it into new trajectories of exploration.

In April 2017, Cassini was running low on that fuel. It was time for its most daring maneuvers of all before its command death dive. The mission scientists of Cassini, some of whom had been working on the project since the 1980s, when it was no more than a dream, knew that Cassini must be completely destroyed. It would be too dangerous to let it wander aimlessly. It might crash into one of the moons in the Saturn system where life might be hiding. Even after 20 years in space, it remained conceivable that life from Earth could still be lurking on the spacecraft. This would violate NASA's planetary protection conventions on quarantine in the book of space laws. If left to chance, Cassini could alter the possible biological destiny of Titan or Enceladus.

A terrible command had to be given, one that would violate every other command programmed into the spacecraft. Cassini was so far from home, it would take the message, traveling at the speed of light, more than an hour to reach it. The same engineers who designed the spacecraft to protect itself in every situation now ordered it to plunge to its death.

The "little spacecraft that could" heroically rallied, rising one last time before plunging toward Saturn. It fought off the immense forces by struggling to right itself one last time. It fired its thrusters at 100 percent, all the time faithfully sending back more data than its designers ever hoped it would. Cassini fought the brutal atmospheric resistance until its fuel tanks were empty, and there was no more fight left. The spacecraft began to break apart and ended its remarkably productive life as a meteor shower on a distant world. On September 17, 2017, the scientists and engineers back at JPL on Earth hugged each other and wept as they marked its official time of death: 11:55 Universal time.

Among Cassini's accomplishments was the discovery of dozens of previously unknown moons of Saturn, evidence for liquid water on the moon Enceladus, and the mapping of Saturn's magnetic and gravitational fields. A mission like Cassini-Huygens affords our species one of those rare occasions for human self-esteem. How quickly have we acquired and perfected an entirely new skill set. Think of it, from Sputnik to Cassini's suicide and all that we've accomplished in space in between, a mere 60 years. It gives me so much hope about what we might learn about the cosmos in the future.

SOMETIMES YOUR DREAMS die with you, but sometimes the scientists of another age pick them up, and take them to the moon, and far beyond. Yuri Kondratyuk may have been forgotten and his contributions to space exploration may have become a matter of dispute. But there was one who remembered and did what he could to ensure that Kondratyuk be given his due.

The year after Neil Armstrong returned from his trip to the moon, he made a pilgrimage to Kondratyuk's humble cottage in the Ukraine. He knelt down and scooped up some of the unpromising soil there and took it away with him. When he returned to Moscow, he appealed to the leaders of what was then the Soviet Union to honor Kondratyuk for making his mythic voyage possible.

CHAPTER NINE

MAGIC WITHOUT LIES

I call our world Flatland, not because we call it so,
but to make its nature clearer to you, my happy readers,
who are privileged to live in Space.
—EDWIN A. ABBOTT,
FLATLAND

I think I can safely say that nobody
understands quantum mechanics.
—RICHARD FEYNMAN,
THE CHARACTER OF PHYSICAL LAW

This delicate visualization of electrons in a two-dimensional electrical landscape is an example of the unique art of chemist and physicist Eric Heller. As he puts it, he paints with electron flow. The electrons enter at several points and then spread over the landscape, resulting in random systems, chaotic motion, and stunning imagery.

OPTICKS:

OR, A

TREATISE

OF THE

Reflections, *Refractions*,
Inflections and *Colours*

OF

LIGHT.

The FOURTH EDITION, *corrected.*

By Sir *ISAAC NEWTON*, Knt.

LONDON:

Printed for WILLIAM INNYS at the West-
End of St. *Paul's*. MDCCXXX.

Nature writes her most intimate secrets in light. The light from our star, the sun, powers all life on this world. Plants eat light to make sugar. Light is the yardstick of the universe, stitching diamond buoys into the fabric of space and time. Imprisoned light defines black holes. It's the absence of light that prevents us from knowing what dark matter and dark energy are. "Seeing the light" usually refers to a religious epiphany. But no one is more light-obsessed than astronomers. And as soon as they began studying light, it baffled even the very best of them.

Take Isaac Newton, for example. As a young man in the winter of 1665–66, he worked tirelessly in his bedroom at Woolsthorpe, his ancestral home in Lincolnshire, England, trying to figure out the physics of light and color. So desperate to understand their nature, he was willing to stick needles in his eyes—literally. By the time Newton was in his 20s, he'd already laid the foundations of a new branch of mathematics called calculus, and he had conducted a series of experiments that led him to conclude that color was an aspect of light. Newton wanted to find out which of the things we see are properties of light, and which are caused by our nerves. Was color hiding inside the light, or was it in our eyes?

Sir Isaac Newton's *Opticks: or, A Treatise of the Reflexions, Refractions, Inflexions and Colours of Light* included 30 years of experiments on light, sight, and color. It was first published anonymously in 1704.

With a burning desire to know, Newton summoned up his courage, picked up a needle, called a bodkin, and with grim determination, proceeded to press the needle into the lower part of his own left eye. Newton stoically wrote up "an experiment to put pressure on the eye," replete with illustration in his Opticks notebook. He carefully noted that if he conducted the experiment in a room filled with light, even with his eyes shut, some light would pass through his eyelids and he would see a great broad "blewish circle." It may not sound like much of a result considering the pain he must have experienced, but it was with simple, homemade experiments such as this one that Newton became the first person to explain rainbows, and how white light hides a whole palette of colors inside itself.

Most people thought of the phenomena that Newton studied as being "just the way things are"—the way an apple falls, the way a ray of light shines through a window. Newton's greatness stemmed from his questioning of the "why" and "how" of ordinary things, much as normal four-year-olds do.

Newton asked, for instance: What was light made of? If you could break light apart into its tiniest component parts, what would you see? Newton noticed that light moved in straight lines. How else to explain the edges of shadows? Or the straightness of those inspirational rays of sunlight that poke through clouds? Or the darkness that results from a total solar eclipse? From these observations, Newton reasoned that light must consist of a stream of particles—or "corpuscles," as he called them—that a ray of light was like a stream of bullets striking the retina of the eye.

But there was one man, over in Holland, who vigorously disagreed with Newton's particle theory of light. And it was none other than Christiaan Huygens, the Dutch astronomer who was the first to understand the nature of Saturn's rings and to discover its largest moon, Titan. He shared Isaac Newton's insatiable curiosity about ordinary things, and, despite his lifelong battle with severe depression, when it came to changing the world, he was no slouch himself. Huygens invented the pendulum clock. He worked

In 1659, Christiaan Huygens invented a motion picture projector and sketched the animation for its first feature: Death does a little dance. It would be hundreds of years before anyone else realized the potential of this art form.

out the mathematical formulas necessary to create a pendulum with an arc that would accurately and consistently measure out uniform increments of time, establishing a standard for precise timekeeping that remained unbeatable for three centuries.

Huygens sketched a prototype for a new machine that he thought might have some promise. He called it a "magic lantern." A few hundred years would pass before it evolved into a working motion picture projector, but back in the 17th century, Huygens already had an idea for a movie, possibly influenced by his gloomy disposition. Huygens made a series of pen and ink sketches, cartoons for an animation of Death performing a little dance. Death takes a playful little bow before removing his own skull and tucking it under his arm as if it were a bowler hat. He struts around, headless but cocky, before replacing his skull to its rightful position, bows once again, and just stands there, grinning at us, eerily.

Huygens, like Newton, also invented his own new branch of mathematics, a predictive theory of the outcomes of games of chance. We now call it probability theory. And, like Newton, Huygens had his own theory of light. But it was very different from Newton's. Huygens didn't think light consisted of particles, like bullets firing along a single path. Huygens saw light as a wave spreading out in all directions.

It was already known in his time that *sound* must travel as a wave. A voice could be easily heard around a door when it was slightly ajar. Sound must travel around the door as water would. Strike a tuning fork against something metal and hold it up to watch it vibrate. As you listen to its hum you can almost see the sound waves emanating in all directions. Huygens thought that light moved the same way sound did, spreading out as waves.

So, which genius was right? The answer to the question of whether light was a particle or a wave would prove to be complicated.

NOW, ENTER THOMAS YOUNG, a man who could do just about anything. And Thomas Young did. Born in Somerset, England, in 1773, he was free to follow his curiosity wherever it might lead due to the generous bequest left to him by his uncle. As a result, he made significant contributions to a remarkable variety of fields.

For centuries, many contenders had struggled in vain to decipher coded messages from a civilization whose customs and gods were very different from their own. In the early 19th century, the European public became fascinated by the race between the numerous contenders to decipher ancient Egyptian hieroglyphics. It was

Young who provided the breakthrough in 1819 by identifying six major sounds that the hieroglyphs represented. An avid student of languages, Young was the first to chart the family tree of the "Indo-European" languages, a phrase he coined that refers to the common roots in India, and Europe, of many of the languages we speak today.

Young broke new ground in the physical sciences as well. He was the first to use the word "energy" in its modern context. He was the first to estimate the size of a molecule, which means two or more atoms that share a chemical bond. And considering he was working at the beginning of the 19th century with what we would consider the most meager forms of technology, he came impressively close to the correct answer.

As a physician, he identified a deformity in the shape of the eye, the defect of vision he named astigmatism. I could go on, but it was Young's design of a simple experiment at the dawn of the 19th century that sent physics down the rabbit hole we still live in. And it was accomplished with just a few thin sheets of cardboard.

Young attached one sheet with a single vertical slit to the tabletop. He then placed another sheet with two narrow parallel slits a short distance away. Beyond that, a third piece served as a screen for the light that would pass through the slits. Young dimmed the lights in his laboratory so that the only source of illumination was an Argand lamp, state of the art in the early 1800s because it could get the most intense light out of a lamp wick. He covered the lamp with a green glass shade in order to filter out all the other colors, and ensure that only a single color, or frequency of light, would pass through the slits. Why was that important? Because he assumed that the many overlapping colors would obscure the subtle interference pattern he hoped to observe.

Now, Young placed the green lantern in front of the single slit of cardboard so that it sent its light through the double slits to end up on the vertical piece of cardboard that acted as a screen. Then he forced that single color of light to travel through two separate

Light moving as a wave through the two slits of Thomas Young's haunting
experiment, first performed in 1801

slits—to see what kind of pattern the light would make on that last piece of cardboard. If light were a particle, you would expect to see two distinct pools of light on the opposite wall where the individual particles of light ended up after they passed through the slits. *But that's not what happened.*

Instead, he observed a series of vertical bars. It was a pattern that two waves would make when they propagated outward and overlapped, or interfered with each other. Young had demonstrated that light was actually a wave. It moved like the colliding ripples on a pond, their crests intersecting and creating an interference pattern.

The scientific community did not react well to the results of Young's experiment. They wanted their greatest genius, Isaac

Newton, to be, well, perfect. More like a saint than a scientist. And now this upstart, Thomas Young, had demonstrated that Newton had been half wrong: light was not always a particle, as Newton had confidently proclaimed. There's a reason that arguments from authority hold little weight in science. Nature, and nature only, settles the argument. And she has so many tricks up her sleeve, only a fool would ever consider our understanding of nature complete. Newton was wrong—in part. Young was right—in part. But we haven't gotten to the really disturbing part of the story yet.

YOUNG LEFT A TIME BOMB with a long fuse, one that took 100 years to burn down before it exploded. What Young couldn't know that night is the spookiest thing of all about light. But nobody could see it because it was happening on a scale so small it was far beyond the reach of the most powerful microscopes of that time. It wasn't until the end of the 19th century that science developed the necessary tools to find an opening to a hidden universe of possible worlds of far deeper mystery than the ancient tombs of Egypt.

It happened at Cambridge University in 1897, where a physicist named J. J. Thomson opened a new, wholly unexpected door into the world of particles and waves. In some ways his investigations reached back 2,500 years to the ideas of the ancient Greek philosopher Democritus, who intuited that the material world was made of atoms. But no one had ever seen an atom, and for all those centuries their existence was an article of scientific faith. Thomson discovered something even smaller than an atom, and what's more, he made it possible for everyone to see it.

Instead of a cardboard with a slit, Thomson used a vacuum glass tube through which he passed electricity. He heated up a metal electrode, a conductor of electricity, and watched as a stream of particles passed through the tube. He could even change the

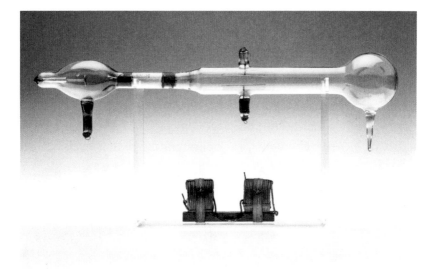

trajectory of those particles by bringing magnets close to the tube. Thomson called the particles electrons.

The American Institute of Physics has made available online an audio recording of remarks Thomson made in 1934: "Could anything, at first sight, seem more impractical than a body which is so small that its mass is an insignificant fraction of the mass of an atom of hydrogen—which itself is so small that a crowd of these atoms equal in number to the population of the whole world would be too small to have been detected by any means then known to science?"

That voice—that particular organization of sound waves frozen in time nearly a hundred years ago—captures something of his astonishment even so many years later. For the first time, an elementary particle of the atom was made visible. Science was breaking into nature's vault, and that's when things got really crazy. If even the smallest units of matter—atoms, say—had even smaller components, such as an electron, then could the same thing be true of light? Scientists, in their never ending fascination with light, set out to devise ways of isolating smaller and smaller units of it. It proved to be the passageway through the looking glass. It was the crossing

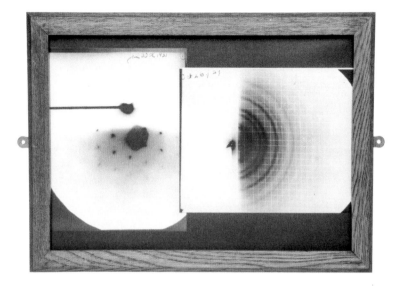

Using devices including a cathode ray tube (opposite), J. J. Thomson showed that atoms contain tiny negatively charged particles—namely, electrons. His son, George Paget Thomson, continued the work and, by shooting electrons through crystals onto gold plates (above), showed that particles move as waves. The ambiguous nature of subatomic particles continues to baffle us.

of a threshold into a wonderland where the established rules of physics do not apply.

In the late 20th century, scientists were able to perform Young's double-slit experiment on a whole new level. Now, they could isolate the tiniest unit of light: a single photon. Individual photons could be fired, one at a time, through Young's notorious double slit. One passed through the slit on the right. Another went through the right slit. The third photon passed through the slit on the left. One after another, they continued in a completely random fashion. If we watched them forever, the pattern would remain random. About half would go through either slit.

And if we rose above the cardboard to see the far wall of the experiment where the photons are hitting, what would we see? Not the interference pattern of the colliding waves, but two clusters of markings of equal size. *Wait a second* . . . Where are the waves?

Where's Young's interference pattern? This is where the weird begins. I cannot explain to you why this happens. That's because no one on Earth understands it yet. If you can't live with that, then you're not going to be happy with what lies up ahead. On this smallest possible scale that we have ever discovered—the quantum universe—the *mere act of observation changes reality.*

Okay, let the photons keep on coming, and this time, we promise not to look. While we're not watching, the photons continue their random passage through the two slits. Open your eyes: There's Thomas Young's interference pattern, the arcing wave fronts colliding in bands of light and darkness! You're not going to believe this, but we can change the pattern on the far wall simply by not watching which slit the photons pass through. I know it sounds crazy, but in every trial of this experiment ever conducted, the outcome depends on whether or not there's an observer. So, the reason the experimenters didn't get the interference pattern wasn't because they chopped the light up into single photons. It was because they were observing which slit the photons passed through.

But how could a photon know if someone's watching? A photon doesn't have eyes; a photon doesn't have a brain. How could it know it was being watched?

You might reasonably conclude that a single photon is such a tiny thing that it's very hard to see without using complex technology. This machinery does violence to the delicate photon. It changes it. But that doesn't explain why photons behave like particles when we're watching but like waves when we're not. If light is fundamentally a particle, then it should never create a wave pattern, whether we're observing it or not. And how can individual photons know where to take their places so that, as a group, they create the interference patterns of waves? This is a maddening conundrum at the heart of quantum mechanics.

Isaac Newton and Christiaan Huygens were both equally right, and equally wrong: Light is both a wave and a particle, and neither.

And this is not just true for photons. All subatomic particles exhibit this behavior. Until we make an observation, the photon, the electron, or any other elementary particle, exists in a state of uncertainty governed by laws of probability. And when we do observe it, it becomes something completely different.

We would be lost in the quantum universe without Huygens. His probability theory provides, even now, the only key we have to grasping the laws of quantum reality. Every particle is at the mercy of random chance and shifting probabilities. Thinking about it is like looking at an optical illusion. You can only grab hold of it for moments at a time before it pops back into something else.

There's an undiscovered frontier where the laws of our world give way to the ones that apply on the tiniest scale we know. They are divorced from our everyday experience. How can you comprehend a world that has different dimensions and rules than ours? It's not easy.

EDWIN ABBOTT'S 1884 MASTERPIECE *Flatland: A Romance of Many Dimensions* is the best introduction I know of for thinking about the challenges of the quantum universe. We recounted it in the first *Cosmos* book and television series to illustrate the concept of the large-scale structure of the universe and the curvature of spacetime, but it's helpful for getting your head around many of the counterintuitive experiences that science and mathematics present. *Flatland* tells the story of the inhabitants of a two-dimensional world, a place that makes it possible for us to conceive of what the leap to an additional next dimension would be like.

Now, imagine that we are flying over a cityscape of flat geometric rooftops and flat oblong vehicles moving along a network of roads. At first glance, this world is perfectly normal except that it just happens to be missing a spatial dimension—the third one.

Everyone, and everything here, and everyone they know and love, is flat. Their houses are flat squares. Some are triangles. Some have more complex shapes, say, octagons. But all are completely flat.

Now, we are close enough to see the citizens of Flatland: tiny vitamin-shaped creatures, riding in little polygons, or strolling down the streets. In their one-dimensional existence, they can turn left and they can turn right. They can move forward and they can move backward. There's just no such thing as up or down.

Now, imagine you were a visitor to Flatland. You call out, your voice reverberating in an otherworldly effect.

No answer. But you hear the patter of footsteps. A Flatlander runs out of the house to search for the source of this disembodied voice. His tiny, flat, oblong self scurries this way and that, confused. Our Flatlander fears he is losing his mind. Your voice feels to him as if it is coming from inside him. That's because nothing can come from above. There is no "above" in this world.

A three-dimensional creature like you can exist on Flatland only where your feet touch the surface of the plane. The Flatlander stops in his tracks, absolutely flabbergasted. The cross sections of the soles of your feet appear to the Flatlander like an apparition.

Maybe you crouch down on your knees, and with the utmost delicacy, pick up the little oblong Flatlander. "Sorry, little guy," you say. "I know how weird this must be for you. Don't worry. You're on a perfectly safe trip to a third dimension. Nothing's going to harm you. But this is your chance to see a whole new perspective on where you live."

Our Flatlander is in shock. But after a while he gets the hang of it. "So this is *above*," he says to himself, as he peers into the flat houses and even into his fellow Flatlanders for the first time. This unprecedented three-dimensional view of his two-dimensional universe is life changing.

This little guy has suffered enough. You gently place him back down in his two-dimensional world. His best friend rushes out to

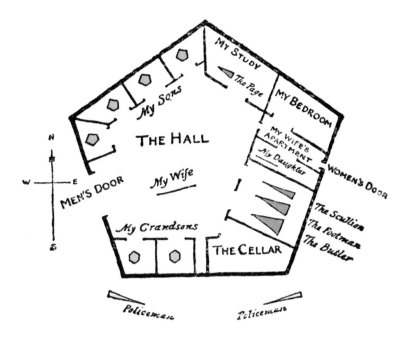

Edwin Abbott's 1884 novel *Flatland* imagined life in two dimensions and houses like this, where a two-dimensional family would live.

greet him. To her, he has inexplicably vanished and then reappeared out of thin air.

We live in a comfort zone of three dimensions. It's easy to imagine a universe in fewer dimensions, but it's very hard to imagine one with more. A zero-dimensional universe is just a point, a dot with no dimension at all. Or a one-dimensional universe where everyone is a line segment. Or the two-dimensional Flatland. Or 3-D, where we all live.

We can laugh at the cluelessness of two-dimensional creatures unable to imagine a three-dimensional world. But when it comes to quantum reality, that inability resembles the problems we ourselves have. We're living in our own Flatland.

WE INHABIT A COSMOS of undiscovered dimensions and para-doxical realities. We live on one level of perception, but there are others all the way up, and all the way down. Every once in a while, a searcher happens upon the doorway to one of these other levels. Newton and Huygens, Thomas Young, Michael Faraday, James Clerk Maxwell, and Einstein are some of the most famous ones. But there was one searcher—less celebrated—who kicked down a door that others thought led nowhere. And it all began because he couldn't bear to live with a cosmic contradiction.

This paradox of light as a wave or a particle had defeated so many others, the scientific community seemed as if they would just rather forget about it. For the first half of the 20th century, it was considered a dead end for scientific careers. Yet John Stewart Bell couldn't let it go. Perhaps you have never heard his name, but he touched your life, and your future, in ways that are difficult to quantify. His revolution still unfolds. But I can't tell you his story without first showing you the mystery that inspired him.

Break a ray of light into its constituent photons, as in the double-slit experiment, and a drama will begin. Lock onto one photon, a quantum packet of light, and divide it in two, splitting its energy. These new photons are married in a profound physical sense—or as quantum physicists say, entangled. And no matter how far they wander from each other, in space and in time, the bond between them will endure. It's a little like Plato's ancient Greek explanation of love: A single being splits into two and separates. For the rest of their existence, each remains the one and only soul mate of the other, exquisitely attuned to the inner life of its partner, even if separated by a whole universe.

Observe the spin of one photon, and its soul mate will instantly change its own spin, too. It's not something special about these particular photons. As far as we know, it's the rule. This kind of

Quantum entanglement—a mysterious relationship that can endure anything but observation—as depicted in this artist's conceptualization

long-distance relationship has been going on for the whole history of the universe. Two photons, born in the early universe—nearly 14 billion years ago—separate and head in opposite directions. They could end up tens of billions of light-years apart. And yet, over all that time and across all that space, the bond between them endures.

What is it about a photon—or an electron or any other elementary particle, once entangled—that makes it capable of such lasting fidelity? And, even stranger, is that all it takes to sever that awesome commitment is someone observing one of them. The simple act of measurement. All I have to do is measure the spin of one of them. Pick a photon, any one. There it is! Half of our cosmic couple. Somewhere, at this very moment, many billions of light-years away from us, its soul mate is suddenly feeling something different. The thrill is gone. The bond has been broken. They are no longer married to each other. Our simple act of observing one of them has ruined a marriage that has lasted since the beginning of time.

How can it be that only one, seemingly innocuous act by a third party can forever sever such a deep and enduring bond? How could one photon, a cosmos away from its partner, send a breakup message across the universe and have the other photon receive it instantaneously? How could two photons communicate with each other faster than the speed of light and carry such a message between them? These are two of the great unanswered questions in science. So don't worry if they bother you. Once he first thought about it, these questions haunted a mind as great as Einstein's for the rest of his life.

There is nothing more intriguing to a scientist than a logical impossibility. If light, the fastest thing there can be, has a cosmic speed limit, then it would be impossible for one photon to communicate with another instantly across such vastness. Einstein found it almost unbearable to live in this kind of universe, where what he called "spooky action at a distance" was possible.

Remember those particles in the double-slit experiment, taking either the left or the right slit? Those choices amounted to nothing more than random chance. But even random chance must obey certain rules—that's the basis for Huygens's probability theory, and for calculating the odds in shooting craps.

When Einstein applied probability theory to the problem of entangled photons, he was horrified. If these photons could brazenly violate the speed of light, then the universe, and all of creation, is nothing more than a casino where the laws of nature can be broken! Einstein dealt with his torment by clinging to the idea that the dice were somehow loaded in a way we didn't yet understand. He invented something he called a "hidden variable," a mechanism that some-how tells the particle how it should behave billions of years from now. That way no faster-than-light communication would be necessary and the disturbing mystery could be explained away.

We had passed this way before. Around a million years ago, our ancestors domesticated fire. They didn't know what fire was, but they used it anyway, to build a civilization. And so it was with quantum physics. We didn't need to understand it in order to exploit its countless practical applications, scientific and otherwise. Much as our ancestors used fire without understanding how it worked, we lived with this particular aspect of the complex quantum mechanical mystery for decades.

But there was this boy, born in 1928 in a working-class neighborhood in Belfast, Ireland, who developed a passionate need to understand quantum fire. John Stewart Bell was determined to find out if Einstein's hidden variables were real. Bell conjured up a thought experiment based on simple arithmetic concepts and probability theory as a way to test Einstein's conjecture. He visualized entangled photons sailing through fences with their pickets tilted, or *polarized*. Some individual photons would glance off the fence posts and others would pass through. He imagined a tallying mechanism to register all those random outcomes.

Suppose every photon knows which way it's polarized before we measure it. Bell proposed that we could set up an experiment to test this idea using filters turned at different angles. He calculated how many photons would pass through the vertical posts of the picket fences. Then he tilted the posts at 45 degrees and fewer photons were able to pass through. He calculated how many would pass through the tilted ones. If the photons were being directed by hidden variables, then the statistics of which ones passed through would be different. But he could not find any of Einstein's hidden variables. If they existed, they would not be near enough to each other to communicate their status at the speed of light but would somehow only occur on a much grander scale—and that would have to be "spooky action at a distance."

As simple as it was, it took scientists another six years to design the actual experiment, one that has been carried out repeatedly ever since. And every time, the photons behave precisely as John Stewart Bell imagined they would, showing both mathematically and experimentally that there can be no hidden variables. The thing Einstein feared most is true: We have entered a territory beyond the reach of classical physics, where a single photon exists in two places at once. Where the elementary particles that make up everything, including us, respond to events they can't possibly know about. In the outlaw casino of the quantum universe, there is no objective reality.

THE BIZARRE QUANTUM UNIVERSE is not only outside there in the quantum universe, tugged on by *undiscovered moons*. It is also inside us, performing its impossible magic on every level of life and experience.

Stare at absolutely anything: the page of this book, a dog, the moon. Whichever object it is, it is sending an image made of light to your eyes. It's arriving at your retina at this very moment. The cells in your retina are changing chemically right now because the object is stimulating some of them with photons. Your retina stores these changes for around four-fifths of a second. Now, it's erasing

John Stewart Bell, the man who succeeded where Einstein failed. It was Bell's refusal to accept a blank page in the book of nature that led to a quantum technological revolution.

them in readiness for the next barrage of photons. Your retina doesn't detect all of them—it can't. It picks up on only a small percentage of photons that come your way. It's impossible to predict which particular cell in your retina will catch a photon. Even when it comes to something as vital as our vision, all we have are our probabilities. But is there really any such thing as certainty? If everything, even our own vision, is governed by probabilities, can there be any absolute reality?

Is there any hope of rescuing our classical idea of reality in the quantum universe? Scientists have come up with one way to preserve our traditional understanding of cause and effect, called the many worlds philosophy. We can't call it a hypothesis because it can't be tested scientifically (yet). But it goes like this: Every probability that can happen does happen in some parallel cosmos that

Another pale blue dot: a single positively charged strontium atom captured between two electrodes. Measuring 215 billionths of a millimeter across, the atom is visible because it absorbed and reemitted laser light.

is foreclosed to us. An infinite number of ever branching realities unfolding at every possible juncture.

Or is probability just an illusion itself, a phantom of our ignorance? It is if we live in a universe where every single event was already foreordained at the beginning of time, something that is called superdeterminism. In a superdeterminist universe, every event no matter how big or small—the catastrophic failure of treaties, a sneeze, one particular bee pollinating one particular flower, you reading this book right now—all were set in lockstep motion at the moment the universe began, when it was all no larger than a marble. Think of it: all of these events—and trillions of others— inscribed in the potential of the first moment of the universe. Since we are made of those same elementary particles as everything else in the universe, we are subject to the same laws that rule the quantum universe.

Superdeterminism has an additional virtue. It can explain the mystery of entanglement: the ability of entangled particles to communicate across the vastness, apparently violating the speed limit of light. In a superdeterministic cosmos, entangled partners, separated by whole galaxies, don't need to hear from each other to change their spin. They were always destined to do so at that precise moment. And so were their partners, and so was the intruder who severed their bond by observing one of them.

Tick ...

And so it is for what will happen next ...

Tock ...

And what will happen after that ...

THE GOOD NEWS IS THAT superdeterminism gives us a solution to the mystery of entanglement. The bad news is that it seems to rob us of all agency, all ability to make decisions and forge our own paths. If we are living in a superdeterministic universe, we are just going through the motions, acting out a script that was written for us nearly 14 billion years ago, all the while telling ourselves how clever we were in that argument, how selfish, how brave. If you could only change that one little thing about yourself ... In a universe devoid of free will, we are nothing more than deterministic robots.

But, at least we're clever ones who have found a way to hitch a ride on the uncertainties, to forge new technologies based on our incomplete understanding. We have built a quantum clock, one that you never have to wind. It will only lose a single second in the next 15 billion years. That's more than all of the time since the beginning of the universe.

For all we know, we may be mere collections of preprogrammed particles in a deterministic universe. But let's not live like we are.

Besides, we have no way of knowing if that's true. And to think that, in some sense, our freedom to explore the quantum realm begins with Thomas Young. Remember, it was Young who also found the key to decrypting the lost language of the ancient Egyptians. He was the first to recognize that the hieroglyphs signified sounds, not just ideas. He did this by studying the Rosetta stone, a royal decree of the 2nd century B.C.E. inscribed in three languages, one of which was ancient Greek, a language he knew.

Young's research led us to quantum encryption, a means of creating codes that vanish the moment someone tries to hack into them. The key to the code can be sent via entangled photons. The observer effect is our insurance policy that no spy can decipher the message without causing the entanglement to break apart, rendering the message unintelligible.

We still don't know how a photon can be both a particle and a wave at the same time. What I love about science is that it demands of us a tolerance for ambiguity. It requires us to live with humility regarding our ignorance, withholding judgment until the evidence comes in. That needn't prevent us from using the little we do know to search for and decrypt new languages of reality.

In this vast cosmos, we are all Flatlanders. Science is the struggle to imagine and then find *above*.

The Rosetta stone, with decrees in three languages including hieroglyphics, was used to decipher the written language of ancient Egypt.

CHAPTER TEN

A TALE OF TWO ATOMS

As we approached St. Pierre we could distinguish the rolling and leaping of the red flames that belched from the mountain in huge volumes and gushed high in the sky . . . There was a tremendous explosion about 7:45 o'clock, soon after we got in. The mountain was blown to pieces . . . It was like a hurricane of fire.
—CREW MEMBER OF THE *RORAIMA*, ANCHORED IN SAINT-PIERRE, MARTINIQUE, DURING THE 1902 ERUPTION OF MOUNT PELÉE

A physicist is an atom's way of knowing about atoms.
—GEORGE WALD, INTRODUCTION TO L. J. HENDERSON, *THE FITNESS OF THE ENVIRONMENT,* 1958 EDITION

Military observers watch a detonation in 1958 as the United States Army returned to Pacific atolls for atmospheric nuclear testing.

The kingdom of matter stores its treasures on many levels. Until recently, we thought there was only one. We had no idea there were others.

When we strike a match, a chemical reaction liberates the energy stored in the molecules. Old chemical bonds break, and new ones are forged. The adjacent molecules begin to move faster, and the temperature increases. Soon, the process becomes self-propagating: a kind of chain reaction. The energy represented by a flame has been locked—perhaps for many years—in chemical bonds between atoms, mediated by the electrons that revolve around their cores. When we make a fire, we release this hidden chemical energy. But there is a deeper level of matter that houses another kind of energy buried inside the atom. And another level, deeper still, inside the heart of the atom: its nucleus.

This hidden treasure was forged billions of years ago in distant stellar furnaces, long before Earth was formed. It is in this microcosmos that the secrets of life can be found. And the human future? It will also be determined on the scale of atoms and nuclei. For better or for worse, science will be the key.

What is an atom? What are they made of? How are they joined together? How could something as small as an atom contain so

Creative and destructive, magnificent and terrifying: Fire has played an essential role in the evolution of human culture.

much power? Where do atoms come from? The answer is: The same place we do. When we seek the origin of atoms, we are searching for our own beginnings. This quest takes us into the depths of space and time. I want to tell you a tale of two atoms.

LONG AGO, BEFORE THERE was an Earth, there was a wisp of cold, thin gas. It was made of the simplest atoms, hydrogen and helium. And they were gravitationally attracted to one another, so they gathered together in clouds that over time whirled, flattened, and contracted.

Gravity pulled them ever closer together, causing the atoms in the interior of the cloud to move faster until the whole thing collapsed in on itself. This collapse raised the temperature so high that the cloud became a natural fusion reactor. Atoms, operating according to the laws of physics, met and fused in the unbroken darkness. And then there was light. In other words, a *star*.

In this froth of elementary particles, the nucleus of one of the atoms—a helium atom—was formed. After billions of years, the star, now elderly, had converted all its available hydrogen fuel into helium. As it approached its death, it resumed the turning inward of its infancy. Our helium atom joined together with two others to become one of our heroes: a carbon atom.

Meanwhile, in another part of the Milky Way galaxy, similar processes were unfolding as stars were born and died. The other atom of our tale was also formed in the heart of a dying star. In the catastrophic process of going supernova, 226 protons and neutrons became fused to a carbon atom, turning it into a uranium atom. And the two atoms wandered through the various realms of the Milky Way.

Our carbon atom traveled far to become part of a small planet. After billions of years, it joined an extremely complex molecule that

This is what happens when you strike a match on the scale of the very small: fire at the molecular level—a rapid, runaway chemical reaction. As existing atomic bonds are broken and new bonds are formed, an avalanche of energy is released in the form of light and heat.

has the peculiar property of making virtually identical copies of itself—the essential life-giving molecule that we call deoxyribonucleic acid, or DNA. In this way, that single carbon atom played its tiny role in the origin of life, becoming part of a one-celled organism at the bottom of the sea and through time, a minute component of the iridescent scale of an ancient fish, the claw of an amphibian making its way out of the ocean onto the land. Through all its incarnations, our carbon atom has had no self-awareness, no free will; it is merely an extremely minor cog in some vast cosmic machinery operating in accord with the laws of nature.

And that other atom, the uranium atom made in the supernova, what has become of it? Our own world was born in fire, and somehow, this tiny atom was drawn to it. Maybe it rode the shock wave of a supernova explosion, or perhaps it was attracted by the gravity of our sun. It plummeted toward the volcanic surface of the early Earth and was pulled down deeper and deeper into the interior.

Over time the surface of Earth cooled, but the interior remained molten rock and metal. The magma slowly circulated, and our uranium atom found itself carried, over the ages, from the deep interior back all the way up to the surface. Despite the high temperatures and pressures deep within the interior, our atom's integrity was never threatened. Atoms are small, old, hard, and durable. Many millions of years ago our uranium atom became part of a rock on the surface of Earth. Over time the rock sunk down into the earth and a tall pine forest grew above it. Everything is made of atoms, including us. But until the last years of the 19th century, no one knew about the frenzied activity inside them.

Our two atoms from opposite ends of the Milky Way galaxy are finally about to meet.

IT HAPPENED IN PARIS. One morning in 1898, a horse-drawn wagon pulling canvas sacks of rocks (including our uranium atom, among trillions of others) from the part of eastern Europe that is now the Czech Republic made its way to the Rue Lhomond. It stopped in front of a ramshackle shed that used to be a storehouse for cadavers at the nearby medical school.

Waiting inside was a scientist who transformed our understanding of matter, Marie Curie, age 31. (Our carbon atom had become part of her retina.) She became strangely elated at the sight of the dumpy, grimy sacks. This was just a few years after the discovery of x-rays. Marie, and her colleague and husband, Pierre, wanted to know how a piece of matter could make it possible to see through skin, and even walls. They knew that these rocks contained pitchblende, now known as uraninite, the substance that gave matter these superpowers. When Marie cut the strings of the coarse cloth sack, the dull brown rocks were still mixed with fragrant pine needles. Now, they faced the extremely labor-intensive task of distilling pitchblende from the large sacks of rocks. The work proved to be all-consuming. She was later to write: "We lived in our single occupation, as in a dream." They worked under difficult conditions to purify the ore into pitchblende, which was 50 to 80 percent uranium. They stored the pitchblende in laboratory vessels on the walls of their shed. This was quite an achievement, but Marie and Pierre were hunting for something far more rare. It took them three years to process tons of ore to isolate a mere fraction of a gram of a substance she named radium.

They experimented on their precious radium and were surprised to find that the radium was entirely unaffected by extreme temperatures. That was strange. Most things subjected to such intense heat would be drastically changed. And there was something else. It spontaneously emitted energy, not through chemical reactions but through some unknown mechanism. Marie Curie called this new phenomenon radioactivity. She and Pierre calculated that the energy that spontaneously flowed from a lump of radium would be much greater than burning the same amount of coal. Radioactivity, to their astonishment, was a million times more potent than chemical energy. They didn't fully understand it at the time, but this was the difference between liberating the energy that resides in molecules and liberating the far greater power stored deeper down.

The beakers and vials that lined the shelves of the shack were filled with pitchblende. Marie wrote of a night when they decided to go to the shed after dinner. Every container was illuminated with a gleaming phosphorescent light. As they entered, Marie put her hand on Pierre's arm to dissuade him from lighting the gas lamp. The shelves glowed with sheer magic: Every bottle, every flask, every tube was illuminated with a gleaming phosphorescent bluish

In her Paris laboratory, Marie Curie worked with her husband, Pierre, and then on her own for years after his death, exploring the nature of uranium and radioactivity.

light. As Marie wrote years later, "They were like earthly stars—these glowing tubes in that poor, rough shack."

Marie leaped to the correct conclusion that the luminescence was due to something happening inside radioactive atoms. For thousands of years, it had been thought that atoms were indivisible—that's literally what the word "atom" means in Greek, "uncuttable." Atoms were thought to be the smallest possible unit of matter. Curie's earthly stars were evidence that the atom was a world where a never-before-seen activity of matter was playing out on a stage that no one knew existed. Curie showed that these atoms could not be affected by chemical reactions. To get at them, whole new strategies, new laws of nature, and new technologies, would be needed.

More than a century later, Marie Curie's notebooks and cookbooks still glow with the radioactivity she discovered. In 1906, Pierre was killed instantly when he was run over by a horse-drawn cart at the age of 46. Marie lived and worked for another 28 years, dying of aplastic anemia at 66, assumed to have been a result of her chronic exposure to radiation.

Convinced as she was of radium's value to medicine and industry, Marie never acknowledged the dangerous aspects of her gift to the world. But it wasn't long before its darker implications dawned in the mind of a visionary, H. G. Wells. He was a genius at turning the new revelations of science into stories that captivated the world. He imagined time machines and alien invasions—and a future world in which atoms were weaponized.

In his book *The World Set Free,* published in 1914, he coined the phrase "atomic bombs" and loosed them on helpless civilian populations. He set his vision in the impossibly distant future of the 1950s. Writing just 10 years after the Wright brothers' first flight, Wells imagined an atomic-powered airplane heading across the English Channel. The goggled and helmeted pilot focused directly ahead, intent on the looming city. His face hardened as he leaned over in the cockpit to lift the heavy bomb. He pulled its firing pin with his teeth, and hoisted it over the side. When the bomb made contact with its target, the tremendous force of the blast hurled his plane sideways. What was once the center of Berlin now resembled the seething caldera of a volcano.

It would take science a mere 20 years to catch up with fiction.

ONE PERSON WHO READ H. G. Wells's novel was a young physicist named Leo Szilard. On September 12, 1933, Szilard, a Hungarian émigré, was staying at the Strand Palace Hotel in London. He had just read an account of a speech by Lord Rutherford in the *Times* of London that really ticked him off. Ernest Rutherford was known as the father of nuclear physics for his discovery, among others, that radiation was produced as one chemical element changed into another. Szilard was offended by Rutherford's statement that the newly won knowledge of atomic structure could never be used to produce energy. He decided to take a walk, his preferred medium for thinking.

As he walked, Szilard thought about how atoms are made of protons and neutrons on the inside, and a skittering veil of electrons on the outside. While stopped at a light at the intersection of Southampton Row and Russell Square, he was struck by a thought: If he could find an element that would emit two neutrons when it absorbed one, it would sustain a nuclear chain reaction. Two would produce four, and four would produce eight, and so forth—until enormous amounts of energy in the nucleus itself could be liberated. Not a chemical reaction, but a nuclear one.

Szilard must have stood among a group of pedestrians waiting for the light to change. Perhaps he thought about H. G. Wells's vision of an atomic bomb. Maybe he froze as the people standing behind him pushed past. I wonder if Szilard knew the legend about the invention of chess, which Carl told me long ago. In all the time since,

Persian chess pieces from around 1000 C.E.—from left, two kings, a rook, and a bishop—are made of ivory, the one piece dyed green to distinguish it from white.

I have never found a better way to convey the power of exponentials, and so I'll recount it here. There are many versions of how the game came to be. Some say India, others say Persia. The most important piece was the king, and the object of the game was to capture him. In Persian, the game was called *shahmat—shah* for king, *mat* for dead—which is where the word "checkmate" comes from.

One version of the legend goes that in seventh-century Baghdad, the king was so delighted by his first game of chess that he offered to grant its inventor, his grand vizier, any wish his heart might desire. Imagine the king's surprise when the grand vizier responded with what seemed to be the most modest of requests: "Your Highness, just give me one grain of rice on the first square of the chessboard, twice that on the second square, twice that on the third, and so on, until each square has its proper amount of rice."

"Rice???" The king could not believe his ears. "I was thinking vast expanses of fertile land, stables filled with mighty steeds, emeralds, diamonds, and rubies." But the grand vizier was adamant. Rice, and only rice, was all he wanted. "So be it," said the king, thinking he had gotten off much too easily.

The king gestured to his courtiers to have a sack of rice brought to the throne room, and a functionary began to count out the rice grains. The first few squares on the board went quickly, but now more sacks were needed. And the counting burden became more complex with each additional square. Too much for one person.

Now, more counters were needed as the number of grains mounted, and the piles of rice on each square grew taller, until they began to bury the people and furniture in the room, even the throne itself! The power of doubling—what is called exponential growth—is so awesome that if the king were to fulfill his promise, there would be *half a billion* grains of rice by only the middle of the fourth row of the chessboard. Before long, rice would be pouring out of every window of the palace until the city itself was buried in rice! Waves of rice would inundate Baghdad and the surrounding terrain.

By the time the king's men got to the last square, the 64th on the chessboard, the grand vizier would have received nearly *18.5 quintillion grains of rice! Seventy billion tons of rice*—that's the equivalent of what everyone on Earth today would consume for 150 years. The fulfillment of the king's pledge bankrupted him. And legend has it that the grand vizier—whose only power was his knowledge of math—now sat upon his throne. Checkmate.

Leo Szilard well knew the power of exponentials, and if a neutron chain reaction could be triggered down there in the world of the atom's nucleus, then something like Wells's imaginary atomic bomb might be possible. He shuddered at the thought of this destructive capability. It was just the latest development on a continuum of violence that began long, long before.

HOW DO YOU JUDGE A CIVILIZATION? Do you know it by its economic system? Its capabilities to communicate and to travel? How much of its wealth is devoted to making war? The kill radius of their weapons—how far their weapons travel to kill the enemy? How many lives they can take with a single weapon? The society's identification horizon—how large a group is deemed worthy of concern? Their sense of the future—how many years ahead are they willing to plan for, and what are they willing to do to protect it?

It is a sad reality that one strand of human history is our ever expanding efficiency in killing one another. Fifty thousand years ago, all humans were roving bands of hunter-gatherers. They communicated over limited areas by calling to each other—that is, at the speed of sound, around 750 miles an hour. But over longer distances, they could communicate only as fast as they could run. It was around that time that they developed the power to kill at a longer distance. Their kill radius expanded to the arc of an arrow propelled by a bow. And the ratio of combatant to victim was 1 to 1—only one person could be killed with a single arrow. Our ancestors were not particularly warlike because there were so few people and so much room back then; moving on was preferable to armed conflict. Their weapons were used almost entirely for hunting. Their identification horizon was likely small—only with the other members of their band of 50 or 100 people.

But their time horizon took a quantum leap with the development of agriculture. They worked long and hard planting crops in the here and now, so months later they could harvest them. They postponed present gratification for later advantage. They began to plan for the future.

By about 2,500 years ago—a mere six seconds to midnight on December 31 on the Cosmic Calendar, humans began to wage a new kind of war. The conquered territories of Alexander stretched from Macedonia to the Indus Valley. There were now many on planet Earth who owed allegiance to groups composed of millions. Over long distances, the maximum speed of both communication and transportation was the speed of the sail and the horse. But advances in weapons technology increased the kill range, and weapon-to-casualty ratio, exponentially—10 times. Now, 10 corpses lay where

one would have been. And the soldier who released the lever on the siege engine likely never saw the faces of his victims. He remained far removed from the carnage on the other side of the city wall.

Archidamus III, king of Sparta in the fourth century B.C.E., was famed for his unflinching courage. He relished taking part in hand-to-hand combat with the enemy. It is said that when he first saw a projectile hurled by a ballista, he cried out in anguish: "Oh, Hercules, the valor of man is lost!"

Today, the maximum speed of transportation is the escape velocity from Earth, 25,000 miles an hour. The speed of communication is the speed of light. The identification horizons have also expanded enormously. For some, it's a billion people or more; for others, it's our whole species; and for a few, it's all living things. The kill radius, in the worst-case scenario, is now our global civilization.

How did we get here? It was the result of a deadly embrace between science and state. And there was one scientist for whom no amount of destructive power was enough. It's hard to pinpoint

The evolution of weaponry: from bows and arrows, shown in Algerian rock paintings (opposite), some dating back 10,000 years, through the well-equipped armies of Alexander the Great, advancing from the left, and the Persian king Darius III, their fourth-century B.C.E. battles depicted in a floor mosaic from Pompeii

the precise moment when the First Nuclear War really began. Some might see it as a continuum tracing it all the way back to that arrow sailing over the treetops. Others might say it started much later, with three messages.

IN 1939, ON APRIL 24, just a few days after Adolf Hitler's birthday, one of Germany's bright young scientists, Paul Harteck, had a special gift in mind for his Führer. He strode through the streets of Hamburg carrying a letter to the Nazi war office. He was excited to inform them that the latest developments in nuclear physics would make it possible to produce an explosive exponentially more powerful than the most destructive conventional weapons. He was trying to give an atomic bomb to Adolf Hitler. But Hitler would never get his hands on a nuclear weapon. He had murdered, imprisoned, or driven out of Europe many of the great physicists in his territories—those who happened to be Jews, or liberals, and many who were both.

On August 2 of that same year, two scientists drove out to Cutchogue, Long Island, on a mission to Albert Einstein. Although both men in the car were Hungarian émigrés, both physicists, they would take radically different paths in life. But today, they were allied in their mission.

One of them was Leo Szilard. Like most everyone else, he could see that war was coming. The physicist who usually chauffeured Leo Szilard on trips out of Manhattan was unavailable that August day in 1939, so Szilard enlisted the services of a young scientist named Edward Teller. Persecution in Budapest sent Teller and his family to take refuge in Munich, where he lost his right foot in a traffic accident. In the early 1930s, Teller and his family were forced to flee once again, eventually coming to the United States. Teller drove Szilard to Cutchogue, where Einstein kept a summerhouse. The great scientist and Szilard sat at a table in a dining room filled with books and papers. Teller lurked restlessly in the adjoining kitchen, a reflection of his junior status.

Just as Harteck felt it was his duty to inform Hitler, Szilard wanted President Franklin Roosevelt to know the awesome potential of such a weapon. There was no scientist on Earth whose prestige and influence was comparable to Einstein's, and Szilard knew that Einstein's signature on a letter about the potential weapon would guarantee the president's attention.

Einstein studied the letter with enormous ambivalence. His nightmare was imagining Hitler with a nuclear weapon at his

Leo Szilard carried this letter to Albert Einstein in 1939, in the hope that the world's most famous scientist would alert President Roosevelt to the destructive potential contained in the atom.

Albert Einstein
Old Grove Rd.
Nassau Point
Peconic, Long Island

August 2nd, 1939

F.D. Roosevelt,
President of the United States,
White House
Washington, D.C.

Sir:

Some recent work by E.Fermi and L. Szilard, which has been communicated to me in manuscript, leads me to expect that the element uranium may be turned into a new and important source of energy in the immediate future. Certain aspects of the situation which has arisen seem
to call for watchfulness and, if necessary, quick action on the part
of the Administration. I believe therefore that it is my duty to bring
to your attention the following facts and recommendations:

In the course of the last four months it has been made probable -
through the work of Joliot in France as well as Fermi and Szilard in
America - that it may become possible to set up a nuclear chain reaction
in a large mass of uranium,by which vast amounts of power and large quantities of new radium-like elements would be generated. Now it appears
almost certain that this could be achieved in the immediate future.

This new phenomenon would also lead to the construction of bombs,
and it is conceivable - though much less certain - that extremely powerful bombs of a new type may thus be constructed. A single bomb of this
type, carried by boat and exploded in a port, might very well destroy
the whole port together with some of the surrounding territory. However,
such bombs might very well prove to be too heavy for transportation by
air.

Yours very truly,

A. Einstein

(Albert Einstein)

disposal. What would be the long-term consequences of this dangerous new knowledge, which, once unleashed, could never be taken back? Einstein would take no role in the U.S. effort to build the atomic bomb, which became known as the Manhattan Project, but he did alert the president to the potential use of atomic nuclei in warfare. Einstein's hand faltered for a moment before he reluctantly signed his name.

After the war was over, he told a reporter that if he had known the Germans would fail in developing an atomic bomb, he never would have signed the letter. Edward Teller had no such ambivalence. He couldn't wait to get started on weaponizing the atom.

The Russian physicist G. N. Flerov had tried repeatedly to alert his leader, Joseph Stalin, to the possible military applications of a nuclear chain reaction. But the Soviet Union was under siege by the Germans in February 1942, and an "atom bomb" project was likely to take years to complete. With their backs against the wall, it seemed too impractical to even think about.

That was, until Flerov visited the Academic Library in Voronezh, a city in northwestern Russia, where he was stationed as a lieutenant in the Soviet Air Force. He had recently published a scientific paper on nuclear physics and he was excited to see what the eminent physicists in Europe and the United States had to say about it. He anxiously turned the pages of the journals without finding a single reference to his paper. Flerov was puzzled. None of the physicists of the international scientific community thought his paper worthy of comment. At first he was hurt, but then he realized what was really happening. American and German scientific journals were being scrubbed of any nuclear physics papers as both nations secretly worked on building the atomic bomb. It was this absence of published data—"the dogs that did not bark"—that moved Flerov to redouble his efforts to convince Stalin to start his own nuclear weapons program.

In all three cases, it was the scientists—not the generals, or the arms dealers—who informed their leaders that a huge increase in kill ratio was possible.

THE U.S. DEPARTMENT OF WAR chose the remote location of Los Alamos, New Mexico, as the headquarters for the atomic bomb research project. It had been recommended by the project's director, physicist J. Robert Oppenheimer, who had spent time there as a teenager, recuperating from an illness. But for Edward Teller, an atomic bomb wasn't big enough. He dreamed of even greater kill ratios, a weapon in which the atomic bomb was nothing more than a match to light a fuse to the nucleus—thermonuclear weapons—what Teller affectionately called the "Super."

If Teller had a polar opposite in this scientific community, it would have been Joseph Rotblat. Rotblat was born in Warsaw to a wealthy family, who, like Teller's, had lost everything. In the summer of 1939, just before the Nazis invaded, he was invited to England to take a research position at the University of Liverpool. At the last minute before his departure, his beloved wife, Tola, had an emergency appendectomy. She was forced to remain behind until she was well enough to travel. Tola insisted that Joseph go on ahead to prepare their new home. It would just be a matter of weeks, she told him.

The challenge for the Manhattan Project scientists was to find a chemical fuse that would light the nuclear chain reaction first imagined by Leo Szilard on his walk through London. All the scientists and engineers told themselves that they would be averting a grave danger by building a bomb of unprecedented destructive power. *Their* government could be trusted. They would never use such a weapon in an act of aggression. Not like those other governments.

These atomic scientists were the first to see building nuclear weapons as a deterrent to using them. The fear of Hitler with an atomic bomb was the rationale that drove them. And yet, when Germany surrendered, and Hitler was dead, of the thousands of Allied scientists who worked on the bomb, only one resigned.

It was Joe Rotblat. In the years that followed, whenever he was asked about his decision, he always rejected any suggestion that he had done so out of moral superiority. He would just smile and say, the truth was that he desperately missed his wife, who had been prevented from leaving Warsaw and lost to him in the chaos of the war. With its end in Europe came his chance to go and search for her. But he never found her, only her name on a list of the dead. Tola had perished in the Holocaust, exterminated at the Belzec concentration camp. Rotblat lived another 60 years. He never remarried and never stopped fighting for nuclear disarmament.

Of the three nations that pursued wartime research into building the bomb, only the United States succeeded before the war's end. Historians believe that one of the reasons for this success was that America had taken in so many immigrants. Of the leading figures in the Manhattan Project, only two were native-born, and only one got his Ph.D. in the States.

The scientists' faith in deterrence was misplaced. U.S. warplanes dropped atomic bombs on the Japanese cities of Hiroshima and Nagasaki, ending the Second World War. Two months later, President Truman invited Oppenheimer for congratulations in the Oval Office. To Truman's dismay, Oppenheimer was in no mood to celebrate. Upon meeting Truman, he blurted out, "Mr. President, I feel like I have blood on my hands."

Truman flashed him a look of disgust and said contemptuously, "Don't be a fool. If anyone has blood on their hands, it's me. And it doesn't bother me at all."

But Oppenheimer persisted. "How long do you think it will be before the Russians get the bomb?" he asked.

Truman answered, "Never!"

When Oppenheimer left, Truman turned to his aide, clearly furious, and said, "Don't you ever let that crybaby scientist anywhere near me again! Do you hear?"

Less than four years later, the Russians exploded their own

Physicist J. Robert Oppenheimer (in the light brimmed hat) and others inspect the remains of the first atomic test, performed in Alamogordo, New Mexico, on July 16, 1945.

atomic bomb. The nuclear arms race, envisioned in those three letters from scientists, had reached a second, more terrifying phase.

After the war, Teller's dreams of greater and greater kill ratios were to come true. In the early 1950s, during the communist witch hunts in the United States, he was perfectly happy to hint that Robert Oppenheimer, his former boss, who had brilliantly run the Manhattan Project, should be stripped of his security clearance, thereby ruining Oppenheimer's career. Oppenheimer was against building Teller's beloved "super." Teller became an effective force in preventing comprehensive treaties to ban nuclear weapons tests. He falsely argued that atmospheric testing was essential to "maintaining and improving nuclear arsenals."

Despite massive reductions in the nuclear arsenals, the specter of nuclear war haunts us still. There are still more than enough in the world to destroy our civilization. How can we sleep so soundly in the shadow of a smoking volcano? In another time, there were others who faced a grave danger, as if immobilized in a dream.

TWO MEN WALKED INTO A BAR in Saint-Pierre on the Caribbean island of Martinique, located between Puerto Rico and Venezuela. It was the night of April 23, 1902, and the two men were police officers, summoned to break up a vicious bar fight. The patrons of the bar had made room for the two combatants. One of them was Ludger Sylbaris, 27, of African descent, so tall and muscular that his nickname was "Samson." He bore the scars of previous fights, and wielded a cutlass sword. His opponent was unintimidated. He broke a bottle on the bar and rushed at Sylbaris, who without flinching, lunged back at him with the cutlass. Sylbaris slashed his opponent badly, just as the authorities arrived. The officers shackled Sylbaris and dragged him off to the Saint-Pierre prison. He was hauled down the stone steps into a horrifying dungeon. Small and fetid, it didn't even have a bed. Despite his terror at being confined in this tomb, Sylbaris remained defiant. He sat on the floor, looking up at the police with contempt as they shut the steel door with only one tiny air hole, leaving him in solitary darkness.

Among the nearly 30,000 inhabitants of this French colonial city of whitewashed houses Fernand Clerc was one of the wealthiest. From his balcony, he had a clear view of his rum distilleries, furniture factories, fields of sugarcane and coffee. They were the economic backbone of the island. Above all of them rose the majestic Mount Pelée, a long-slumbering volcano, one of the many mountain peaks that dotted the island.

But then Clerc noticed something odd: There appeared to be a dusting of frost on everything. How could that be on such a sunny, warm morning? He ran his finger along the balcony rail and realized that it wasn't frost but a kind of dust.

As the bells of the cathedral tolled, Clerc reached for his telescope to examine the town more closely. Everyone was still asleep.

The streets were empty. Just as he turned toward the mountain, there was a deafening boom—like the broadside of a cannon—and a column of ash shot into the sky. Clerc's wife, Véronique, rushed onto the balcony, clutching a crucifix, searching her husband's eyes for an explanation.

When the ash began to fall, Clara Prentiss, wife of the American consul, considered going home to Massachusetts. No, that was out of the question. There was the gala she'd planned for the following week. Postponing it was unthinkable.

Marius Hurard, editor and publisher of *Les Colonies* newspaper, was looking over the latest edition. He was a youngish man of enormous energy. The front page declared that a leading authority on volcanoes was offering reassurance that Mount Pelée posed no threat. The only problem with this statement was that the "leading authority" was Marius Hurard himself. Elsewhere on the front page was the headline "Invitation From the Gymnastic and Shooting Club." It went on to read:

> Please Join Us for a Grand Excursion to the
> Crater of Mt. Pelée for the Best View of the Eruption.
> Picnic to Follow. An Experience You Will Never Forget!

We will never know how many of the anonymous poor had forebodings and were prevented from leaving the island because they lacked the resources. How many were told, as birds fell dead from the sky, "Don't you worry. It may seem frightening, but the city has seen it all before, and nothing much happened then, either. Besides, it says in the newspaper there's nothing to worry about."

The streets filled with ash.

Alone in his office, Mayor Fouché worked late into the evening, drafting the detailed plans for the official Ascension Day banquet and ball. Liveried servants were laying yards of white linen on everything from furniture to fixtures. Linen was laid on the table-tops to cover the silver, crystal, and china place settings. But it was quickly covered with ash that somehow got in through the closed windows. The hotel staff swept through the room, giving the floor a last-minute brushing, and removing the ash from the table; others stood with fans at the ready. The servants exchanged worried expressions, but nobody departed from their duties.

The closest thing to a scientist on the island of Martinique was the elementary school teacher Gaston Landes. He stood in the Botanical Gardens aghast, surrounded by his dead plants and succulents, killed by the volcanic ash. Landes actually made a pilgrimage to the newly awakened volcanic crater, and shared his observations of heightened activity in the newspaper.

The ground had become littered with the corpses of birds who had been choked by the fumes and gases. But Landes was more concerned about his forthcoming trip to Paris. He had planned to display samples of the island's plant life along with the lecture he had been asked to give. With the ash falling at this rate, his specimens were all ruined.

The priest at the cathedral of Saint-Pierre looked over his congregation, their raggedy clothing stained with the soot and dust of the eruption, and recited from Psalm 46:

Therefore will we not fear, though the earth be removed, and though the mountains be carried into the midst of the sea; Though the waters thereof roar and be troubled, though the mountains shake with the swelling thereof.

Now, massive boulders and huge tree trunks were being carried along the expanding mudflow all the way down the mountain to the ocean. From time to time, the volcano roared with the sounds of the earth breaking apart.

Mayor Fouché sat at his desk in despair. He mustered enough resolve to create a poster that read: "Fellow citizens, be not afraid. No lava flows can reach the city in the near future. We have 7 kilometers between us and the volcano. The amount of lava would have to be impossibly huge to cross the two immense valleys and the swamp between us and Mt. Pelée."

And Fouché wasn't wrong . . . about the lava. But the volcano would produce something even more far-reaching, fast-moving, and terrifying than rock, so hot that it flows like water. Some of the people of Saint-Pierre were making what they thought were sound decisions about staying, based on the information available to them. Others were simply in denial. Still others boarded the packet boats for safer places. But none could imagine how the volcano would express all the pent-up pressure contained within it.

Two days later, more than two weeks after the first signs of activity, the first of the *nuées ardentes*—incandescent clouds—were ejected from the volcano, sending white firebrands down on the city below. Volcanic lightning, a phenomenon of even more ferocious lightning than in the greatest storm, combined with the glowing red and yellow lava dome of fire to make the scene even more hellish. The horrendous "burning cloud" arced over the valleys and began torching the city below.

At dawn on May 8, dozens of sailors stood on the deck of a schooner, looking toward Martinique. They smiled with relief, and joked with each other, as the volcano began to simmer down. The danger must have passed. The volcano became utterly calm. The air was cool and fresh, and the sea like glass. The view of Saint-Pierre from the deck of the ship was lovely. All of a sudden, with a blinding flash, Mount Pelée exploded, sending a towering cloud of fiery debris almost two miles high.

The sailors' amazement turned to horror. Some of them were blown back against the bulkheads; others were blasted off the deck by the shock wave and sent flying into the sea. When Mount Pelée erupted at 8:02 a.m., on May 8, 1902, the explosion produced a sound so loud it was heard 500 miles away in Venezuela.

Now Mount Pelée puked up a nimbus of burning gas, rocks, and dust that moved with hurricane force and speed. The burning cloud raced down the mountainside and rampaged across the valleys into

the city, carrying its rolling lightning storm along with it. The massive death cloud of superheated gases crossed the valleys to the city in minutes. Morning became night as the city was devoured by the death cloud, which only stopped when it reached the sea.

Nine thousand years ago, when the artist at Çatalhöyük made those few magical strokes representing wispy smoke, the earliest image of an eruption we have yet found, she or he initiated our conscious, recorded relationship with volcanoes. The complete destruction of Saint-Pierre within minutes began another new phase. It led to a new science called volcanology and to a phrase that would replace the festive-sounding phrase *nuées ardentes* with the more clinical "pyroclastic flow." It was the pyroclastic flow that incinerated Saint-Pierre. The explosion was the equivalent of just a single strategic nuclear warhead.

Three days after the eruption, men from another part of the island combed the still smoking streets of Saint-Pierre to collect the bodies, and burn what the volcano had failed to consume completely. Suddenly, they heard muffled cries. The men looked at each

Saint-Pierre, Martinique, after the 1902 eruption of Mount Pelée

other in disbelief before rushing toward them. As they neared the ruins of the prison, the cries grew louder, more desperate.

In the history of the world few have ever experienced what Ludger Sylbaris endured and lived to tell about it. When the volcano erupted, he heard the screams of his captors briefly before a terrifying silence. And then, a fierce heat came blasting through the tiny vent in his cell. He hopped and jumped around to avoid it, but he was still severely burned up to his shoulders. For three days, he suffered in agony, with no other sustenance than the moisture on the walls of his cell. His sentence to solitary confinement in the thick-walled dungeon had saved his life.

He was one of only two survivors of the 30,000 citizens of Saint-Pierre. After being nursed back to health he became a major attraction in the Barnum & Bailey Circus, touring the world and bearing witness to his hair-raising story of improbable survival.

What about us? Are we underestimating nature's power? Are

NASA'S Chandra X-ray telescope captured this image of the rapidly expanding supernova G292.0+1.8, one of only three in the Milky Way with ample oxygen, thus representative of the star birth that provided Earth with elements necessary for life: oxygen (yellow and orange), magnesium (green), silicon, and sulfur (blue).

we smart enough to anticipate all the scenarios that pose a danger to us? Would we know when to flee? What if there is no means of getting off the island in time?

LET'S RETURN TO THE TRAIL of one of our two atoms—the uranium atom. Its nucleus begins to throb. A uranium atom is inherently unstable. Sooner or later, it decays. A particle from its nucleus breaks away, transforming the uranium atom into an entirely different element—thorium. Subatomic particles move like bullets through the fine structures of life, shearing electrons from their molecules. This is how ionizing radiation affects living things. This is why atomic weapons are so much more dangerous than conventional ones. Radiation is all around us, and even inside us. At low levels, it poses no threat. But at higher levels, it's a different story. In the near term, exposure to lethal levels of radiation can cause a runaway reaction of the cell that makes it multiply exponentially—cancer. But its power to harm can also echo down the corridors of time. When the radiation tore into the chromosomes, it left a trail of destruction in its wake that changed the destiny of the unborn offspring: a mutation in its genes. The damage is passed on, vandalizing our future.

We are made of atoms that were born in stars thousands of light-years away in space and billions of years ago in time. Our search for our own origins has carried us far from our epoch and our world. We are starstuff deeply connected with the rest of the universe. The matter that makes us up was generated in cosmic fire.

And now, we—ambulatory collections of seven billion billion billion atoms, evolved over eons—have devised a means to tap that cosmic fire hidden in the heart of matter. We cannot unlearn this knowledge.

And tragically, insanity runs in our family.

The letters that the scientists wrote to begin this nightmare were followed by another in 1955, this one a letter to the planet stating that this new understanding of physics demanded a new way of thinking. "Shall we . . . choose death, because we cannot forget our quarrels? We appeal as human beings to human beings: Remember your humanity, and forget the rest." This manifesto, written by Bertrand Russell, announced by Joseph Rotblat, and signed by Albert Einstein, was the last public statement of the great scientist, who died only days later.

And what of our other atom, the carbon atom?

It's inside you.

CHAPTER ELEVEN

THE FLEETING GRACE OF THE HABITABLE ZONE

When Spring returns
Perhaps I will no longer be in the world.
Today I wish I could think of Spring as a person
So that I could imagine her crying for me
When she sees that she's lost her only friend.
But Spring isn't even a thing:
It's a manner of speaking.
Not even the flowers or green leaves return.
There are new flowers, new green leaves.
There are new balmy days.
Nothing returns, nothing repeats,
because everything is real.
—FERNANDO PESSOA,
"WHEN SPRING RETURNS"
(translated by Richard Zenith)

An imaginary travel poster of the future beckons us to vacation on TRAPPIST-1e,
the fourth exoplanet of the seven worlds circling its red dwarf sun.

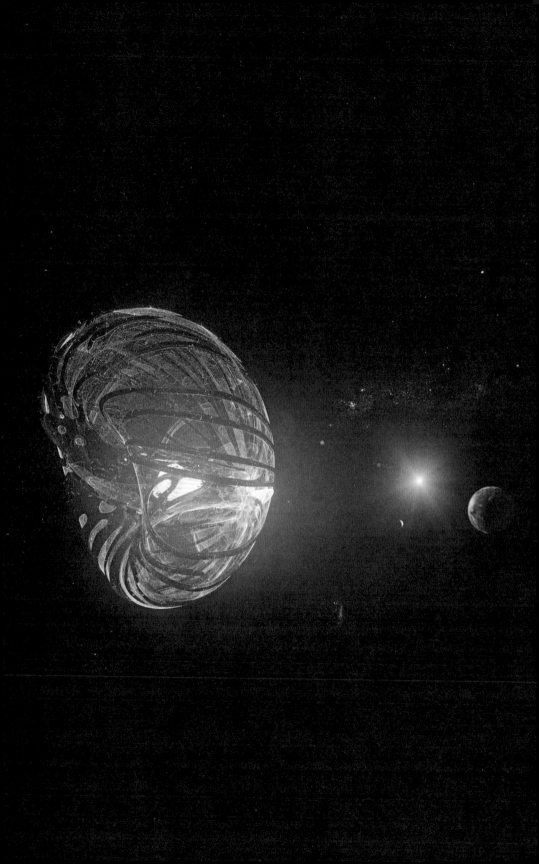

In our galaxy, there may be ships of other worlds that dare to venture into the cosmic deep. When I imagine them, they are nothing like the extraterrestrial spacecraft in our movies. In my fantasies they are more . . . biological. Something not built recently out of urgent necessity but instead the evolutionary result of a long tradition of spacefaring. Perhaps they travel from star to star on survey missions, searching for worlds where life has taken hold to get a closer look at the emergent properties of living things that even they can't predict.

Imagine an alien vessel on just such a survey mission. Tiny podlike probes adhering to the craft's surface like randomly scattered freckles depart to reconnoiter this molten, battered world. They cruise low just above the seething atmosphere as the mother ship performs its own analysis. Veins of fire criss-cross the planet's incandescent surface. If we ourselves were to spy on this hell, would we think it had great prospects for life? Would we see puppies and orchids in its future? The pods return as a swarm to reattach themselves to the mother ship just as it turns away from the infernal planet to head in the direction of its star.

An artist's conception of an alien craft on a survey mission of the third planet of an ordinary yellow dwarf star. The ship is imagined to have a buzzing transparent skin of cosmic radiation.

In its infancy, Earth held little apparent promise. The crew of our imaginary reconnaissance mission of four billion years ago would have bet on Venus, blue with oceans and sprawling landmasses back then, and perhaps, even life. This long ago epoch was Venus's moment to flourish, its time in the habitable zone. For any world, that's a period when its relationship to its star means that it's not too hot, and not too cold. It's a time in a world's existence when it can foster and sustain life. But the grace of the habitable zone is a fleeting thing, and no world lasts forever.

We are fortunate to reside in the inner edge of our star's habitable zone, but it is moving outward at the rate of about three feet per year. Earth has already passed through 70 percent of the time it has in the sun's most hospitable zone. But no need to worry, that still leaves us hundreds of millions of years to plan and execute our exit strategy. Where will we go when the sun's grace leaves us behind for other worlds, and Earth is no longer a garden for life? Will our species have set sail for distant islands in the vast ocean of the Milky Way? There is no refuge from change in the cosmos, no safe place to hide for more than a few billion years.

Look around you at the beauty of our home planet. Someday, all of it will surrender to the churning cycles of birth, destruction, and rebirth mandated by the laws of nature. The universe evolves beautiful things, and then smashes them to bits before making new ones out of the shattered pieces. Neutron stars collide, and spew gold throughout the cosmos. Any species that wants to survive long term on any possible world will have to learn how to engineer interplanetary and, ultimately, interstellar mass transit.

How do we know this? The little we have learned about the universe allows us glimpses of the future. I'm not talking about the near term, where climate change caused by human activity poses a danger to our civilization. If we want to endure for thousands, millions, even billions of years, we'll have to stop dumping all that carbon dioxide into the atmosphere, right now. But let's give us the benefit of the doubt, and take the long view.

Our own star a billion years from now—still a yellow dwarf but with a hotter surface as it begins to exhaust its nuclear fuel

THE SUN IS AGING just like the rest of us. Someday, it will exhaust the hydrogen fuel at its core. Five or six billion years from now, the zone of hydrogen fusion will slowly migrate outward, an expanding shell of thermonuclear reactions, until the temperatures are less than about 10 million degrees. Then the hydrogen fusion reactor at the sun's interior will shut itself off. Over the course of hundreds of millions of years, the self-gravity of the sun will force a renewed contraction of its helium-rich core. The ash of hydrogen fire will become fuel, and the sun will be triggered into a second round of fusion reactions. This will give the sun a new lease on life for some hundreds of millions of years more. It will generate the elements

The Mars landscape, 3.5 billion years ago, as the sun set over the Kasei Valles. Craters and erosion patterns observed on the planet's surface today indicate that water flowed there in those days—and it may once again as our star ages.

carbon and oxygen and provide additional energy for the sun to continue shining.

Our sun will lose gas as its atmosphere expands into space in a kind of stellar tempest. It will go from being a yellow dwarf to a red giant. This will diminish its gravitational hold on Venus and Earth, allowing them to migrate to a safer distance—for a little while. This red giant sun, ruddy and bloated, will envelop and consume the planet Mercury. The grace of the habitable zone will be moving outward, farther and faster. If we play our cards right, so will we. Solar evolution is inevitable, but we have a billion years to go house hunting. Plenty of time to seek those worlds in the cosmos that could become our new homes. Human beings will almost certainly evolve into something quite different by then. Who knows? Perhaps our distant descendants will be able to control or moderate the very destiny of the stars themselves.

Stellar evolution will also transform Mars, the world next door. This will not be the first time that Mars has been graced with liquid water on its surface. There was a time, three or four billion years ago, when waves crashed on Martian beaches, and the nights were warm and sultry. Mars was a strangely familiar, Earthlike world with wispy white clouds shading the red landmasses and the blue oceans. A small white polar ice cap sat rakishly atop its northern hemisphere.

This ancient Mars reminds me of home. But these comforting, familiar features mask—from a human's point of view, anyway— one fatal flaw. Mars just wasn't big enough. At only about half the diameter of Earth, it couldn't generate enough heat at its iron core to render it molten, generating a life-protecting magnetic field. When the streaking fingers of the solar winds clawed at Mars, its clouds and its oceans leaked away into space, leaving the desert planet that we know today.

Scientists think this life-friendly Mars only lasted a couple of hundred million years. We do not yet know if life ever had a chance to get started there. But if it did, that was long ago when the sun was young. In the sun's late middle age, it will give Mars a second chance. One or two billion years from now, Mars will return to the sun's good graces. This second golden age will last only as long as the first—just a few hundred million years. Not enough time for complex Martian life to evolve, but more than enough time for our descendants to set up camp, as they contemplate their next move. But ultimately, the life cycle of the sun will send us so much farther. It will be time to hit the road again. The sun's aging will continue to move the habitable zone outward, scorching Mars, and making the planet too hot for the likes of us. The distant descendants of wanderers will be wanderers still.

The sun's atmosphere will continue expanding, reddening, bloating until it fully bakes the Martian surface, which will crack and char. So where to next?

By now, the intense light and heat of the sun's expansion will reach all the way out to the Jupiter system. Its clouds of ammonia and water will escape, and be lost to space as vapor. And for the first time, the more drab hidden layers down beneath Jupiter's gaudy upper atmosphere will be exposed. Could we make a home on one of Jupiter's frozen moons? The thick layers of ice encasing Europa and Callisto will defrost, exposing the liquid oceans beneath to harsh sunlight, *thousands of times* stronger than before. This will liberate large amounts of water vapor, starting a runaway greenhouse effect.

Cracks on the surface of the moon Ganymede, another ice ball, will begin to spread as geysers of newly liberated water shoot up thousands of feet from the surface. They will arc outward into space before raining down on the increasingly liquid-covered moon. Ganymede's once thin atmosphere will become steamy and dense. If life was swimming in those oceans all along, here is a new chance for it to flourish and evolve. Then Ganymede will belong to those beings. It's just as well, because we'll want our next home to be at a safer distance from the sun.

Not Saturn, now stripped of its glory by the newly raging sun, its rings stolen. Nor its moon Titan, robbed by the same culprit of its water and atmosphere. Not Uranus, not Neptune, their cloudy surfaces tormented by relentless lightning strikes.

Just when it might look like we're running out of possible worlds, here comes Triton, one of Neptune's moons. Named for the son of the Roman god of the sea, Triton will benefit mightily, at least from our point of view, from the sun's transformation into a red giant star. Right now, Triton looks something like a cantaloupe, but when the sun expands outward, Triton will transform into a place of alpine mountaintops, covered with snow tinted pink by the giant red star in the sky that now looms seven times larger than our sun did in our own time. When the heat of the red giant sun melted the ammonia and water ices of this once frigid moon, it created a great ocean.

Voyager 2 passed by Triton, Neptune's largest moon, and sent pictures of its gnarled surface with active ice volcanoes, likely formed of nitrogen, dust, and methane compounds.

If our distant descendants can make a go of it on Triton, they will live to different rhythms than we do. A day on Triton will be 144 hours long. The winters will be brutal. They'll be nearly 50 years long. But still, the Triton of a few billion years from now could be a great home for us. It will have everything: an atmosphere, water oceans, the chemical building blocks that would make life possible. Okay, it's chilly, but not much worse than upstate New York in January. And that means great skiing year-round. And with the much lighter gravity, the ski jumps will crush all records.

But one day, the sun will exhaust itself completely, and the fleeting grace of the habitable zone will end here, too. When the sun's torrid red giant phase is over, it will be stripped naked, revealing the small white dwarf beneath, a star without even enough energy left to warm its few surviving children. The moons of the outer solar system will freeze once again.

So, if we're looking for a long lease on a new home—say, more than just a couple of hundred million years—we'll have to travel even farther out. We'll have to leave our solar system and brave the vast ocean of interstellar space.

I know what you're thinking: Are *we* to venture to the distant stars? We once made a few baby steps to the moon before we lost our will and scurried back to the safety of our Mother Earth. What makes us think that we could survive a voyage between the stars, the nearest of which is a hundred million times farther than our moon? Wouldn't our tiny ships be swallowed up by the great unknown?

I think we can do it. Why? Because we've done it before.

WE DREAM OF SAILING AMONG the island worlds of the Milky Way, catching photons with our light sails, daring to go tetherless beyond the point of no return. We have passed this way before. Once, there was a group of people who chose the unknown. They risked everything to go forth on uncharted seas and their courage was rewarded. They found paradise. We call these people the Lapita, but that was never their name. It was just the result of a misunderstanding made decades ago when we first began to discover the broken shards of their pottery. To me, they're not the Lapita. They are the Voyagers, a name far more worthy of them. About 10,000 years ago, when the population of settlements in southern China began to swell, these Voyagers chose to pioneer the frontier farther south to what is now Taiwan. They settled there happily for thousands of years until the place began to get too crowded again.

Just as we, of this planet, came of age in a kind of cosmic quarantine, cut off from any hope of knowing about, much less reaching, the other worlds of the cosmos, our distant ancestors were, to some extent, prisoners of the land. If you wanted to travel a great distance, you had to walk there. And after you walked as far as you could you would be hemmed in at the water's edge. This was before the age of the great seafaring civilizations—the Phoenicians of the Middle East, and the Minoans of Crete. And for most of their history, they hugged the shore; their fishing and trading expeditions were careful to keep land in sight. For our ancestors, this was the edge of the cosmic ocean.

We do not know what first inspired the Voyagers to attempt the seemingly impossible. They were living on a tectonic plate where earthquakes and volcanic eruptions were common. Could they no longer trust the earth? Or did hostile neighbors make life intolerable for them there? Did a change in climate threaten their livelihood? Were there new population pressures? Did they begin to exhaust the resources of their island by overhunting and overfishing? Or was it simply something innately human in them that made them want to know what was out there? To reach for the mysterious distance, no matter how dangerous that might be? Whatever their motives, over time, they conquered their fear and embarked on a daring odyssey.

I imagine a morning when everyone in the village, young and old, is busy with preparations for a voyage like no other. Men strip bark off the trees, while others lash together logs and weave sails out of reeds. Women fashion fishhooks out of bones and stones. In my fantasy, the whole village gathers at the water's edge. Twenty or so double-hulled canoes line the beach, partly in the sand, partly in the shallow waters. They are being loaded with small, domesticated animals, including dogs, pigs, and chickens; potted rice plants, breadfruit, piles of sweet potatoes; and peeping baby frigatebirds in cages.

The sky in the east begins to change color, as the first sign of the sun appears on the horizon. This is the cue for the Voyagers to board their boats and set sail. As they push off, the elderly villagers (and others who have chosen to stay at home), wave them on with encouragement and pride. All 20 dugouts now unfurl their palm sails, marked with the same geometric designs as their tattoos and pottery. As the sails whip in the wind, the ships move majestically into the great unknown, disappearing over the horizon.

WEEKS LATER, THE FLEET has still seen nothing but water. Now, only 15 craft bob on the ocean swells. Thirsty and hungry, the people look thinner and burned by the sun. Their eyes reflect a faraway look of fatigue and fear. A navigator on one of the boats stands on the prow, using the outstretched fingers of his hand as a sextant to navigate by the stars. He points his index finger at the bright star that we call Canopus and his thumbnail downward to the horizon to take a reading of the boat's position. He looks to a woven map on the deck, where seashells and bits of stone and bone have been artfully arranged into compass points.

Clouds gather to obscure the stars, and I can imagine the worry on our navigator's face. His glance falls on the frigatebirds in their cages. They have grown since they left home.

A few mornings later, still no sign of land. The lips of the Voyagers are blistered with sunburn and thirst. Finally, a bolt of lightning, and it begins to rain. The Voyagers joyfully make certain that their pottery can catch as much rain as possible. But the sea begins to swell with the storm. Huge waves rise up and come crashing down on the boats. Before long, they lose sight of three of the boats—never to be seen again.

Days later, only a dozen boats remain. The seas are calm again, but water bowls lie shattered, and much of their provisions have been washed overboard. And still no sight of land. Some of the Voyagers are fishing listlessly with their bone hooks; others are

Pacific wayfinders marked the locations of far-flung islands with coconut fiber and shells. The shells signified islands and atolls; the intersections of sticks, ocean waves and currents. A navigator would study the configuration and leave the stick chart behind, following it by memory.

mending the pandanus leaf sails with bone needles and plant fibers. One man trails his hand in the water purposefully, seeking changes in the current or temperature. A frigatebird hops fitfully in its cage, and the navigator stares at it, his mind working. Suddenly, a mountain of sea rises up between the boats—blue whale! A moment of awe and terror as a geyser blasts forth from the whale's blowhole. And then, just as fast, it's gone again, the great whale returning to the deep.

Another week passes. The navigator eyes the frigatebird once again. He's made up his mind. He reaches down forcefully and picks up the cage, the frigatebird hopping manically inside. He unlatches

Magnificent frigatebirds, their wingspan more than seven feet, can stay aloft for months. The first explorers of the Pacific, Lapita and Polynesian, partnered with them to find land.

the door, grabs the bird in both his hands. At the top of his lungs, he yells in his language: "Show us the way!" He reaches upward to release the frigatebird. All eyes follow the bird's trajectory.

The Voyagers used the careful observations of their ancestors, over generations, to develop navigational techniques that are still viable today. The seasonal, migratory flight patterns of the birds were their GPS. The Voyagers could read water, feeling the ocean currents in their fingertips, and the messages written in the clouds. They were scientists, and all of nature was their laboratory.

I can imagine a time when the survivors must have been ready to abandon all hope. The people on the eight remaining boats were slumped in despair, when one of the women among them happened to look up at a cloud in the distance. To us, it would have looked like any other. But she saw that the underside of the cloud was tinted slightly green. For a moment, maybe she was speechless with excitement, and then she managed to let out a cry that aroused everyone from their stupor: "Land!" The Voyagers adjusted their sails, and started to paddle frantically in the direction of the cloud. Mavulis, the verdant, northernmost island of the Philippines, came into view.

The surviving Voyagers dragged the canoes ashore. The Philippine Islands was where they settled first. After lingering there for a thousand years, they were ready to set sail again. New generations of Voyagers, Polynesians, mounted successful missions of exploration to Indonesia, the Melanesian Islands, Vanuatu, Fiji, Samoa, and on to the Marquesas. And then to the most isolated island group on Earth, the Hawaiian Islands, and on to Tahiti, Tonga, New Zealand, and Pitcairn and Easter Islands. Their empire of water covered nearly *20 million square miles* of sea. And they accomplished this without a single nail or metal tool of any kind.

As time passed, contact between the islands became less frequent. The language the Polynesians brought with them evolved into different tongues in isolation. Many words changed, but one word remained the same in all the languages of the wide Pacific: *layar*—the word for "sail."

If we could sail the cosmic ocean as skillfully as our ancestors navigated the Pacific, I know what I'd do. I wouldn't head for any particular world, but to an empty place 50 billion miles from our sun.

WE'VE BEEN STUDYING LIGHT for millennia and gravity for centuries. Among Einstein's many insights was an understanding of how one could affect the other. The way gravity bends light makes it possible to turn any star, including our own, into a kind of lens for a cosmic telescope, one 50 billion miles long. Our most powerful space-based telescopes of the present can only see the worlds of other suns as mere dots. A cosmic telescope could give us detailed images of the mountains, oceans, glaciers, and maybe even the cities of these worlds.

How would it work? A cosmic telescope's detector array collects the light bouncing off a distant world. It then sends a signal back to Earth, becoming, in effect, the "eyepiece" of our cosmic telescope. And that brightest star in our sky, our sun, is its lens. In its entirety, if we could see it all at once, the telescope would look like a piece of jewelry, with its silver tethers and a yellow diamond (our sun) at its center. So how can a star, which you can't see through, be turned into a lens? When all the rays of reflected light from a distant planet pass very close to the sun, the sun's gravity bends those rays ever so slightly. Where they converge in space is called the focal point because that's where the object you're looking at comes into focus.

What can you see through a 50-billion-mile-long telescope? Virtually anything you want. Galileo's best telescope could magnify an image 30 times, making a world like Jupiter appear 30 times closer. Our cosmic telescope can make things appear 100 billion times closer. And we can aim it in almost any direction. Our detector array moves 360 degrees around the sun. There's only one part of the cosmos that's off-limits to us, and that's the heart of our own Milky Way galaxy, which is just too bright, its radiance blinding. But with a telescope like this one, so much else that has been foreclosed to us would be made visible.

We could look at the gases in the atmosphere of a distant world and would be able to tell if life is there. Molecules have specific color signatures. If we look at the atmosphere through a spectroscope—that instrument that breaks down light into its constituent colors—we'll be able to identify the molecules that make up the atmosphere. The presence of oxygen and methane would be a telltale sign of life.

And our cosmic telescope could give us a complete picture of a distant world's entire surface.

It's not just an optical telescope, one that can only see visible light—it's also a *radio telescope*. Just as it can magnify light from distant worlds 100 billion times, it can do the same for radio signals. There's something astronomers call a "water hole." It's named after that place where the lions and the water buffalo gather to drink and bathe. It's a bit of a scientific pun because this is between the oxygen and hydroxyl emission lines on the spectrum. These are the constituents of water, aka H_2O. The cosmic water hole is a region of the radio spectrum where interference is at a minimum, where we can eavesdrop on even the faintest transmissions between far-flung civilizations. We would need to use all of our computing power to decrypt the signals hidden in the noise. I imagine they would be something like . . . *hydrogen atom . . . resonant frequency 1420 megahertz . . . help us, please . . . 3.1415926 . . . welcome . . . plasma density . . . love you . . . stellar flare warning . . . rendezvous coordinates 163, 244 . . .*

This vast telescope is also a means for *seeing back in time*. You can't look across space without seeing an object in the past. That's because light travel time is finite. In the morning, look up at the sun and see it as it was eight minutes and 20 seconds ago. You'll never see it any other way. That's because the light from the sun takes that long to travel the 93 million miles to Earth. And when we look at any world through this telescope, we're seeing it in the past.

Now, imagine the cosmic telescope of another civilization. Say, one that's 5,000 light-years from Earth. The astronomers of that world could witness the building of the pyramids in Egypt, or follow the Polynesian Voyagers as they bravely made their way across the Pacific. But perhaps the most important use of this cosmic telescope would be our search for new Earths.

What I can't understand is why we haven't built one. We already know how to do it. We have the technology—right now. When would you like the future to begin?

WE'VE GOT BIG DREAMS of putting our eyes on other worlds, traveling to them, making them our home. But how do we get there? The stars are so far apart, we would need sailing ships that could sustain human crews over the longest of all hauls. The nearest star is four light-years away. That's 24 trillion miles to Proxima Centauri. And again, just to give you some idea of how far away that point of light really is, if NASA's Voyager 1 spacecraft—which moves at a pretty good clip, 38,000 miles an hour—was headed for Proxima Centauri, it would take 73,000 years to get there. And that's only the nearest star out of the *hundreds of billions* in our galaxy alone.

If we want to endure as a species beyond the projected life of our own planet, we need to act like the Polynesians. We need to take what we know of nature and build sailing ships that can ride the light as they once rode the wind. Imagine a flotilla of sailing ships, not the lentil-size nanocraft of chapter 1, but great sailing ships with masts many miles high. When a photon of light strikes their magnificent sails, it gives it a little push. The sails are enormous, but they're very thin. This means that in the vacuum of space, even the tiniest push from a photon will propel them ever faster, until they're moving at a significant fraction of the speed of light. When the ships get so far from home that the sun becomes just another star in the sky, the ships can drop powerful lasers like buoys in their wake. I can imagine them bobbing for a moment before their nuclear thrusters fire, stabilizing them. Beams of laser light issue forth from them, and slash through space to land on the sails. It's a cosmic light show. When you get too far from your star, and the light dwindles, lasers can do the trick.

The watery surface of Proxima b, as imagined by an artist; in the distance, the yellow dwarf stars Alpha Centauri A and B

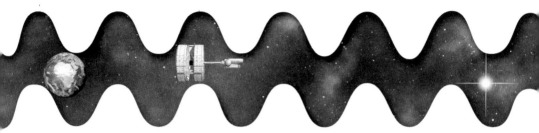

If we were to light-sail to Proxima Centauri this way, it would take not 73,000 years but 20. Proxima Centauri, a red dwarf star, has two stellar siblings, Alpha Centauri A and B. Proxima Centauri also has at least one planet, Proxima b. It lies in the habitable zone of its star, but we don't yet know if it could support life. Does it have the kind of protective magnetic field that has sheltered the evolution of life on our world? Can it retain its atmosphere in the face of such gale-force solar winds, 2,000 times more powerful than the ones our sun sends Earthward?

Because it's so close to its parent star, a year on Proxima b flies by in only 11 Earth days. This closeness to its star bodes well for life because red dwarfs give off just a fraction of the heat that our sun does. But if the planet's magnetic field is weak or intermittent, life may not have had a chance to get going. Another consequence of Proxima b's close location to its star is that the planet is tidally locked. One side perpetually facing the star; the other doomed to endless night.

These red dwarf stars may be lukewarm, but they have a long future ahead of them—trillions of years. Just to give you an idea of how long that is, the universe itself is only 14 billion years old, less than one percent of the life span of these red dwarfs, the most common stars in the universe. Their worlds can bask in the habitable zone for as long as these stars live. Think of the continuity and growth potential of a civilization with a future measured in trillions of years.

A graphic illustration of how an Alcubierre warp drive spaceship would expand space behind it and compress space ahead of it as it travels faster than the speed of light

It's always "magic hour" on the strip of land that lies between day and night on this tidally locked world. If Proxima b were habitable, its life would be confined to this twilight zone. It could be a home for the indigenous life here, or a possible campsite for our descendants. The gravity on Proxima b is about 10 percent greater than ours on Earth. No real problem for us, just a little like exercising with weights on.

For those longer trips, far beyond the nearest star, we're going to need a faster boat. Let's say we found a system located about a hundred light-years from home, one with several potentially habitable worlds. For light-sailers, that would be a 500-year-long trip. Is it possible to build a ship that could break the cosmic speed limit?

A mathematical physicist, Miguel Alcubierre, of Mexico—inspired by the original *Star Trek* television series—conceived the calculations for a ship that could theoretically travel faster than the speed of light. If successful, it could cut the travel time between our sun and this distant star system down to a single year or even less. But wait a minute, isn't it a cardinal rule of science that "Thou shalt not travel faster than light"? It is. But here's the thing about the Alcubierre drive: *It doesn't move, the cosmos does.* The ship itself would be enclosed in its own spacetime bubble, where it needn't violate any laws of physics. Harold White, of the United States, ironed out some of the kinks, such as the prohibitively enormous energy requirements to fly it, and concluded that a faster-than-light starship is at least theoretically possible. But it remains far beyond our immediate grasp.

The Alcubierre drive ship is a gravitational wave–making machine that compresses the ocean of spacetime in front of it, and expands that ocean in its wake. While the Alcubierre drive appears to be stationary, the ripples on the fabric of spacetime are squeezed tighter in front of it, as they stretch out behind it. Jet Skis for joy-riding through the galaxy. Six hundred trillion miles in the blink of an eye. Before you know it, you're in the planetary system of a distant star. Let's call it the Hoku system, a red dwarf star surrounded by a retinue of rocky and ice giant planets. Somewhere among them is a world that we have come to call home. Our imaginary (for the time being) cosmic telescope sifted through all the stars within a radius of a hundred light-years, and pointed the way to this one.

All seven of these imaginary planets huddle closer to their star than Mercury is to our sun. The outermost planet, Haumia, is spruce green at the upper latitudes of the northern and southern hemispheres with a lighter shade of green at the mid-latitudes, and lengthy, meandering white horizontal clouds. Haumia is just on the outskirts of Hoku's habitable zone. Those warm green colors seem inviting, but we're not seeing the tops of forests. That green comes from methane and ammonia. Even at a distance of only 27 million miles, the star Hoku is too weak to keep this planet warm.

In the very far distance to the right is Tawhiri, a stormy gas giant planet with dozens of moons. On the left side is the planet Oro, with its black sand surface and red veins of iron magma. We are now in the sweet spot of Hoku's habitable zone. Straight ahead is a blue-green world with two major continents. This is the planet Tangaroa, where the latest chapter in the saga of our species is playing out.

As we descend through the cloud cover, it dissipates, and emerging through the morning mist is an Earthlike landscape covered with trees and rivers and rolling green hills. It took a few hundred years for humans to terraform this lifeless world. But now, the air tastes as sweet as home. As we get a closer look at the surface, we realize that there are many dwellings, but they are so well integrated into the natural environment as to be almost invisible.

IN OUR GREAT COSMIC VOYAGE, this is only the equivalent of Indonesia, one of the early stops on our nomadic odyssey throughout the Milky Way. There are still so many islands that lie ahead. In this dream future of ours, one that contains a ship that can travel faster than light, there could come a time when we could place our cosmic telescope far enough away from our home planet that we could witness the ancient story of our world and its life and see those of our nameless ancestors who first set sail on unknown seas.

CHAPTER TWELVE

COMING OF AGE IN THE ANTHROPOCENE

*The human race is challenged
more than ever before to demonstrate our mastery,
not over nature but of ourselves.*
—RACHEL CARSON,
SILENT SPRING

Hurricane Michael, October 10, 2018, was the worst storm on record to strike the Florida Panhandle. Warmer ocean and atmospheric temperatures generate deadlier hurricanes: one of many characteristics of the new geologic age called the Anthropocene.

Human civilization may be seen as a gift of the Holocene, that balmy interglacial period that began about 11,650 years ago, at the start of the last 30 seconds in the Cosmic Calendar year. Scientists who study Earth, the geologists, are not generally viewed as an excitable group. But they have looked at the evidence, and many have decided that it is time to give our age a name that better reflects our species' global impact. They believe our era should be known as the Anthropocene, from the Greek words *anthropos* for "human" and *-cene* for "recent." It reflects our species' global impact on the environment and the life it sustains.

When did the age of the Anthropocene begin? It's debatable. Some could argue that it actually started when the Holocene did, when we overhunted the first of the other species we rendered extinct. I wonder, Did our ancestors paint images on cave walls of mammoths and giant lemurs to somehow keep their memory alive after slaughtering the last of them? Human-caused extinction is nothing new. But we can't really blame our ancestors. They couldn't see the big picture. It was a matter of survival for them. How could they know that this or that kill meant the end of an entire species? They knew only what was happening in their immediate vicinity.

Aurochs, wild Eurasian oxen now extinct—but soon to be on the way back thanks to genetic engineering—grace the ceiling of France's Lascaux cave. Carrying massive horns, they were probably the progenitors of today's cattle.

Maybe the Anthropocene started with the first seed that was planted in the ground, and the agricultural revolution that followed. Before that time, the world had twice as many trees absorbing Earth's carbon dioxide and releasing oxygen. With the invention of agriculture, our ancestors stopped wandering to settle down in farms and cities. Forests were cleared to make room for construction, and to build the ships that, for good and ill, transformed humanity into a global intercommunicating organism.

Did the Anthropocene begin with the domestication of animals? Cattle convert wild grasses into methane, another gas that changes the climate. It happens inside them when they're digesting their meals. But nobody would figure this out until the modern scientific era. How could a few head of cattle do any harm, let alone change Earth so radically? Our ancestors wanted to feed their families, and make sure that the little ones would not go hungry, that they would live.

Those hearths, those fires that warmed the small dwellings of our ancestors—were they the beginning? In China, around 4,000 years ago, a revolutionary discovery was made: Certain rocks burned longer and more efficiently than wood to drive away the cold and the damp. These rocks were actually the carbon remains of plants and trees that had died millions of years before and lay buried in the earth. Was the discovery of coal the beginning of the Anthropocene? As the forests were cut down for lumber, coal became increasingly important to power forges and foundries and homes. The smoke from those small fires did little to alter the atmosphere. But over thousands of years, our numbers grew exponentially until we were burning so much wood and coal that we were cranking out enough carbon dioxide into the atmosphere to warm the whole world.

Or did the Anthropocene really get going about 1,000 years later, when people all over Asia began to grow rice? They devised an ingenious technique called "puddling," which involved transplanting seedlings into flooded paddies. There was no way for these hardworking farmers to know that this particular method of growing rice,

Geologists place a golden spike, literally and figuratively, between geologic strata, marking the boundaries between different eras.

like the cattle, would someday produce hundreds of millions of tons of methane. The flooded soil loses oxygen, and then tiny, invisible creatures—microbes—digest the plant matter and produce methane. And to compound this problem, the leaves of the rice plants release more methane into the atmosphere. These early farmers had no way of seeing what was happening on the scale of the very small. Nobody would figure this out until the modern scientific era. Again, they were just trying to feed themselves and their families.

Time writes in the rocks of Earth. If you know how to read time's alphabet, you can reconstruct events in the story of the planet. The most dramatic passages in this saga are not written in the brightest colors. All over the planet, there's a pale white layer in the rocks that is a kind of epic poem. It tells the saga of the death of titans. It's made out of an otherwise rare metal called iridium that signifies the end of the Cretaceous chapter some 66 million years ago. This is when the dinosaurs, and three-quarters of all the plants and animals, became extinct.

The geologists have a custom: When they find a layer in the earth that indicates the boundary of the first or last time that the fossils of any species can be found—it is marked with a golden spike. They drive it into the rock with a hammer. If we are living in the Anthropocene, the age of human-caused extinction, where do we drive *our* golden spike?

Maybe it should be in *me*. In the first year of my life, there were two great superpowers fighting over the planet. They were both willing to endanger everything to assert their dominance. In 1945, the United States had invented a weapon that could liberate the energy locked inside the atom. Four years later, during the summer I was born, in 1949, their Soviet rivals reached a new level of madness. Both nations exploded even more fiendish weapons, those that unlocked the energy of nuclear fusion, the awesome power inside the stars. Both sides tested these nuclear weapons in the atmosphere just to show how strong they were. Before it was over, they had detonated thousands of them over a period of decades. The bombs gave off strontium-90, an atom made unstable by its excess nuclear energy. These radioactive isotopes polluted mother's milk all over the planet. Mothers nursing babies refused to live with this horror. They joined together in protest until a treaty banning the atmospheric testing of nuclear weapons was signed in 1963.

I, and my whole generation, carry an excess of another radioactive isotope in the tissues of our bodies. It's called carbon-14. Every radioactive atom has a half-life, which is for an atom like the rings of a tree—you can count them to know the tree's or the atom's age. The arms race doubled the amount of carbon-14 in the atmosphere. If I ever lose my mind, and forget how old I am, the echoes of those nuclear explosions the summer I was born would tell you my age. Does that "golden spike" inside me signify the beginning of the Anthropocene? Is that when it began?

The atmospheric testing ended, but we just kept on trashing our home—all the while knowing that the day would come when it would all fall down. What good is it to know of a danger if you don't do anything about it? Maybe it's better not to know. *Knowing can be a curse.*

THE STORIES THAT LIVE THE LONGEST are those that never were and always will be . . . myths. One of them is many thousands of years old. Even back then, there were rivalries that blinded men into acts of unspeakable destruction.

Apollo, the ancient god of light, fell in love with Cassandra, the favorite daughter of Priam, the king of Troy. She rebuffed him, so Apollo bribed her with the gift of prophecy. Apollo's revenge for his rejection was that Cassandra would foresee the future, but she was condemned to be ignored. When her brother, Paris, asked their father if he could visit Sparta, Cassandra knew where it would lead—to Paris's abduction of Helen, the wife of the Spartan king, and ultimately, the destruction of Troy. But no one paid any attention to what Cassandra said. To the Trojans, and even to the Spartans, she was just a prophet of gloom and doom.

Cassandra's horrific vision unfolded as she said it would: The once proud towers of Troy crumbled as the Greek armies moved in. The city was in flames. The iconic Trojan horse stood empty, having served its purpose. Apollo had his satisfaction. Cassandra's grim prophecies had gone unheeded, and now it was too late for Troy.

For Cassandra, knowing was a curse. But it can also be the greatest of blessings. Let me tell you another story. Once upon a time, there were no refrigerators. It used to be hard to keep food from spoiling in the summertime. There was a person called the iceman. He carried a big block of ice in a horse-drawn truck, and he would come to your house and sell it to you. He would use a chisel to break off a large chunk, pick it up with a huge pair of calipers, and with great difficulty, bring it around to the entrance on the side of the building below street level. It would be kept in something called an icebox, and the ice would preserve the kinds of food that spoil quickly. In the hot weather, water would soon drip from the lower corners of the icebox door. It would drip all over the floor.

In a 16th-century tapestry, Cassandra pleads with Priam to avoid the future catastrophe only she can foresee.

So somebody thought up another way to keep food cold. It was a gas-powered system that used ammonia or sulfur dioxide as a coolant. No more lugging blocks of ice. What could be bad about that?

Well, for one thing, the chemicals were poisonous and smelled terrible. When there were leaks, the coolant was dangerous to children and pets. A substitute coolant was badly needed—one that would circulate inside the refrigerator but not poison anyone if the refrigerator leaked, or pose a danger if it was sent to the junkyard. Something that wouldn't make you sick, wouldn't burn your eyes, or attract bugs, or even bother the cat. But in all of nature, no such material seemed to exist. So chemists in the United States and Germany invented a class of molecules that had never existed on Earth before. They called them chlorofluorocarbons, or CFCs, because they were made up of one or more carbon atoms and some chlorine and/or fluorine atoms.

These new molecules were wildly successful as coolants, far exceeding the expectations of their inventors. CFCs became the chief coolant in not only refrigerators but also air conditioners. There were so many other things you could do with CFCs, too. They were used to propel great fluffy mounds of shaving cream. And to protect your hairdo from wind and rain. They were also the propellant used in fire extinguishers, foam insulation, industrial solvents, and cleansing agents. CFCs were what made spray paints so much fun. The most famous brand name of these chemicals was Freon, a trademark of DuPont. Freon was used for decades and no harm seemed ever to come from it. Safe as safe could be, everyone figured.

That was until, in the early 1970s, two atmospheric chemists at the University of California, Irvine, were studying Earth's atmosphere. Mario Molina was a Mexican immigrant, a young laser chemist. Sherwood Rowland was a chemical kineticist, a scientist who studied the motions of molecules and gases under varying conditions. He was from a small town in Ohio. Molina wanted to grow as a scientist. He was looking for a project that would take him as far from his previous research experience as possible. He wondered, What happens to those Freon molecules when they leak out of the air conditioner? Back then the Apollo astronauts were still making regularly scheduled trips to the moon. NASA was contemplating weekly launches of the space shuttle. Would all that burning rocket fuel pose a danger to the stratosphere, that place where Earth's atmosphere meets the blackness of space?

This is how science works a lot of the time. You set out to solve one problem, and you happen on a completely different, unexpected phenomenon.

Rowland and Molina discovered that those wonderfully inert, supposedly "harmless" CFCs—the magic molecules of shaving cream and hair spray—didn't simply vanish when we were done with them. They had an afterlife at the edge of space, where they accumulated in the trillions. They were silently congregating high above Earth, and they were up to no good. To their horror, Molina and Rowland realized that the CFCs were thinning the layer that shielded us from the sun's harmful ultraviolet radiation. And the protective layer was getting thinner all the time. Later research confirmed that it was happening at an alarming rate.

When UV light hits a CFC molecule, it strips away the chlorine atoms. Once that happens, the chlorine atoms start devouring the precious ozone molecules, so essential to our existence. It wasn't until our planet developed an ozone layer, about two and a half billion years ago, that it was safe for life to leave the ocean for the land. A single chlorine atom can destroy 100,000 ozone molecules. But back in the 1970s, CFCs were in everything, and the manufacturers couldn't imagine a world without them. Even when the decrease in the ozone layer was confirmed, the corporate response to this danger was that the science hadn't been settled.

People had a hard time believing that we had become powerful enough as a species to endanger life on the planet. They looked for nonhuman causes for the giant hole in the sky. One executive suggested that everyone just wear more sunblock and put on a hat and sunglasses. But the scientists pointed out that the plankton, those tiny plants at the base of the global food chain, and the larger plants, were unlikely to do so.

Molina and Rowland tirelessly worked to warn the world. But Rowland wondered, "What's the use of having developed a science well enough to make predictions if, in the end, all we're willing to do is stand around and wait for them to come true?" Rowland and Cassandra would have had a lot to talk about. But then something amazing happened.

In 1974, when chemist Sherwood Rowland, right, and post-doc Mario Molina showed that CFCs damaged the atmosphere, the idea was derided by corporations and governments. Now it is known to be scientific fact.

There was a global outcry. People all over the world got involved. In the 1960s, the women of the world demanded an end to atmospheric nuclear testing because they didn't want to nurse their babies with poisoned milk. In the 1980s, consumers demanded that the corporations stop manufacturing CFCs. And then remarkably, the governments listened. CFCs were banned in 197 countries. That's just about as many countries as there are on this planet. And that's why this is one danger we can cross off our worry list. The damage to the ozone layer has been healing since. It fluctuates, but it's expected to be fully restored by the year 2075, around the centennial of Rowland and Molina's discovery.

What would have happened if Rowland and Molina hadn't been curious about the stratosphere, or if their warnings had been ignored as Cassandra's were? The vital protection of the ozone layer would have vanished in 40 years. Our grandchildren would never have been able to take their children to bask in the sunshine. Most of the herbivores, those who live exclusively off the plants, would have died out. The carnivores would subsist on their corpses for a while, but ultimately they, too, would be doomed. We dodged that existential bullet, but there are others.

ONE LAST STORY. It's about another person who had the power to foresee the future. His life and work remain unknown outside the scientific community. But even Apollo would have envied his gift of prophecy. He foretold an epic tale of things to come with astonishing accuracy. And every one of us is in his debt.

He was born in a rural part of Japan named Ehime, which means "lovely princess." A place of unspoiled natural beauty. But he spent much of his boyhood buried beneath the surface of the earth. The Second World War had forced the boy and the people of his small town to hide in an underground bomb shelter.

At first, Syukuro Manabe wanted to be a doctor, like his father and grandfather. But as a teenager, he became enchanted with physics, although he worried that he couldn't do the math. His grades were poor, until he began to concentrate on the question that interested him most: Why is the atmosphere and climate of Earth the way that it is?

Manabe knew that the temperatures fluctuate in the seasons, but he wondered why Earth maintained the same average global temperature year after year. What was keeping the planetary thermostat set at that particular temperature? Was it possible to take all the variables of the planet's climate—its atmosphere, pressure, cloud cover, humidity, surface conditions, ocean and wind currents—and create a climate model for the planet? One that had the power of prophecy? Now remember, this was before climatologists in Japan had any access to computers. He did the brain-numbing calculations by hand.

In 1958, Manabe was invited to immigrate to America by the U.S. Weather Service. Five years later, he was given access to one of the first supercomputers. It was the most powerful computer of its day, but the great volume of data about Earth's climate that he fed into it crashed the entire system. It took Manabe another four years to assemble the evidence for a bold and tragic prediction.

Sometimes prophecy comes as a cry from the heart of a Trojan princess, but it can also be the dry-as-dust title of a scientific paper: "Thermal Equilibrium of the Atmosphere With a Given Distribution of Relative Humidity." It doesn't sound like "the sky is falling, the sky is falling!" But that's what it said. Manabe and his colleague, Richard Wetherald, predicted how the temperature of the planet would change as a function of the increased greenhouse gases humans pumped into the atmosphere. The scientists foresaw precisely how the looming catastrophe would unfold. They saw far. Into our own time, and beyond. Some people still claim the science is unsettled, but if that's so, how was it possible for Manabe and Wetherald to correctly predict the rise in Earth's temperature across more than 50 years? And if it wasn't caused by us, where was all that carbon dioxide coming from?

The larger community of climate scientists predicted these impacts of climate change. Heightened flooding of coastal cities, *check*. The mass death of coral reefs by ocean warming, *check*. The increase in intensity of catastrophic storms, *check*. Lethal heat waves, droughts, and runaway wildfires of unprecedented magnitude, *check*. The scientists warned us.

The corporations with vested interests in the fossil fuel industry and the governments they supported acted just like the tobacco companies. They pretended the science was unsettled and stalled for precious years.

The last time there was this much carbon dioxide in Earth's atmosphere was at least 800,000 years ago. The rate of change back then was relatively slow, so most species had time to adapt. We are taking carbon that took hundreds of millions of years to accumulate in the earth, and blowing all that carbon dioxide into the atmosphere in a matter of decades. Two scientists stood up in 1967 and told us how Earth would change if *we* didn't. And that's exactly what happened. Science has given us a gift of seeing a future catastrophe as only the gods could confer in the past. But as Rowland lamented, *"What's the use of having developed a science well enough to make predictions if, in the end, all we're willing to do is stand around and wait for them to come true?"*

The fates of coral reefs and tree frogs may leave most of us unmoved. But what about *your* future, *your* life, the lives of *your* children?

Imagine the child whose first day of kindergarten may be postponed until the thermometer drops below the lethal temperature level. When the wildfires come, her family may be forced to flee with nothing from her childhood home. Water may be the champagne at her wedding. An outbreak may begin when a virion, a mega-virus, dormant for over 100,000 years, is awakened as the permafrost of the Arctic melts away.

This doesn't have to be. It's not too late. There's another future, another possible world. The Anthropocene could become the age of human awakening, when we rise to the challenge of our newly acquired powers and learn to use science and high technology in harmony with nature. There is a global community of people who are alert to the danger and committed to averting it. And thanks to the internet, we know how to get in touch with each other.

Come with me into that future we can still have.

A snorkeler surveys the wreckage of a bleached coral reef. Corals depend on microscopic algae that live inside them and provide food and color. In warmer water, or water made more acidic by carbon dioxide emissions, the algae die, leaving the corals a ghostly white and turning the reef into a graveyard.

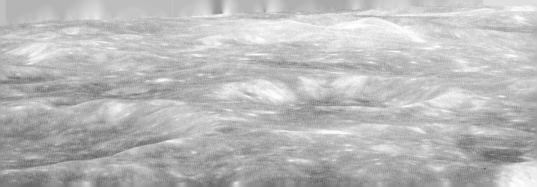

CHAPTER THIRTEEN

A POSSIBLE WORLD

*A map of the world that does not include Utopia
is not worth even glancing at, for it leaves out the
one country at which Humanity is always landing.
And when Humanity lands there, it looks out,
and, seeing a better country, sets sail.*
—OSCAR WILDE,
"THE SOUL OF MAN
UNDER SOCIALISM"

A book must be the axe for the frozen sea inside us.
—FRANZ KAFKA, IN A LETTER
TO OSKAR POLLAK, JANUARY 27, 1904

A new "Earthrise," created for the 45th anniversary of the Apollo 8 mission by
combining the original image with a much sharper lunar landscape, computer-
generated with recent data from NASA's Lunar Reconnaissance Orbiter

Our planet's polar ice caps shrink and the permafrost, solid as granite for eons, turns to mush, but the frozen sea inside us seems unbreakable. We have known about the dangers we pose to ourselves for decades and yet we continue sleepwalking toward a grim future, somehow numb to what it will mean for our children and theirs. Almost every depiction of our world's future in popular culture is a dystopian vision of a planet piled high with garbage, a ruined wasteland. They are accurate reflections of the fear in our hearts. But if dreams are maps, could a great dream of our future possibly help us find our way out of this nightmare?

Where is the scientific basis for that dream? How can confidence in the human future be anything more than the blind faith of religion, or a bad case of denial?

This is a question that my son, Samuel Sagan, a prospective citizen of the future and one of my esteemed collaborators on the companion television series to this book, posed to me throughout this project. He is like his father. He prefers reality to reassurance. Sam's persistent probing has inspired me to do some soul searching. Can there be solid scientific and historical reasons for hope for our species? Or is optimism just a coping mechanism, a form of wishful thinking that science evolved to guard against?

Tourists pack the interior of the Tree of Life colossus in New York Harbor, on April 30, 2039. It affords the best view of the opening of the New York World's Fair.

In 1961, Carl's close friend, fellow astronomer Frank Drake, created an equation for calculating the number of intelligent civilizations in the galaxy:

$$N = R_* \cdot f_p \cdot n_e \cdot f_l \cdot f_i \cdot f_c \cdot L,$$

where

N = the number of civilizations in our galaxy with which communication might be possible,

R_* = the average rate of star formation in our galaxy,

f_p = the fraction of those stars that have planets,

n_e = the average number of planets that can potentially support life per star that has planets,

f_l = the fraction of planets that could support life that actually develop life at some point,

f_i = the fraction of planets with life that actually go on to develop intelligent life (civilizations),

f_c = the fraction of civilizations that develop a technology that releases detectable signs of their existence into space, and

L = the length of time for which such civilizations release detectable signals into space.

Frank, and Carl, knew that there were a huge number of stars in our galaxy, and reasoned correctly, more than three decades before the discovery of the first exoplanet, that the number of planets would be high, too. They thought that a smaller number of them would support life, and on a still smaller number of those possible worlds, intelligent life would evolve to develop world-altering technology.

That last value of L in the Drake equation signifies the length of time any one of those civilizations could be expected to survive what Carl called our "technological adolescence," that dicey period when a young civilization devises the technical wherewithal to destroy itself, but has yet to attain the maturity and wisdom to prevent such a catastrophe from happening. Frank and Carl knew that they were projecting L based on the dreary prospects for our own civilization during the depths of the nuclear arms race. This was also the period when Manabe and Wetherald were creating the first accurate climate models that factored in the large-scale dumping of greenhouse gases into the atmosphere.

So, why do I think we'll make it? Well, for one thing, show me a person who didn't seem or feel hopeless for at least some part of their adolescence.

I sure did and mine lasted long beyond the usual teenage years. I was reckless and irresponsible. I caused my parents countless sleepless nights with my failure to call or show up as promised. My emotions were unpredictable. My room, and later my apartment, was usually a mess. I started things I didn't finish. I would lose my possessions with disturbing regularity. I experimented with substances of unknown potency, flirting with danger to my brain and my life. I was careless with the facts. I was gullible because I had yet to internalize a means for thinking critically. I was selfish and couldn't be trusted to keep my promises or to do the hard work that would get me the future I wanted. The future had no reality for me. In fact, reality had no reality to me. I couldn't get a hold of it until I started to grow up.

And that didn't fully happen until I began to know Carl. It was a subtle change at first. We knew each other as colleagues and friends for the first couple of years. He didn't lecture me or ridicule me for my unexamined beliefs. He would ask the perfect question— the kind of question that would stay with me and act later as a time-release capsule on my thoughts. He gave me new standards of evidence to judge those beliefs I cherished the most. The glibness that had taken me a long way was no longer sufficient. Carl was really listening and he had follow-up questions.

When we fell in love, it was like discovering a new world. It was one that I had hoped was possible but had never been to before. On this new world, reality exceeded fantasy in every way. Above all, it mattered what was true. Just as you could never lie your way to the

The possible world two people can make together. Carl Sagan and Ann Druyan share a laugh on Ann's 40th birthday.

moon or to the other planets because every single one of the tens of thousands of steps in every mission would have to be true in order to succeed, there could be no lies in this new world that we shared. We both knew that our happiness depended on our oneness with each other and even a small lie would be a form of separation, no matter how tiny. Everything we did together became another form of making love.

Is there an equation for the propagating effect of goodness in a true love relationship? Carl made me want to be the best human being I could be. Every loving thing that one of us did made the other want to go higher. My writing, which had been precious and agonizing, became liberated from my often crippling self-consciousness. I no longer strived to impress. I only wanted to communicate, to connect with the reader. And from *Cosmos: A Personal Voyage* onward, my work became a daily love offering to

Carl. When we wrote together, I would watch him read my day's output. Sometimes he would burst out laughing, or gesture as if tipping his hat to me, and my heart would soar. I know he felt the same way about my joy in his work.

One starry night, as we lay together on the deck of a ship in the Pacific, we spotted a dolphin couple riding the wave off the hull. We watched them for about 10 minutes, when suddenly in a single graceful motion they peeled off the wave at a right angle and disappeared into the deep. They moved in unison as if they had been communicating in some mysterious way. Carl looked at me and smiled: "That's us, Annie," he said.

We had 20 years until his death made me a permanent exile from that world we discovered together. I was suicidal. But our children were still young and as their mother I had no choice but to live. So I carried what I learned with Carl inside me and have done my best to keep his flame burning. I rededicated my life to continuing the work we had done together.

I HOPE WHAT I LEARNED from my two decades on that world is part of everything I do now, more than two decades later. From chapter 1 onward, this book is the story of how we, as a species, invented agriculture for a future that, at the time, could only have been an abstraction. How the worst of us, as in the life of Asoka, can learn to change. How the tenacity of life enables it to survive the apparently insurmountable challenges the environment poses. How we can endure unbearable suffering, as Vavilov and his colleagues did, to preserve a livable future for our descendants. How we have courageously used the lens of science to see unflinchingly into our own selves. How science has weaned us of our infantile need to be the center of the universe, empowering us to embrace our true circumstances on a pale blue dot among a trillion other worlds. How we have begun to awaken to the consciousness of the other life-forms that we have exploited and tortured. How we are finally ending our long cosmic quarantine and venturing into the deeper parts of the cosmic ocean. How science teaches us to live with the mysteries of nature without leaping to the false but comforting explanation. How it can help us to foretell coming dangers to our habitat, long in advance, so that we may do the hard work that will allow us to migrate elsewhere in the distant future. How science can endow us with the power of prophecy to protect the human enterprise. And finally, how a young child, in the most modest of circumstances, on a planet where nothing has ever escaped its own gravity, can dream of the unfolding of interstellar flight and grow up to become a leader on his planet's very first mission to the stars.

So permit me my optimism and let me tell you my dream of the future.

Imagine it's the year 2029. There's a girl somewhere. Maybe she's 10. She inhabits a future that still has room for improvement. My mind's eye floats into her apartment. She is stretched out on a shabby living room rug, for a long afternoon. She draws her own vision of how the future will unfold on the 21st-century equivalent of Carl's childhood drawing pad. We can tell from her surroundings and clothing that there are still latchkey children in 2029. From the rug print on her arm and elbow, we know she's been at this for some time, and yet she remains totally absorbed.

The title across the top of the poster reads "HOW THE EARTH GOT WELL" and her drawing is also a composite of headlines and dates from her own imaginary future. The first of her headlines is dateline 2033. It reads "AMAZON RAIN FOREST TRIPLES IN SIZE!"

Other dates and headlines from other made-up websites are splashed across the page, casually overlapping each other so that some words are incomplete.

A celebration on the Eiffel Tower in 2034 heralds, "ITER FUSION REACTOR ON-LINE! ENTIRE CITY OF PARIS POWERED BY A TEASPOON OF WATER!"

The colossal Tree of Life in New York Harbor. Built out of limestone created by drawing carbon dioxide out of the atmosphere, it serves as a symbol of the human capacity to rise to even the greatest of challenges.

2035: "FIRST CONTACT WITH BLUE WHALES! SONGS TRANSLATED! THEY'RE FURIOUS!!"

2036: A frozen wasteland dotted by futuristic structures: "INTERPLANETARY SEED BANK OPENS AT LUNAR SOUTH POLE!"

2037: "TRANSPORTATION MUSEUM ACQUIRES LAST INTERNAL COMBUSTION ENGINE!"

2049: "COSMIC TELESCOPE REVEALS ARTIFICIAL OBJECT OF IMMENSE PROPORTIONS!!"

2051: 1,000,000TH TREE PLANTED ON MARS!"

All the headlines are arranged around a large circle with a completely unfamiliar structure at the center. It towers over New York Harbor. This is our Tree of Life, a colossus made of calcium carbonate, made from the same material nature uses to fashion seashells and pearls. But this amazing structure was constructed from the carbon dioxide redeemed from our planet's atmosphere and turned

to alabaster stone. All the myriad life-forms on this planet are exquisitely represented almost as if they have found a perch on its spectacularly broad branches. This soaring tree of life is firmly rooted in the Hudson Shelf Valley depths of the Atlantic Ocean.

This new colossus is one of many erected in each of Earth's greatest harbors. These future wonders of the world not only signify that our species has found a way to use science and high technology to avert the worst consequences of climate change, but also that we declare our ambition for the kind of human greatness that lives in peace with our fellow Earthlings. The Statue of Liberty was a step in that direction, and for more than a century it lit up the world with hope.

The waters below have changed, too. Vast schools of fish, seahorses, crabs, lobsters, ruffled flatworms, eels, squid, dolphins, and seals swim in and out of the tree's roots that extend into the

The 2039 New York World's Fair with its grand pavilions

grand Hudson Canyon, where a pod of humpback whales are at play. Sea-based squads of ghost-net hunters have rid the oceans of the abandoned fishing nets that have killed so many rare species of marine life. They have been replaced with countless vertical lines laden with enormous clusters of mussels, oysters, and clams. The growth of shellfish aquaculture, which depends on clean waters, has been extremely beneficial for the world's oceans. The shellfish themselves act as water filtration systems.

And on the land, in the same place where Carl found his bliss as a five-year-old, a 2039 New York World's Fair. Visitors pour into the entrance, awed by the vision of the five sweeping, futuristic pavilions surrounding the vast ellipse-shaped reflecting pool. They all share a kind of biological aesthetic—each one an homage to nature. It feels as if we are entering a lost world, an optimistic future that has been foreclosed to us since the days when humans last walked on the moon.

First stop on our tour of the fair is the Pavilion of Searchers. We enter through an opening that looks like a giant unblinking eye to find the atrium filled with old friends—the greatest heroes in the history of science now coming to virtual life, each one ready to recount, on a one-on-one basis, how they deciphered nature's secrets. These aren't just robots whose heads are filled with recorded messages. We've found a way to reproduce the neural networks in their brains—their ideas, memories, and associations—their connectomes. They tirelessly answer every conceivable question you might have. Here, there is no such thing as a dumb question, no shame in asking anything you really want to know.

Imagine a world where the still unfolding story of the universe was told to every child as naturally as the nursery rhymes and fairy tales we fill their heads with today. How many fresh neurons and how much precious time do we waste when we busy our children's minds with nonsense during their most retentive years?

Next is the Pavilion of the Fourth Dimension—time. The entire Cosmic Calendar is yours to explore. It's a place where anyone can set their coordinates in space and time, and visit any moment in the 13.8-billion-year history of cosmic evolution. We only started doing science systematically four centuries ago, and yet we've already been able to reconstruct so much of what happened billions of years before we even got here.

The upper part of this vast interior space is filled with the dynamic astronomical objects of the universe—comets soar, stars assemble into pinwheel galaxies, worlds coalesce out of the accretion disks surrounding newborn stars. The entire floor of the massive building is our Cosmic Calendar, divided into year-at-a-glance months and days, but with one striking difference: All the dates and times are portals through the floor for entering a deeper experience of the events of cosmic evolution.

The crystal Palace of Life at the 2039 New York World's Fair, a temple consecrated to the heroic four-billion-year continuity and staggering diversity of life

What event in the history of the universe would you most like to witness? We could go to that time when the first stars turned on. Or to that last perfect day of the dinosaurs, creatures who had dominated the planet for hundreds of millions of years. Or to pay our respects to the mitochondrial Eve, the mother of us all, the woman to whom all humans can trace their lineage. Or, what about a day trip to Jericho to see the Tower when it was new? Just take your pick.

The next pavilion is the crystal Palace of Life. Its towers, filled with seawater, shoot up into the clouds. The entire structure is transparent, but as you enter, a great darkness descends. And out of the darkness looms something brooding, terrifying. It seems to be part animal, part architectural wonder: the Maw of Eternity, the palace entryway.

This phantom is so alien, so frightening, and yet we recognize it as *Saccorhytus coronarius,* our earliest common ancestor, who we met in Chapter 7, with other animals. We can trace the evolution of our own DNA all the way back across more than 500 million years. That's half a billion years of life somehow managing to squeak through whatever the environment could throw at it. Discovering our direct connection to this ancestor is one of the surpassing achievements of science. What form will life's shape-shifting genius take hundreds of millions of years in the future? The real *Saccorhytus coronarius* was actually quite small, just a black dot to our eyes, but it looms large in our personal story. As far as we know now, "Sacco" is a founding life-form of the animal kingdom. So how did life, the sculptor, carve us out of *that*? Evolution, given world enough and time, makes possible those more complex and completely unexpected qualities that can arise from simpler things.

THE LOWER "JAW" of the Maw of Eternity slowly drops down, revealing a ramp that leads into the Palace of Life, where nature's staggering diversity is on display. Orchids and butterflies and hummingbirds give the scene a feeling of vibrant, quivering life.

Life, a thread four billion years long, has survived at least five mass extinction events and come back from each of them stronger and more diverse than ever before. Life demonstrates that we are more than the sum of our parts, and even when we find ourselves with our backs to the wall, life can find a way into the future.

Even apparently insoluble problems can be solved if we apply our knowledge to nature wisely. The world is infested with *110 million* land mines left over from now forgotten conflicts. Every year they kill or maim many thousands of civilians, among them farmers and children at play with their friends. So, what to do? Think of the global effort that would be required to find and defuse 110 million explosive devices buried in the earth. Hopeless, right?

In the Palace of Life there are fields of wildflowers. Among them are thale-cress plants with delicate white flowers. There are two or three plants with bright red leaves among the expanse of green ones. Botanists have bioengineered an ingenious way to reveal the presence of these dangerous explosives beneath our feet. They have bioengineered the thale-cress plant, whose roots can detect the nitrogen dioxide gas that these land mines and improvised explosive devices (IEDs) emit. If the plant puts out red leaves, beware: land mine below. But if its leaves are green, then you can play there in peace with your friends. We can use our understanding of nature to spring the traps that we've set for ourselves.

With our wars and our lifestyle, we have dumped a lot of garbage on this world. Not just land mines and IEDs, but the toxins from our fossil fuels, the waste from our consumer civilization, nuclear power plants, weapons, and the electronic toys that we discard at an alarming rate, laden with lethal heavy metals—lead, cadmium, beryllium, and other e-wastes. I have moments of despair when I try to wrap my mind around the enormity of the problem. But life and science even provide a way out of this nightmare. It's called bioremediation.

Poplars naturally transform trichloroethylenes—known as TCEs, carcinogenic solvents that are common by-products of industry—into harmless chloride ions. Simple salts. Microbiologists discovered that they could crossbreed two different species of poplar trees to enhance their power to neutralize TCEs. The massive planting of these trees has not only rid the land of its poisonous threats to human and other life, but has also added to the number of trees that consume the greenhouse gas carbon dioxide and give off oxygen.

Yeast, which has given us bread and beer, can help us clean up the world. It's a means to neutralize the most dangerous garbage we have produced. One particular kind of yeast, *Rhodotorula taiwanensis,* and a plant called *Deinococcus radiodurans* are especially effective against gamma radiation, acids, and toxic heavy metals. They capture these poisons and prevent them from contaminating the water supply and the rest of the environment. Nature offers us second chances, a means of undoing the damage done.

But how do we keep from doing it again? What on Earth is designed by humans to protect the distant future? We don't have a single institution that even acknowledges the long-term danger we pose to ourselves, let alone one designed to plan for it. Our time horizon ends at three months from now, the next fiscal quarter, or four years—the next general election. But science is telling us that life's timescale measures in the billions of years. How do we maintain awareness of the continuity of life's past, and our personal role in being a link to its future, so that it actually makes a difference?

Science, as of now, has no means of making us wise and far-sighted. But science can create a reminder of just how long the future is.

In the Palace of Life gift shop, they sell pieces of quantum jewelry, wristwatches, and charms for necklaces that contain a three-dimensional lattice of laser light to keep isolated atoms of the element strontium suspended in space. These atoms are so perfectly attuned to the quantum rhythm of the universe that they will keep time for the next 15 billion years without losing a single second. And those 15 billion years are but a tiny fraction of forever.

How many civilizations have lost the battle that we fight now? How many worlds lie buried beneath the surface of this one? Maybe we'll never know. But at the fair of my dreams, there's a pavilion where long-dead civilizations come roaring back to life: the Pavilion of Lost Worlds.

In the fifth century B.C.E., in Greece, Herodotus, the father of history, wrote of the opulent lifestyle of the Tartessians on the Iberian Peninsula. Their wealth came from the silver and gold they extracted from the earth. They had their own language, culture, dances, music—and yet very little survives of them besides a handful of objects of marvelous design. Theirs is one of the lost worlds of planet Earth—yet in this pavilion we can walk among them as they lived when their civilization was at its most vibrant.

We can meet the nameless people who once thrived in what is now Nigeria, in a place called Nok. For 1,500 years, their engineers were on the cutting edge of technology, forging new ways to work with iron. Just as with the Tartessians, they had their own unique civilization, and yet all that remains of them are some ceramic statues in a style unlike any other. But here, in this pavilion, their ways, long thought devoured by time, come back to life.

When the Indus Valley civilization was at its high point in 2500 B.C.E., it was a vast network of cities with a population of five million. At a time when the Greeks wandered in small tribes, just a band of itinerant merchants, these people planned and laid out their most famous city, Mohenjo Daro. They even installed modern plumbing in their homes, something most people didn't have until the late 20th century. And they mastered other forms of hydro-engineering— underground pipes, sewage management, kitchens with running water. They had dentistry, and standardized measures for the tiniest quantities. They were great sculptors who introduced natural reality into the three-dimensional depiction of the human form.

They had writing, and hung signs on buildings, but we have yet to understand their meaning. They used dice to play games of chance and whiled away their evenings with board games. And there's something curious about them. They left no depictions of war in their art, nor large caches of weapons. There's no evidence that their meticulously planned cities were ever burned to the ground by enemy invaders. In the study of their contemporaries, and human history generally, this is most unusual.

In my Pavilion of Lost Worlds, the mothers of Mohenjo Daro lean out their windows and summon their children to dinner. The children sullenly dawdle home as the sun sets on one of our lost worlds. They were as real as we are. Their moment as real as this one.

JUST BEYOND THE PAVILION OF LOST WORLDS, there's another one, the Pavilion of Possible Worlds, of those worlds still to come. It's as if the Milky Way galaxy has been brought down to earth, a huge, slowly rotating pinwheel structure of lights and multicolored mists that suggest the gas and dust between the stars. At its center is a core of incandescent light. It rotates gently, completely surrounded by a moat. As it spins, the spiral arms link up with pedestrian bridges that span the surrounding waters.

In our own time, we have launched five ships to the stars. They are backward and primitive craft, moving with the slowness of a race in a dream compared to the immense interstellar distances through which they travel. But in the future we will do better. We will find our way to the stars at far greater speeds. We've already located and begun to study thousands of worlds that circle other suns—all this from our remote confinement on Earth—all this in just 400 years since Galileo's first look through a telescope. The Milky Way has hundreds of billions of stars, and likely even more worlds.

When Carl wrote *Cosmos: A Personal Voyage,* he imagined an *Encyclopedia Galactica*—a reference work that includes all the worlds of all the stars. He was bravely writing at a time before a single exoplanet had been discovered and long before the internet. In the decades since, we have located thousands of planets orbiting other stars. His dream of the *Encyclopedia Galactica* is a little closer to reality now.

Our vague perceptions and inferences of several thousand exoplanets will someday give way to a more intimate degree of knowledge of some half a million worlds. Imagine, as Carl once did, a huge galactic database, a Library of Alexandria for the Milky Way, a means for our small world to attain some measure of cosmic citizenship.

Imagine that we are stepping inside one of the spiral arms of the spinning Pavilion of Possible Worlds. It's surprisingly dark. There's a light at the end of the corridor. As we get closer to it, we realize it's a star, a member of a binary system. As the holographic display rotates, the first world swings into view. It's a crackled ice

For the original *Cosmos* book, Carl Sagan composed entries for the imaginary book he desired most to read, the *Encyclopedia Galactica.* They were scientifically derived digests about the civilizations of possible worlds, including our own. Here we quote two of Carl's creations from *Cosmos,* plus a new entry.

"We Who Flower in Darkness"

Civilization Type: 1.1R.
Society Code: 2Y6,
  Inter-planetary subterranean communities, emergent cooperative philosophies
Civilization Age: 4.4×10^{11} s
First locally initiated contact: 6.3×10^{10} s ago
Receipt first galactic nested code:
  3.1×10^{10} s ago
  Source civilization, high energy neutrino channel bursts
  Local Group polylogue.
Biology: C, H, O, N, Fe, Ge, Sl.
  Noctosynthetic lithotrophs
Genomes: 5×10^{14}
  (semi-nonredundant bits/mean genome: $\sim 3 \times 10^{17}$).
Probability of survival (per 1000 yr): 72.1%

"We Who Survived"

Civilization Type: 1.8L.
Society Code: 2A11,
Star: FOV, spectrum variable,
  r = 9.717 kpc, theta = 00°07'51",
  phi = 210°20'37".
Planet: sixth, a = 2.4×10^{13} cm,
  M = 7×10^{18} g, R = 2.1×10^9 cm,
  p = 2.7×10^6 s, P = 4.5×10^7 s.
Extra-planetary colonies: none.
Planet age: 1.14×10^{17} s.
First locally initiated contact:
  2.6040×10^8 s ago.
Receipt first galactic nested code:
  1.9032×10^8 s ago.
Biology: C, N, O, H, S, Se, Cl, Br,
  H_2O, S_8, polyaromatic sulfonyl halides. Mobile photochemo-synthetic autotrophs in weakly reducing atmosphere.
  Polytaxic, monochromatic.
  m $\sim 3 \times 10^{12}$ g, t $\sim 5 \times 10^{10}$ s.
  No genetic prosthesis.
Genomes: $\sim 6 \times 10^7$
  (nonredundant bits/genome: $\sim 2 \times 10^{12}$).

Technology: exponentiating, approaching asymptotic limit.
Culture: global, nongregarious, polyspecific (2 genera, 41 species); arithmetic poetry.
Prepartum/postpartum: 0.52 [30],
Individual/communal: 0.73 [14],
Artistic/technological: 0.81 [18].
Probability of survival (per 100 yr): 80%.

"Humanity"

Civilization Type: 1.0J.
Society Code: 4G4,
Star: G2V, r = 9.844 kpc, theta = 00°05'24", phi = 206°28'49".
Planet: third, a = 1.5×10^{13} cm,
  M = 6×10^{27} g, R = 6.4×10^8 cm,
  p = 8.6×10^4 s, P = 3.2×10^7 s.
Extra-planetary colonies: gestating.
Planet age: 1.45×10^{17} s.
First locally initiated contact:
  3.07×10^9 s ago.
Receipt first galactic nested code:
  application pending.
Biology: C, N, O, S, H_2O, PO_4.
  Deoxyribonucleic acid.
  No genetic prosthesis.
  Mobile heterotrophs, symbionts with photosynthetic autotrophs.
  Surface dwellers, monospecific, polychromatic O_2 breathers.
  Fe-chelated tetrapyroles in circulatory fluid. Sexual mammals.
  m $\sim 7 \times 10^4$, g, t $\sim 2 \times 10^9$ s.
Genomes: 4×10^9.
Technology: exponentiating/fossil fuels/nuclear weapons/organized warfare/environmental pollution, inadvertent climate modification, planet-wide bio-remediation efforts underway.
Culture: ~ 200 nation states, ~ 6 global powers; cultural and technological homogeneity underway.
Prepartum/postpartum: 0.21 [18],
Individual/communal: 0.31 [17],
Artistic/ technological: 0.14 [11].
Probability of survival (per 100 yr): 50%.

planet with no obvious signs of life or civilization. Another world comes around into view. When we see its dark side, we realize it's spiderwebbed with a network of lights, clearly the signature of an intelligent civilization. And there, before us, is this world's entry in the encyclopedia, a variation on Carl's vision in the original *Cosmos* book. These guys, who call themselves "We Who Survived," are only a little more advanced than we are. If we could only communicate with them, maybe they could tell us how they managed to get through their stormy adolescence.

As the spiderweb world transits out of view, we walk farther down the spiral arm until we come to an orange K-type star with a retinue of worlds orbiting around it. We focus on the fourth one out, which has a deep violet atmosphere, and auroras shining above the northern polar cap.

What about a civilization more advanced than ours? There may be worlds with engineering on a scale that dwarfs our proudest achievements. We walk farther down the hall, past other stars and worlds and moons, until we come to a blue-white F-type star slightly brighter than the sun. The worlds of this system are passing in front of us, when a world with green landmasses and bright orange oceans appears on the horizon. It has a prominent ring.

As the ringed planet gets closer, we realize that, unlike Saturn, this ring is composed of a solid artificial structure. It appears to be fashioned from platinum with well-spaced windows and ports. There may be cultures that disassemble other planets in their system and reassemble them around their world to make a ring, buying them more room and more resources. We are now close enough to the surface of this world to see enormous platforms floating above the giant orange waves.

Well, their future looks bright. We walk on to a red dwarf star with a small number of planets and moons orbiting close in, all of them dotted with lights and dense with structures. The little bit of land that is undeveloped is strangely cratered. The poor beings of this world have only a 1-in-3 chance of making it through. There's something happening on their star: Enormous spacecraft in stellar orbit appear to be erecting a massive scaffolding. Could this be their attempt to solve a solar system–wide energy crisis? They depend on solar power, but their star is only a feeble red dwarf incapable of providing enough energy for their multiplanetary civilization. Maybe they've used up all their fuel. We move on to see the artificial scaffolding around the star more clearly: It's a completely unfamiliar object, a star partially encased in an artificial shell. They must be building a shell to surround their star and harvest every photon of sunlight.

HOW WOULD WE FRAME our own entry in the *Encyclopedia Galactica*? Perhaps, even now, someone somewhere in our galaxy has written it for us—a planetary dossier garnered from our television broadcasts or from some discreet survey mission. They might summon up the index of blue worlds in our province of the Milky Way until they came to the listing for Earth, which includes the statistic "Probability of survival (per 100 years): 40 percent."

I look at that 40 percent, which is of course nothing more than a guess, and I hear the skittering dice on the sidewalk of Mohenjo Daro at dusk, the buzzing of those dancing bees debating where their next home should be. I feel the hunger of Vavilov and his colleagues and the weight of all the thoughts, from those undulating stromatolites through Einstein and all the way to us. The words Einstein chose to open the 1939 World's Fair echo in my brain: "If science, like art, is to perform its mission truly and fully, its achievements must enter not only superficially but with their inner meaning into the consciousness of the people."

Here is what I think he meant by that *inner meaning*.

Our universe began some 14 billion years ago when matter, energy, time, and space burst forth.

And the darkness was cold, and the light was hot, and the union of these extremes gave shape to matter and there was structure.

And there were great stars hundreds of times the mass of our sun. And these stars exploded, sending oxygen and carbon to the worlds to come and adorning them with gold and silver. And in their deaths, the stars became darkness and the weight of their darkness anchored the light. And new stars were born from their death shrouds. And they began to dance with each other and now there were galaxies.

And the galaxies made stars. And the stars made worlds. And on at least one of those worlds there came a time when heat shot out from its molten heart, and it warmed the waters. And the matter that had rained down from the stars came alive and that starstuff became aware.

And that life was sculpted by the earth, and its struggles with the other living things.

And a great tree grew up, one with many branches, and six times it was almost felled. But still it grows and we are but one small branch, one that cannot live without its tree.

And slowly, we learned to read the book of nature, to learn its laws, to nurture the tree. To find out where and when we are in the great ocean, to become a way for the cosmos to know itself and to return to the stars.

A necklace of dewdrops. Biology, chemistry, and physics collaborate to create this natural jewelry.

ACKNOWLEDGMENTS

When Carl Sagan died in 1996, it was not only a tragedy for my family and me but also a grave blow to our planet. We lost a pathfinder in science, a poet who could connect with every kind of person, a conscientious planetary citizen who fearlessly defended our future, one who was tireless in his search for truth. I am keenly aware of just how big the shoes I am walking in here are. I would not dare to attempt to do so without the help of a multitude.

As with the original, the Cosmos book and television series are tightly interwoven and so my debts extend to both sides of the Cosmos family.

I wish to first thank Steven Soter, co-writer with Carl and me, of the original 1980 series, *Cosmos: A Personal Voyage,* and on the treatment for *Nucleus,* a project that was never produced and from which Chapter 10 of this book was adapted. I am additionally indebted to him for bringing me up to date on the current thinking about the eruption of Mount Pelée. There are echoes of my collaboration with Carl and Steve in all the Cosmos that has come after. Their scholarship, originality, and goodness reverberate throughout this book and series.

Throughout my career I have been consistently blessed with brilliant and generous creative partners. Brannon Braga contributed much to *Cosmos: A SpaceTime Odyssey,* the series that Steve and I co-wrote. And now, for the third *Cosmos* television series, I have had the enormous pleasure of sitting in a room thinking and writing with Brannon for a couple of years and then directing and producing the episodes with him. I cherish those times and thank him for his saintly patience with me and his manifold contributions to both the *Cosmos* book and show.

For part of that time we were joined in the writers' room by Andre Bormanis and Samuel Sagan. Andre, who also serves as our on-site science adviser, is a model of erudition and graciousness. Sam pointed us to some of the best stories in both seasons, inspired us with his knowledge of ancient civilizations, and performed other roles in the production.

During the final weeks of shooting, Sam suffered a nearly fatal brain hemorrhage. I am most profoundly indebted to Dr. Nestor Gonzalez and the doctors and nurses of Cedars-Sinai Neurology ICU for Sam's recovery and for the preservation of Sam's irreplaceable Samness. I thank Dr. Ron Benbassat in particular for his vigilance on Sam's behalf and many kindnesses to us during Sam's weeks in the ICU. Jennice Ontiveros's and Sasha Sagan's thoughtfulness made those harrowing weeks bearable. The always loving Jonathan Noel and Laurie Robinson made it possible for Sasha to be there for us. Jennice lent her beautiful voice to the audiobook, and Sasha brought her own grandmother, Rachel Sagan, back to life by gracefully portraying her in the show.

If not for Seth MacFarlane, there would likely never have been another season of Cosmos on television after the original one. Everything Cosmos since flows from Seth's passionate commitment to bringing it to a new generation. It was his advocacy to Peter Rice, then CEO of the Fox Networks Group, and Peter's vision of what prime-time commercial network television could be, that resulted in the wherewithal and freedom to make *Cosmos: A SpaceTime Odyssey* in 2014. At Fox, I also wish to thank Shannon Ryan, Rob Wade, Phoebe Tisdale, and Alex Piper. It was the National Geographic Channel's willingness to join equally with Fox that helped to make our second season the largest rollout in global television history. National Geographic has continued to be, with Fox, the best of possible partners. For National Geographic's generous support at all times, I feel an enormous debt of gratitude to Gary Knell, Courteney Monroe, Chris Albert, Kevin Tao Mohs, Heather Danskin, and Allan Butler. They have gone above and beyond.

Cosmos: Possible Worlds, the 13-part television series, is the work of more than 1,000 people over a period of five years.

Jason Clark, my fellow executive producer, has been an invaluable partner from the earliest days of the two most recent Cosmos seasons through their completion and global distribution. Through two seasons of *Cosmos* I have watched Joe Micucci grow from an assistant to producer of the series. The show could not have been in more able, or more conscientious, hands. I thank Neil deGrasse Tyson for his performance. We were blessed to have the distinguished director of photography Karl Walter Lindenlaub to paint the series in light and shadow, award-winning maestro Alan Silvestri to create our music, Kara Vallow to lead the team that made our animation sequences a series of jewels, and Jeff Okun, dean of VFX supervisors, to make manifest our wildest dreams.

The hugely creative and hardworking Cosmos family includes but is by no means limited to Sabrina Corpuz Aspiras, Andrew Brandou, Ruth E. Carter, Marjorie Chodorov, Ryan Church, Kimberly Beck Clark, Alexandria Corrigan, Jane Day, Alex de la Peña, Hannah Dorsett, Adam Druxman, John Duffy, Jack Geist, Gail Goldberg, Lucas Gray, John Greasley, Coby Greenberg, Neil Greenberg, Zack Grobler, Rachel Hargraves-Heald, Connie Hendrix, Mara Herdmann, Julia Hodges, David Ichioka, Sheila Jaffe, Duke Johnson, Matthew Keller, Gregory King, Tony Lara, Carlos M. Marimon, James Oberlander, Scott Pearlman, Clinnette Minnis Sagan, Nick Sagan, Safa Samiezadé-Yazd, Eric Sears, Joseph D. Seaverton, David Shapiro, Elliot Thompson, Max Votolato, and Brent Woods.

Central to the fulfillment of our mission has been the willingness of distinguished scientists to allow us to pepper them with questions for both book and show. The errors that may have crept in are purely mine. I am grateful to Jonathan Lunine, David C. Duncan Professor in the Physical Sciences, director of Cornell Center for Astrophysics and Planetary Science, Cornell University; Michael Allen, emeritus professor of plant pathology and professor of biology, director of Center for Conservation Biology, University of California, Riverside; Dr. Kenneth Carpenter, Hubble Operations project scientist, NASA Goddard Spaceflight Center; David Anderson, Seymour Benzer Professor of Biology, California Institute of Technology; Toby Ault, assistant professor of earth and atmospheric sciences, Cornell University; Peter Bellwood, emeritus professor, School of Archaeology and Anthropology, Australian National University; Robert Byer, William R. Kenan, Jr., Professor, School of Humanities and Sciences Department of Applied Physics, co-director of Stanford Photonics Research Center, Stanford University; Sean Carroll, Theoretical Cosmology, Field Theory, and Gravitation, California Institute of Technology; Alexander Hayes, assistant professor of astronomy, Cornell University; Lisa Kaltenegger, associate professor of astronomy, director of Carl Sagan Institute, Cornell University; Barrett Klein, associate professor of biology, University of Wisconsin; Peter Klupar, Director of Engineering, Breakthrough Starshot; Abraham (Avi) Loeb, Frank B. Baird, Jr., Professor of Science, chair of Astronomy Department, director of Institute for Theory and Computation, founding director of Black Hole Initiative (BHI), chair of Breakthrough Starshot Advisory Committee, vice chair of Board on Physics and Astronomy, National Academies, Harvard University; David A. B. Miller, W. M. Keck Foundation Professor of Electrical Engineering, professor of applied physics, Stanford University; Dr. E. C. Krupp, director of Griffith Observatory; Mason Peck, associate professor of mechanical and aerospace engineering, Cornell University; Thomas D. Seeley, Horace White Professor in Biology, Cornell University; Pete Worden, executive director of Breakthrough Starshot, former director of NASA Ames Research Center; and Stephen Zinder, professor of microbiology, Cornell University.

I am especially grateful to Dario Robleto, esteemed artist and friend, for telling me the stories of Angelo Mosso, Giovanni Thron, and Hans Berger, and for the pleasure of his friendship. All along, it was Sam Sagan's idea for us to tell the story of Asoka. Writer Gita Mehta's stirring account of his life reawakened me to its power. I thank Gita for her gracious response to my interest in retelling his story.

I owe a special debt to Pam Abbey for two decades of dedication and diligence, to Vanessa Goodwin for her expert assistance in preparing the manuscript of this book and her generosity to me throughout the production of the series, to Kathy Cleveland for holding the fort and for her friendship, and to Patty Smith for her kind assistance. My trust in them has made it possible for me to focus on this work.

I would not have undertaken to write this book if I had not had two inspiring encounters, one with Susan Goldberg, editor in chief of *National Geographic* magazine, and the other, the first of many, with Lisa Thomas, publisher of National Geographic Books. I wish to thank them both for their trenchant editorial input and all their dedication to shepherding this book to completion. Working with Lisa from the first chapter to this page has been a joy. I also wish to thank Susan Tyler Hitchcock, senior editor; Hilary Black, deputy editor; Allyson Johnson, senior editorial project manager; Melissa Farris, creative director; Susan Blair, director of photography; Jill Foley, photo editor; Jennifer Thornton, managing editor; and Judith Klein, senior production editor. This manuscript could not have been in better hands, and I thank them also for the visual beauty and mindfulness that went into the selection of images for this book.

I am indebted to my two lifelong friends, Jonathan Cott and Ernie Eban, for some of this book's most provocative and fitting epigrams. And I am fortunate to have had the benefit of David Nochimson's and Joy Fehily's always wise counsel.

And finally my love and admiration to Lynda Obst. It was the profundity and hilarity of all those conversations on various balconies that made my time in Los Angeles during the making of these shows and the writing of this book so much fun.

FURTHER READING

CHAPTER 1
- *Catal Huyuk: A Neolithic Town in Anatolia* by James Mellaart (McGraw-Hill, 1967).
- *Çatalhöyük: The Leopard's Tale: Revealing the Mysteries of Turkey's Ancient "Town"* by Ian Hodder (Thames and Hudson, 2011).
- *Inside the Neolithic Mind: Consciousness, Cosmos and the Realm of the Gods* by David Lewis-Williams and David Pearce (Thames and Hudson, 2005).

CHAPTER 2
- *Ashoka: The Search for India's Lost Emperor* by Charles Allen (Overlook Press, 2012).
- *Shadows of Forgotten Ancestors: A Search for Who We Are,* by Carl Sagan & Ann Druyan (Random House, 1992; Ballantine Books, 2011).

CHAPTER 3
- *The Vital Question: Energy, Evolution, and the Origins of Complex Life* by Nick Lane (W. W. Norton, 2015).

CHAPTER 4
- *Lysenko and the Tragedy of Soviet Science* by Valery N. Soyfer, translated by Leo Gruliow and Rebecca Gruliow (Rutgers University Press, 1994).
- *The Murder of Nikolai Vavilov: The Story of Stalin's Persecution of One of the Great Scientists of the Twentieth Century* by Peter Pringle (Simon and Schuster, 2008).
- *The Vavilov Affair* by Mark Popovsky (Archon Books, 1984).

CHAPTER 5
- *Angelo Mosso's Circulation of Blood in the Human Brain,* edited by Marcus E. Raichle and Gordon M. Shepherd, translated by Christiane Nockels Fabbri (Oxford University Press, 2014).
- *Broca's Brain: Reflections on the Romance of Science* by Carl Sagan (Random House, 1979; Ballantine Books, 1986).
- *Fatigue (1904)* by Angelo Mosso, translated by Margaret Drummond (Kessinger Publishing, 2008).
- *Fear* by Angelo Mosso (Forgotten Books, 2015).

CHAPTER 6
- *Solar System Astronomy in America: Communities, Patronage, and Interdisciplinary Science 1920-1960* by Ronald E. Doel (Cambridge University Press, 1996; 2009).

CHAPTER 7
- *The Dancing Bees: An Account of the Life and Senses of the Honey Bee* by Karl von Frisch (Harcourt Brace, 1953).
- *Honeybee Democracy* by Thomas D. Seeley (Princeton University Press, 2010).
- *The Power of Movement in Plants* by Charles Darwin (CreateSpace Independent Publishing Platform, 2017).

CHAPTER 8
- *The Saturn System Through the Eyes of Cassini* by NASA including Planetary Science Division, Jet Propulsion Laboratory, and Lunar and Planetary Institute (e-book, https://www.nasa.gov/ebooks, 2017).

CHAPTER 9
- *The New Quantum Universe* by Tony Hey and Patrick Walters (Cambridge University Press, 2003).
- *The Quantum World* by J. C. Polkinghorne (Longman, 1984; Princeton University Press, 1986).

CHAPTER 10
- *Joseph Rotblat: Visionary for Peace* by Reiner Braun, Robert Hinde, David Krieger, Harold Kroto, and Sally Milne, eds. (Wiley, 2007).
- *The Making of the Atomic Bomb* by Richard Rhodes (Simon and Schuster, 1987; 2012).

CHAPTER 11
- *First Islanders, Prehistory and Human Migration in Island Southeast Asia* by Peter Bellwood (Wiley-Blackwell, 2017).
- *Polynesian Navigation and the Discovery of New Zealand* by Jeff Evans (Libro International, 2014).
- *Polynesian Seafaring and Navigation: Ocean Travel in Anutan Culture and Society* by Richard Feinberg (Kent State University Press, 1988; 2003).

CHAPTER 12
- *The Sixth Extinction: An Unnatural Extinction* by Elizabeth Kolbert (Henry Holt, 2014).

CHAPTER 13
- *Cosmos* by Carl Sagan (Random House, 1980; reprint Ballantine, 2013).
- *The Demon-Haunted World: Science as a Candle in the Dark* by Carl Sagan with Ann Druyan (Random House, 1996; Ballantine Books, 1997).
- *Pale Blue Dot: A Vision of the Human Future in Space* by Carl Sagan (Random House, 1994; Ballantine Books, 1997).

ILLUSTRATIONS CREDITS

Cover, Courtesy of Cosmos Studios, Inc.; endpapers, Rogelio Bernal Andreo, DeepSkyColors .com; 1, NASA/Ames/SETI Institute/JPL-Caltech; 2-3, Nathan Smith, University of Minnesota/ NOAO/AURA/NSF; 6, Howard Lynk—VictorianMicroscopeSlides.com; 8-9, Courtesy of Cosmos Studios, Inc., LLC; 10-11, Courtesy Cosmos Studios, Inc.; 12-13, Courtesy Cosmos Studios, Inc.; 14, Poster by Joseph Binder, photo by Swim Ink 2, LLC/CORBIS/Corbis via Getty Images; 16, Model designed by Norman Bel Geddes for General Motors, photo by Library of Congress/ Corbis/VCG via Getty Images; 21, David E. Scherman/The LIFE Picture Collection/Getty Images; 22 (BOTH), NASA; 24, Tony Korody, Courtesy of Druyan-Sagan Associates; 28, NASA/JPL-Caltech/ SSI; 30, Babak Tafreshi/National Geographic Image Collection; 34, Frans Lanting/National Geographic Image Collection; 35, Copyright Carnegie Institute, Carnegie Museum of Natural History/ Mark A. Klingler; 39, Image use courtesy of Christopher Henshilwood, photo by Stephen Alvarez/National Geographic Image Collection; 40, Album/Alamy Stock Photo; 43, Vincent J. Musi/ National Geographic Image Collection; 44, Courtesy of Cosmos Studios, Inc.; 47 (LE), Ann Ronan Pictures/Print Collector/Getty Images; 47 (RT), Courtesy of Dr. Rob van Gent/Utrecht University; 52, Eric Isselee/Shutterstock; 53, Craig P. Burrows; 55, The Simulating eXtreme Spacetimes (SXS) project *(http://www.black-holes.org);* 56, Illustration courtesy Tatiana Plakhova at *www .complexity graphics.com,* created for Stephen Hawking's project in Breakthrough Initiatives (a flight of nano-spacecraft to Alpha Centauri); 60, The doors to the Zoroastrian fire temple, Chak Chak (photo)/Chak Chak, Iran/© Julian Chichester/Bridgeman Images; 62, John Reader/Science Source; 64-5, SATourism/Greatstock/Alamy Stock Photo; 68, Courtesy of Cosmos Studios, Inc.; 71, David Mack/Science Source; 74 (UP LE), The Natural History Museum, London/Science Source; 74 (UP CTR), Lawrence Lawry/Science Source; 74 (UP RT), Francisco Martinez Clavel/ Science Source; 75 (UP LE), Francisco Martinez Clavel/Science Source; 75 (UP CTR), Francisco Martinez Clavel/Science Source; 75 (UP RT), The Natural History Museum, London/Science Source; 80, Chronicle/Alamy Stock Photo; 83, Album/Alamy Stock Photo; 84, Asif Ali Khan/ EyeEm/Getty Images; 85, The Art Archive/Shutterstock; 86, Insights/UIG via Getty Images; 88, Memory, 1870 (oil on mahogany panel), Vedder, Elihu (1836-1923)/Los Angeles County Museum of Art, CA, USA/Bridgeman Images; 90, NASA/CXC/JPL-Caltech/STScI; 93, Bob Gibbons/ Science Source; 97, Danita Delimont/Getty Images; 98 (ALL), John Sibbick/Science Source; 102, Science & Society Picture Library/SSPL/Getty Images; 104, Gary Ombler/Dorling Kindersley/ Getty Images; 108, NASA/JPL-Caltech/SETI Institute; 112, Courtesy of Cosmos Studios, Inc.; 114, sbayram/Getty Images; 116, DEA Picture Library/De Agostini/Getty Images; 120, Fine Art Images/Heritage Images/Getty Images; 123, Universal History Archive/Getty Images; 128, Mario Del Curto; 131, From *Where Our Food Comes From* by Gary Paul Nabhan. Copyright © 2009 by the author. Reproduced by permission of Island Press, Washington, DC.; 132, Russia/Soviet Union: "There Is No Room in Our Collective Farm for Priests and Kulaks," Soviet propaganda poster, Nikolai Mikhailov, 1930/Pictures from History/Woodbury & Page/Bridgeman Images; 136, akg-images/Universal Images Group/Sovfoto; 142, Courtesy of Cosmos Studios, Inc.; 144, Pasieka/Science Source; 146, Dan Winters; 151, Marble relief depicting Asclepius or Hippocrates treating ill woman, from Greece/De Agostini Picture Library/G. Dagli Orti/Bridgeman Images; 152, The Print Collector/Alamy Stock Photo; 155, Apic/Getty Images; 159, Photo: Photographic collections, Scientific and Technologic Archives, University of Torino. Reference: Sandrone, S.; Bacigaluppi, M.; Galloni, M. R.; Cappa, S. F.; Moro, A.; Catani, M.; Filippi, M.; Monti, M. M.; Perani, D.; Martino, G. Weighing brain activity with the balance: Angelo Mosso's original manuscripts come to light. *Brain* 137 (2), 2014: 621-33; 164, Courtesy Ann Druyan; 167, Wild Wonders of Europe/ Solvin Zankl/naturepl.com; 168 (LE), David Liittschwager and Susan Middleton; 168 (RT), Jurgen Freund/NPL/Minden Pictures; 169 (BOTH), Jurgen Freund/NPL/Minden Pictures; 172, Pasieka/ Science Source; 174, NASA, ESA, H. Teplitz and M. Rafelski (IPAC/Caltech), A. Koekemoer (STScI), R. Windhorst (Arizona State University), and Z. Levay (STScI); 176, Babak Tafreshi/ National Geographic Image Collection; 179, The Print Collector/Alamy Stock Photo; 180, Carl Iwasaki/The LIFE Images Collection/Getty Images; 183, Courtesy of Cosmos Studios, Inc.; 185, Haitong Yu/Getty Images; 186, David Parker/Science Source; 188, Bettmann/Getty Images; 190, Courtesy of Druyan-Sagan Associates; 195, Sovfoto/UIG via Getty Images; 196, NASA; 198, Babak Tafreshi/National Geographic Image Collection; 200, Imaginechina via AP Images; 203, Emmanuel Lattes/Alamy Stock Photo; 205, Amy Toensing/National Geographic Image Collection; 206, vlapaev/Getty Images; 209 (BOTH), SPL/Science Source; 212, Dirk Wiersma/Science Source; 215, Jack Garofalo/Paris Match via Getty Images; 218, Tim Graham/Robert Harding World Imagery; 222 (LE), Science Source; 222 (RT), The Natural History Museum, London/Science Source; 223 (LE), The Natural History Museum, London/Science Source; 223 (RT), Science Source; 224, Courtesy of Cosmos Studios, Inc.; 226, NASA/JPL-Caltech/Space Science Institute; 228, Courtesy of Cosmos Studios, Inc.; 231, Courtesy of Cosmos Studios, Inc.; 232, NASA/Science Source; 237, The British Library/Science Source; 243, Album/Alamy Stock Photo; 245, NASA/LARC/Bob Nye/PhotoQuest/Getty Images; 247, NASA/JPL-Caltech/USGS; 248-9, NASA/JPL-Caltech; 252, Eric Heller/Science Source; 254, David Parker/Science Photo Library/Getty Images; 257, Leiden University Libraries, sgn. HUG 10, fol. 76v; 260, Russell Kightley/Science Source; 262, Science & Society Picture Library/Getty Images; 263, Science & Society Picture Library/Getty Images; 267, From *Flatland: A Romance of Many Dimensions* by Edwin Abbott Abbott, 1884. London: Seeley and Co.; 269, David Parker/Science Source; 273, CERN PhotoLab; 274, David Nadlinger, Ion Trap Quantum Computing group, University of Oxford; 277, Universal History Archive/Universal Images Group/Shutterstock; 278, U.S. Army; 280, Henrik Sorensen/Getty Images; 283, Courtesy of Cosmos Studios, Inc.; 286, Science History Images/Alamy Stock Photo; 289, Image copyright © The Metropolitan Museum of Art. Image source: Art Resource, NY; 292, De Agostini/M. Fantin/Getty Images; 293, Universal History Archive/UIG via Getty Images; 295 (UP), © CORBIS/ Corbis via Getty Images; 295 (LO), MPI/Getty Images; 299, RBM Vintage Images/Alamy Stock Photo; 304-305, Library of Congress/Corbis/VCG via Getty Images; 306, NASA/CXC/SAO; 308, NASA-JPL/Caltech; 310, Courtesy of Cosmos Studios, Inc.; 313, Courtesy of Cosmos Studios, Inc.; 314, Kees Veenenbos/Science Source; 317, NASA/JPL/USGS; 321, Walter Meayers Edwards/ National Geographic Image Collection; 322, Frans Lanting/National Geographic Image Collection; 326, Mark Garlick/Science Source; 328-9, Mikkel Juul Jensen/Science Source; 332, NOAA via AP; 334, Sisse Brimberg/National Geographic Image Collection; 337, Courtesy of Cosmos Studios, Inc.; 340, Colleción Banco Santander/HIP/Art Resource, NY; 343, AP Photo/FILE; 346, Rainer von Brandis/Getty Images; 348, Scientific Visualization Studio/NASA; 350, Courtesy of Cosmos Studios, Inc.; 354, Courtesy of Druyan-Sagan Associates; 357, Courtesy of Cosmos Studios, Inc.; 358-9, Courtesy of Cosmos Studios, Inc.; 361, Courtesy of Cosmos Studios, Inc.; 371, Thomas Marent/Minden Pictures/National Geographic Image Collection.

Whirlpool galaxy art used throughout the book courtesy Cosmos Studios, Inc.

INDEX

Boldface indicates illustrations.

A

Abbott, Edwin 265–267
Abrahamson, Seymour 192
Acacia trees **206,** 206–207
Agriculture
 agricultural revolution 42, 117–118, 291
 Anthropocene and 54, 336–337
 pollination 51–54
 Russia 124–125
 as science 121–123, 125, 126–129, 135–136, 139–142
 seed banks 128–130, 138, 140–142, **142,** 143
 Soviet Union 130–143, **131, 132, 136**
 see also Wheat
Ahura Mazda (god) 67–69
Alcubierre, Miguel 329–330
Alexander II, Tsar (Russia) 133
Alexander III, Tsar (Russia) 124
Alexander the Great 77–78, **293**
Alien spacecraft (imagined) **310,** 311–312
ALMA telescopes, Chile **198**
Alpha Centauri A and B **326,** 328
Amsterdam, Netherlands 46–51
Anaerobes 96
Angra Mainyu (archetype for evil) 67–69, **68**
Animal kingdom
 coevolution with plant kingdom 51–52, 213
 common ancestor **224,** 225, 361–362
 genetic drivers of behavior 73–76
Anthropocene 332–347
 agriculture and 54, 336–337
 CFCs 341–344
 climate change 143, 312, 344–347, **346,** 351
 defined 335
 mass extinction events 55, 73
 onset 335–338
 solutions to problems created by 362–363
Apollo missions **196,** 196–197, 240, 244–245, 349
Archidamus III, King (Sparta) 292
Arecibo Observatory, Puerto Rico 202, 209
Armstrong, Neil 196, 251
Arteriovenous malformation (AVM) 147–148
Arthropods **98,** 210
Artificial selection 121
Asoka (Hindu emperor) 78–87, **80**
Astrology 235–236
Atacama Desert, Chile **30**
Atacama Large Millimeter Array (ALMA) radio telescopes, Chile **198**

Atomic bombs *see* Nuclear weapons
Atoms 19–20, **274,** 278–307
Australopithecus robustus **62**
AVM (arteriovenous malformation) 147–148

B

Barton, W. H., Jr. 18
Barulina, Yelena 130
Bateson, William 122–123, 126
Bees
 dance language 208, 214–217, **215,** 220
 death pheromone 73–74
 human-centered view of 214, 222
 political process 217, 219–221
 as pollinators 52, **52,** 54, 213
 queen's role 217, 219, 221
 sleep 221
 swarm 217–221, **218**
Beetles **73–74,** 74, 76–77
Bell, John Stewart 268, 271–272, **273**
Berger, Hans 147, 161–162
Beta Lyrae (binary star system) 181–184, **183**
Bindusara (Hindu emperor) 78–79
Biodiversity **98–99,** 99–100, 127–128, 210
Bioremediation 363
Black holes 56–57, **57**
Blombos Cave, South Africa 38, **39,** 41
Blood pressure gauge 158
Blue-green algae *see* Cyanobacteria
Bok, Bart 178
Braga, Brannon 12
Brain, evolution of 35, 165–169
Brain, human **155**
 "Broca's area" 155
 Broca's brain 156
 dreaming and 157–158, 160
 EEG **146,** 147, 162
 epilepsy 149–151, 153, 154–155
 mapping 155
 nerve fibers **144,** 145
 neurochemistry 170
 New York as metaphor for 169–170
 phrenology **152,** 153–154
 psychic powers 161–162
 Sam Sagan's crisis 147–149, 173
 as seat of consciousness 151
Breakthrough Starshot project **58,** 58–59
Broca, Paul 154–157
"Broca's area" 155
Broca's Brain (Sagan) 156, 171
Bruno, Giordano 46
Buddhism **80,** 81, 82, 84, **84, 85,** 87
Burgess Shale fossils, Canada **98–99**
Burial practices *see* Death, cultural practices surrounding

C

Callisto (Jupiter's moon) 316
Cambrian explosion **98–99,** 99–100
Carbon atoms 282–283
Carbon dioxide 98, 99, 312, 345–347, **357,** 357–358
Carina Nebula **2–3**
Cartography, first 46
Cassini, Giovanni Domenico 235–239
Cassini-Huygens spacecraft 248–249
Cassini spacecraft 226–251, **248–249**
 accomplishments 251
 Enceladus mission 112
 gravitational assist 245, 250
 images from **28, 226,** 227, **247**
 mission team **228,** 228–230, 250–251
 Saturn observations 239, 245–251
 size 239
 suicide 230, 250–251
Çatalhöyük (ancient city) 42–46, **43, 44,** 304
Catalogue of Nebulae and Clusters of Stars (Herschel) 111
Cave art **40,** 41–42, **334,** 335
Cave of the Spider, Valencia, Spain **40,** 41–42
CFCs (chlorofluorocarbons) 341–344
Chak Chak grotto **60,** 61
Chandra X-ray telescope 306
Chandragupta (Hindu warrior) 78
Chemistry, 19th century 101–104, **102**
Chess 288–290, **289**
China
 FAST telescope **200,** 202
Chlorofluorocarbons (CFCs) 341–344
Cities, early proto-cities 42–46, **43, 44**
Civilizations, vanished 364–365
Clerc, Fernand 300–301
Clerc, Véronique 301
Climate change 143, 312, 344–347, **346,** 351
Coevolution 51–52, 213
Cold War 194–195, **195,** 338
Comets 185–186
Concentration camps 103, 104, 298
The Conquest of Interplanetary Space (Kondratyuk) 241–242, 244–245
Consciousness 151, 165–166, 207
Contact binary star systems 183
Copernicus, Nicolaus 236
Coppens, Yves 156
Cosmic Calendar **8–9,** 9, 33–42, 95
Cosmic rays 18–19, 20, 34
Cosmic telescopes 324–325
Cosmos: A Personal Voyage (1980) 23, 148, 169–170, 265, 366–368, **367**

Cosmos: A SpaceTime Odyssey (2014) 25
Cosmos: Possible Worlds (2019) 25, **44,** 156–157
Cosmotheoros (Huygens) **47**
Curie, Marie 284–287, **286**
Curie, Pierre 284–287
Cuzzi, Jeff **228**
Cyanobacteria 95–96, 98–99, 100, 165

D
Darius III, King (Persia) **293**
Darwin, Charles 121, 222–224
De Sitter, Willem 178
Death, cultural practices surrounding **44,** 45–46, 119
Democritus (Greek philosopher) 261
Descartes, René 75–76, 178, 179
Diatoms **6**
DNA 34, 73–77, 94, 100, 283
Dogs 68–70
Domestication, agricultural 42, 117–118, 291
Drake, Frank 209, 352–353
Dreaming 157–158, 160
Druyan, Ann
    adolescence 353
    Cosmos: A Personal Voyage (1980) 23
    Cosmos: A SpaceTime Odyssey (2014) 25
    Cosmos: Possible Worlds (2019) 25, 156–157
    dream of future 356–366, 368
    hope for future 351, 353–356, 369–370
    prologue by 15–27
    Sagan and 21–22, **24,** 156, 163–164, 353–355, **354**
    Shadows of Forgotten Ancestors 63
    Voyager mission golden record 163, **164**

E
Earth (planet)
    evolution of life on 33–38, **34, 35,** 99–100
    explorers 318–323
    first global winter 98
    formation of 33, 284
    in habitable zone 312
    human impact (*see* Anthropocene)
    magnetic field 107
    moon (*see* Moon)
    NASA's planetary protection protocols for 106–107
    origin of life on 33–34, 92–95, 104, 192–193
    ozone layer 100, 342, 343–344
    search for intelligent life on 198–225
    solar evolution and 314–315
    from space 22–23, **28**
    transformed by life on 95–99
EEG *see* Electroencephalograph
Egypt, ancient **116,** 157, 258–259, 276, **277**
Einstein, Albert
    atomic bomb and 294–295, 307

collaboration with de Sitter 178
contributions to science 19–20
on cosmic rays 18–21
on God 51
on gravitational waves 57
gravity and light studies 323
New York World's Fair (1939) 18–21, **21,** 369
photon research 270–272
Spinoza and 50–51
theory of relativity 187
underestimating human potential 55–56
Electrocardiograph (EKG) 158, **159**
Electrochemical communication 203, 207
Electroencephalograph (EEG) **146,** 147, 162
Electrons **252,** 253, 261–262, **262, 263**
Elements 101–103, **102**
Enceladus (Saturn's moon) 111–113, **112, 226,** 250
Encyclopedia Galactica (Sagan) 366–368, **367,** 369
Epilepsy 149–151, 153, 154–155, 159–161, 166
Ethiopia: agriculture 129
Europa (Jupiter's moon) 107, **108,** 109, 316
European Space Agency 32, 235, 248–249
Evil: religious explanations for 67–70, 72
Evolution
    of the brain 35, 165–169
    carbon atoms and 282–283
    coevolution of plants and insects 51–52, 213
    common ancestor **224,** 225, 361–362
    of consciousness 165–166
    as lacking purpose 222–223
    Lamarck on 126
    of life on Earth 33–38, **34, 35,** 99–100
    "The Evolution of Interstellar Flight" (Sagan) **190**
Extinctions 54–55, 73

F
Famine 117, 119–121, **120,** 123–124, 133–135, 140, 142, 143
FAST telescope, China **200,** 202
Fatigue (Mosso) 158
Fear (Mosso) 158
Fire: humans and **64–65,** 65–67, **280,** 281, 336
Five-Hundred-Meter Aperture Spherical Radio Telescope (FAST), China **200,** 202
Flatland (Abbott) 265–267, **267**
Flatworms 168–169, **168–169**
Flerov, G. N. 296
Forests 202–207, **205,** 224
Fouché, Mayor 301–303
Freon *see* Chlorofluorocarbons
Frigatebirds 319–322, **322**
Frisch, Karl von 214–217, **215**
Funeral practices **44,** 45–46, 119
Future
    Druyan's dream of 356–366, 368

Druyan's hope for 351, 353–356, 369–370
possible world 348–371

G
G292.0+1.8 (supernova) **306**
Galaxies
    formation of 91, 370
    Hubble Ultra Deep Field **174**
Galileo 46, 75–76, 234–235, 324
Galileo spacecraft 109
Ganymede (Jupiter's moon) 316
Geese 74, 76
Geminid meteor shower **185**
Genetics
    artificial selection 121
    behavior driven by 73–77
    Darwin's contributions 121, **222–223,** 223–224
    Lamarckism 126, 133
    Mendel's contributions 121–122, **122,** 125
    Vavilov's contributions to 127, 137
    see also DNA
Geochemistry 103, 105
Geological boundaries **337,** 337–338
George III, King (England) 110
Germany *see* Nazi Germany
Giraffes **206,** 206–207
Global warming *see* Climate change
God *see* Religion
Godunov, Boris 120
Golden record 21–22, **22,** 163–164, **164**
Goldschmidt, Victor Moritz 101, 103–105
Gonzalez, Nestor 148–149, 173
Goodricke, John 181–182
Göring, Hermann 103
Grand Prismatic Spring, Yellowstone National Park, U.S. 96, **97**
Gravitational assist 242, 245, 250
Gravitational waves 57–58
Gravity 20, 323–324
Great Ordovician Biodiversification Event 210
Greece, ancient 149–151, **151,** 153, 339, **340,** 364
Greenhouse gases *see* Carbon dioxide; Climate change; Oxygen
Gruber, Rachel Molly 189, 191, 192

H
Habitable zone 308–331
    defined 312
    Earth in 312
    interstellar travel 318, 323, 327–331, **328–329**
    Mars in 315
    Proxima Centauri system 59, 328–329
    solar evolution and 312–318
    Venus in 312
Haile Selassie, Emperor (Ethiopia) 129
Harteck, Paul 293–294
Heller, Eric, art by **252,** 253
Herodotus 364
Herschel, Caroline 110–111
Herschel, John 111
Herschel, William 110–111
Hertzsprung, Ejnar 178

Index

Hess, Victor 18, 20
Hieroglyphs 258–259, 276, **277**
Hippocrates 150–151, **151**
Hitler, Adolf 103, 139–142, 293–294, 297
Holocaust 104, 298
Homo erectus **62**, 66
Homo habilis **62**
Honeybees *see* Bees
Hooke, Robert 237
Houbolt, John Cornelius 244, **245**
Huaynaputina volcano, Peru 119–120
Hubble, Edwin 187
Hubble Ultra Deep Field **174**
Human brain *see* Brain, human
Human Connectome Project **144**, 145
Human impact on Earth *see* Anthropocene
Human nature 37–38, 63, 73–74, 77
Humans, early
   art by **39, 40,** 41–42, 45, 46
   evolution 36–41, **39, 40, 62**
   hearths **64–65,** 65–67
   memory of 63–64
   science conducted by 38, 41
Hunter-gatherer societies 37–38, 54, 291
Hurard, Marius 301
Hurricane Michael (2018) **332,** 333
Huygens, Christiaan 46–48, 235, 256–258, 264, 265, 271
Huygens spacecraft 235, 248–249

I
Icarus (journal) 197
India: early leaders 78–87, **80**
Insects
   behavior driven by DNA 73–77
   evolution 210, 211
   as pollinators 51–52, **52,** 211–213
   see also Bees
Intelligent life, search for
   Drake equation 352–353
   on Earth 198–225
   extraterrestrial 201, **209**
   see also Interstellar messages
Interstellar messages 21–22, **22,** 163–164, **164, 209**
Interstellar travel 318, 323, 327–331, **328–329,** 366, 368–369
   see also Planetary travel
Ivanov, Dmitri 140

J
J1407b (exoplanet) 230, **231,** 233
Jellyfish 166–168, **167**
Jericho 118–119
Jet Propulsion Laboratory **228,** 228–230, 250–251
Jews
   Amsterdam community 48–50
   Nazi persecution of 103–105, 298
Johnson, Torrence **228**
Juno spacecraft 107
Jupiter (planet)
   Cassini's observations 237–238
   formation of 92, 184
   gravity 109
   Kuiper's observations 187
   Late Heavy Bombardment 33

magnetic field 107, 109
   moons 107, **108,** 109, 238, 316
   NASA's planetary protection protocols for 107
   rings 234
   solar evolution and 316

K
Kalinga (region), India 81–83
Kameraz, Abraham 140
Karamzin, Nikolay 120
Kepler-186f (exoplanet) 7
Khvat, Aleksandr Grigorievich 139
Kilp, Yelena 140, 141
Kondratyuk, Yuri (Aleksandr Shargei) 240–245, **243,** 251
Korolyov, Sergey 243
Kovalesky, G. 140
Kriyer, Georgi 140
Kuiper, Gerard Peter
   binary star research 181, 182–183
   chemical nature of solar system 187–189
   childhood and adolescence 177–178
   contributions to planetary science 197
   eyesight 177
   in Leiden 178–179
   Mars observations 187, 194
   at McDonald Observatory **180,** 181, 194
   moon missions and 196
   Sagan and 192, 194, 196
   Urey and 188–189, 196–197

L
Lamarck, Jean-Baptiste 125–126, 133
Land mines 362–363
Landes, Gaston 302
Lapita people 318–323
Lascaux cave, France **334,** 335
Laser Interferometer Gravitational-Wave Observatory (LIGO) 56–57
Leakey, Richard 63
Leborgne, Louis "Tan" 154–155, **155**
Lederberg, Joshua 106
Leeuwenhoek, Antoni van 47, **47**
Leningrad, Siege of 139–142
Life
   Cambrian explosion **98–99,** 99–100
   elements necessary for **306**
   on Enceladus 113
   evolution on Earth 33–38, **34, 35,** 99–100
   NASA's planetary protection protocols 106–107
   origin of 33–34, 92–95, 104, 192–193
   transforming Earth 95–99
Light
   17th-century scientific inquiry 46–47
   gravity and 323–324
   Huygens's studies 256–258, 264
   Newton's studies **254,** 255–256, 260–261, 264
   polarized 271–272
   speed of 238
   wave or particle paradox 256, 258, 260–261, 263–264, 276

Young's studies 259–261, **260,** 263–264
   see also Photons
LIGO observatories 56–57
Lomas Rishi Cave, India **86,** 87
Louis XIV, King (France) 236–237, 238–239
Luna 3 spacecraft 242
Lunine, Jonathan 228
Lysenko, Trofim Denisovich 130, 133–138, **136,** 143
Lyssavirus 69–70, **71**

M
Malygina, A. 140
Manabe, Syukuro 344–345, 353
Manhattan Project *see* Nuclear weapons
Many worlds philosophy 273–274
Mars (planet) 107, 181, 187, 194, 238, **314,** 315
Mass extinctions 54–55, 73
Mauryan Empire 78–86
McDonald Observatory, Texas **180,** 181, 194
"Memory" (Vedder) **88**
Mendel, Gregor 121–123, 125
Mendeleev, Dmitri 101–103
Mercury (planet) 314
Meteor showers 185, **185**
Meteorites **186,** 186–187
Meteors **176**
Methane 96, 98, 187, 336, 337
Microbes
   communication 165–166
   consciousness 165–166
   disease microbes 69–70
   Grand Prismatic Spring 96, **97**
   Leeuwenhoek's studies 47, **47**
   origin of life and **34,** 94
Microscopy 47, **47**
Milky Way galaxy **2–3, 30,** 31, 91–92, **198**
Miller, Stanley 193
Mohenjo Daro 365
Molina, Mario 341–344, **343**
Molotov, Vyacheslav 136
Moon (Earth's)
   Cassini's map 236, **237**
   Luna 3 photographs 242
   missions to 31, **196,** 196–197, 240, 244–245, 349
   NASA's planetary protection protocols for 106
Mosso, Angelo 157–161, **159**
Muller, H. J. 192–193
Mushrooms 204, 210
Mycelium **203,** 203–204

N
Nanocraft **58,** 58–59
NASA (National Aeronautics and Space Administration)
   founding 195
   planetary protection protocols 106–107, 109–111, 250
   see also specific missions and spacecraft
Navigation 214–216, 320, **321,** 321–322, **322**

Nazi Germany
    atomic bomb efforts 293–294, 296, 297
    Holocaust 298
    invasion of Soviet Union 139–142, 243–244
    treatment of Jews 103–105, 298
    weaponized rockets 191
    weaponry 293–294
Neptune (planet) 233, 316–317, **317**
Neurochemistry 170
Neurons 166, 168, 170
New General Catalogue (Herschel) 111
New York World's Fair (1939) **14,** 14–21, **16, 21,** 369
New York World's Fair (2039) **350, 358–359,** 359–366, **361,** 368–369
Newton, Isaac 20, 178, 255–256, 260–261, 264
NGC 602 star cluster **90**
Nikbanu, Sassanian Princess 61
Nok civilization 364–365
Nuclear reactions 282, **283,** 288, 290
Nuclear weapons
    Anthropocene and 338
    destructive capability 290, 306–307
    as deterrent 297
    Einstein and 294–296
    in fiction 287–288
    Nazi efforts 293–294, 296, 297
    Soviet efforts 296, 298–299
    testing **278, 299,** 338
    U.S. efforts 294–298

O
Observation: changing reality 264–265, 268, 270
Oceans: limestone towers 92–94, **93**
Ocher 38, **39,** 41, 45, 46
Oleic acid 73–74
Olivine 92, 104, **104,** 105
Oort, Jan 178
Oppenheimer, J. Robert 297, 298, 299, **299**
Opticks (Newton) **254,** 255, 256
Ordovician period 210
Oxygen 66, 96, 98, 100
Ozone layer 100, 342, 343–344

P
Pattern recognition 150
Pelée, Mount, Martinique 300–305, **304–305**
Periodic table of elements 101–103, **102**
Perseid meteor **176**
Persepolis 68, **68**
Philosophy 75–76
Photons 20, 263–265, 268, 270–272, 276
Phrenology **152,** 153–154
Pigott, Edward 181
Pir-e Sabz grotto, Iran **60,** 61
Pitchblende 285
Planck satellite 32
Planetary travel
    alien spacecraft **310,** 311–312
    contamination concerns 106
    gravitational assist 242, 245

imperialism concerns 106
    planetary protection protocols 106–107, 109–111
    travel poster **308**
    see also Interstellar travel
Planets: formation of 92
Plant kingdom
    coevolution with animal kingdom 51–52, 213
    forests 202–207, **205,** 224
    future 362–363
    pollination 51–54, **52,** 211–213
    sex 51–52, 211–213
    see also Agriculture; Wheat
Plato 268
Pleiades (asterism) **176,** 177
Pollination 51–54, **52,** 211–213
Pollution 363
Popovsky, Mark 136
Porco, Carolyn **228**
Prentiss, Clara 301
Probability theory 258, 265, 271
Proxima b **326,** 328–329
Proxima Centauri (star) 59, 327–329
Psychic powers 161–162
Putin, Vladimir 143

Q
Quantum encryption 276
Quantum entanglement 268–271, **269,** 275, 276

R
Rabies 69–70, **71**
Radio astronomy 178–179, **198, 200,** 202, 325
Radioactivity 285–287
Radium 285, 287
Ras Tafari 129
Red dwarf stars 328
Refrigeration 339–344
Religion
    ancient Egypt 157
    Buddhism 80, 81, 82, 84, **84, 85,** 87
    Einstein on 51
    evil explained by 67–70, 72
    fire in 67
    Galileo and 46, 75–76
    Huygens on 48
    Jewish community of Amsterdam 48–50
    medicine and 150–151, 153
    no room for doubt in 75–76
    Spinoza on 48–51
    Zoroastrians 61, 67–69, **68**
Ringed planets 230–235, **231, 232**
    see also Jupiter; Saturn; Uranus
Roche, Édouard 246
Roche limit 246, 248
Rodina, Liliya 135–136, 140
Rømer, Ole 238
Roosevelt, Franklin D. 294–296
Rosetta stone 276, **277**
Rotblat, Joseph 297–298, 307
Rotblat, Tola 297, 298
Rowland, Sherwood 341–344, **343,** 347
Russell, Bertrand 307
Russia
    agriculture 124–125

famines 120, **120,** 123–124
    Russian Revolution 127, 133, 241
    see also Soviet Union
Rutherford, Ernest 288

S
Saccorhytus coronarius **224,** 225, 361–362
"Sacred Disease" (Hippocrates) 151, 153
Sagan, Cari 191
Sagan, Carl
    Apollo missions and 196–197
    Broca's Brain 156, 171
    childhood **190,** 191–192
    children 147–149, 173, 351
    contributions to planetary science 197
    Cosmos: A Personal Voyage (1980) 23
    Druyan and 21–22, **24,** 156, 163–164, 353–355, **354**
    education 193–194
    Encyclopedia Galactica 366–368, **367,** 369
    as inspiration 148–149
    on intelligent civilizations in the galaxy 352–353
    on invention of chess 288–289
    Kuiper and 192, 194, 196
    Muller and 192–193
    New York World's Fair 15, 17–19
    on origins of life 192–193
    planetary protection protocols 106
    on salt 171
    Shadows of Forgotten Ancestors 63
    Titan observations 249
    Urey and 192, 193, 196
    Voyager missions and 21–23, 163
Sagan, Rachel Molly Gruber 189, 191, 192
Sagan, Sam (Carl's and Ann's son) 147–149, 173, 351
Sagan, Sam (Carl's father) 189, 191
Sakharova, Katya 126, 127, 130
Salt 171, **172**
Saturn (planet)
    Cassini's observations 239, 245–251
    Galileo's observations 234–235
    Huygens's observations 47, 235
    Late Heavy Bombardment 33
    moons 47, 110–113, **112,** 187, **226,** 248–250
    NASA's planetary protection protocols for 110
    rings **28,** 47, 234, 235, 239, 245–246
    solar evolution and 316
Schwartz, Delmore 105–106
Science
    agriculture as 121–123, 125, 126–129, 135–136, 139–142
    approach to nature 25–26
    collaboration between disciplines 184, 186–187, 192, 197
    by early humans 38, 41
    Einstein on 21, 369
    Einstein's contributions 19–20

as evidence-based 26, 137, 138, 261, 276, 370
of fatigue 158
Lamarck's contribution to 126
openness to change 32
redemptive powers 27
united with philosophy 75–76
Sea jellies 166–168, **167**
Search for extraterrestrial intelligence 201, **209**
Search for intelligent life on Earth 198–225
Selassie, Haile, Emperor (Ethiopia) 129
Seleucus I Nicator 78
Sex 51–52, 204, 211–213
Shadows of Forgotten Ancestors (Sagan and Druyan) 63
Shargei, Aleksandr (Yuri Kondratyuk) 240–244, **243,** 251
Shark Bay, Australia **34**
Sleep 157
Small Magellanic Cloud (SMC) **90**
Solar system
Cassini's observations 236–237
Descartes's model **179**
Kuiper's speculation concerning 184
Solar systems: formation of 197
Soter, Steven 23, 25
Sound waves 258
Soviet Union
agriculture 130–143, **131, 132, 136**
famine 133–135, 140, 143
German invasion (1941) 139–142, 243–244
labor camps for scientists 242–243
logic of 242
nuclear weapons 296, 298–299, 338
Russian Revolution 127, 130, 133, 241
scientific institutes 129
Sputnik 1 satellite 194–195, **195**
see also Russia; *specific missions and spacecraft*
Space race 194–195, **195**
Spectroscopy 182, 231, 324
Sphygmomanometer 158
Spinoza, Baruch 48–51
Sputnik 1 satellite 194–195, **195**
Stalin, Joseph
atomic bomb and 296
German invasion and 139, 140
Kondratyuk and 242
Russian admiration for 143
Vavilov and 129, 134–138
Stars
binary stars 181–183, **183**
birth of 91–92, 282, **306,** 370
Milky Way galaxy 31, 91–92
reconnaissance missions to 58–59
red dwarf stars 328
solar evolution **313,** 313–318
Starshot nanocraft **58,** 58–59
Stchukin, Alexander 140
Strobel, Darrell **228**
Sun
birth 91–92
evolution **313,** 313–318
Superdeterminism 274–275

Supernovae 282, **306**
Svalbard Global Seed Vault **142,** 143
Sylbaris, Ludger 300, 305
Symbolic languages 208, **209,** 214–217, 220
Synapses 168
Szilard, Leo 288–290, 294–295

T
"Tan" *see* Leborgne, Louis "Tan"
Tardigrades 225
Tartessians 364
TCEs (trichloroethylenes) 363
Telepathy 161–162
Teller, Edward 294, 296–297, 299
Theological-Political Treatise (Spinoza) 49–50
Thomson, George Paget 263
Thomson, J. J. 261–263
Thron, Giovanni 159–161
Tidal flexing 109
Titan (Saturn's moon)
Cassini observations **247,** 248–249
Huygens's discovery of 47, 235
Kuiper's observations 187
NASA's planetary protection protocols for 110, 250
solar evolution and 316
Tower of Jericho 118–119
Tree of Life **350, 357,** 357–358
Trees
assisting one another 204–205
bioremediation 363
communication 204, 206–207
Darwin's studies 224
evolution 210–211
parenthood 205–206
see also Forests
Trichloroethylenes (TCEs) 363
Trilobites **98,** 100
Triton (Neptune's moon) 316–317, **317**
Truman, Harry S. 298
Tufa (limestone towers) 92–94, **93**
Two-dimensional world 265–267, **267**

U
Ukraine: agriculture 133–134, **136**
Uranium atom 282–285, 306–307
Uranus (planet) 110, **232,** 233–234, 316
Urey, Harold Clayton **188,** 188–189, 192, 193, 196–197

V
Vavilov, Alexandra 124
Vavilov, Lydia 124
Vavilov, Nikolay Ivanovich 123–143, **131**
arrest and imprisonment 139–141
background 123–125
contributions to genetics 127
friendship with Muller 192–193
Lysenko and 130, 133–138
marriage 126, 127, 130
Russian Revolution 127
scientific approach 125, 127
scientific reputation 143

Soviet agriculture and 127
travel adventures 128–130
wheat research 126–127, **128**
world seed bank 128–130, 138, 140–142
Vavilov, Oleg 127
Vavilov, Sergei 124, 130
Vedder, Elihu: painting by **88**
Venus (planet) 107, 312, 314
Vernalization 133, **136,** 138
Viruses 69–70, **71,** 100
Volcanoes 98–99, 119–120, 300–305, **304–305**
Voskresenskaia, Olga 140
Voyager missions
Enceladus observations 111
golden record 21–22, **22,** 163–164, **164**
gravitational assist 242
images from 22–23, **317**
Jupiter's rings 234
longevity 59
Neptune observations 233
speed 31, 59
Uranus observations 233
Voyagers (Lapita) 318–323

W
Wasps 211–213, **212**
Water
on Enceladus 111–113, **112**
on Mars **314,** 315
Weaponry, evolution of 290–293, **292, 293,** 296, 307
Weather 119–120
see also Climate change
Wells, H. G. 287–288
Wetherald, Richard 345, 353
Wheat **114, 116,** 126–127, **128,** 135, **136**
White, Harold 330
Wonderwerk Cave, South Africa **64–65,** 65–67
The World Set Free (Wells) 287–288
World's Fair (New York, 1939) **14,** 14–21, **16, 21,** 369
World's Fair (New York, 2039) **350, 358–359,** 359–366, **361,** 368–369

X
X-rays 284–285

Y
Yeast 363
Yeats, W. B. 105–106
Yellowstone National Park, U.S. 96, **97**
Yosemite National Park, California **176**
Young, Thomas 258–261, 263–264, 276

Z
Zoroastrians 61, 67–69, **68**

ABOUT THE AUTHOR

Ann Druyan was the creative director of NASA's Voyager Interstellar Message Project and program director of the first solar sail deep space mission, launched on a Russian ICBM in 2005. With her late husband, Carl Sagan, she co-authored the original 1980s Emmy Award– and Peabody Award–winning TV series *Cosmos: A Personal Voyage* and six *New York Times* best-sellers. Additionally, Druyan was co-creator and co-producer of the Warner Bros. feature film *Contact,* starring Jodie Foster and directed by Bob Zemeckis. Druyan was the lead executive producer, a director, and co-author of *Cosmos: A SpaceTime Odyssey,* produced for Fox and the National Geographic Channel, for which she won Peabody, Producers Guild, and Emmy Awards in 2014. The show, which received 13 Emmy nominations, has been seen in 181 countries. She is an executive producer, writer, director, and creator of *Cosmos: Possible Worlds,* first broadcast in 2020. The asteroids Sagan (2709) and Druyan (4970) are in perpetual wedding ring orbit around the sun.